RESEARCH DESIGN
for
PROGRAM EVALUATION

CONTEMPORARY EVALUATION RESEARCH
A series of books on applied social science

Series Editors:
HOWARD E. FREEMAN, *Department of Sociology, University of California, Los Angeles*
RICHARD A. BERK, *Department of Sociology, University of California, Santa Barbara*

The CONTEMPORARY EVALUATION RESEARCH series meets the need for a monograph-length publication outlet for timely manuscripts on evaluation research. In the tradition of EVALUATION REVIEW (formerly EVALUATION QUARTERLY), studies from different disciplines and methodological perspectives will be included. The series will cover the full spectrum of substantive areas, including medical care, mental health, criminal justice, manpower, income security, education, and the environment. Manuscripts may report empirical results, methodological developments, or review an existing literature.

Volume 1: ATTORNEYS AS ACTIVISTS: Evaluating the American Bar Association's BASICS Program
by Ross F. Conner and C. Ronald Huff

Volume 2: AFTER THE CLEAN-UP: Long-Range Effects of Natural Disasters
by James D. Wright, Peter H. Rossi, Sonia R. Wright and Eleanor Weber-Burdin

Volume 3: INEFFECTIVE JUSTICE: Evaluating the Preappeal Conference
by Jerry Goldman

Volume 4: REFORMING SCHOOLS: Problems in Program Implementation and Evaluation
by Wendy Peter Abt and Jay Magidson

Volume 5: PROGRAM IMPLEMENTATION: The Organizational Context
by Mary Ann Scheirer

Volume 6: RESEARCH DESIGN FOR PROGRAM EVALUATION: The Regression-Discontinuity Approach
by William M. K. Trochim

RESEARCH DESIGN
for
PROGRAM EVALUATION
the regression-discontinuity approach

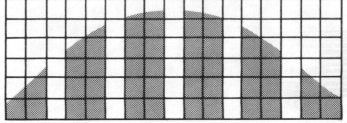

WILLIAM M. K. TROCHIM

Foreword by DONALD T. CAMPBELL

CONTEMPORARY EVALUATION RESEARCH
A series of books on applied social science edited by
HOWARD E. FREEMAN and RICHARD A. BERK

6

SAGE PUBLICATIONS Beverly Hills London New Delhi

For information address:

SAGE Publications, Inc.
275 South Beverly Drive
Beverly Hills, California 90212

SAGE Publications India Pvt. Ltd.
C-236 Defence Colony
New Delhi 110 024, India

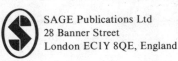

SAGE Publications Ltd
28 Banner Street
London EC1Y 8QE, England

Printed in the United States of America

Library of Congress Cataloging in Publication Data

Trochim, William, M. K.
  Research design for program evaluation.

  (Contemporary evaluation research; v. 6)
  Bibliography: p.
  1. Social Sciences—Methodology. 2. Regression
analysis. Evaluation research (Social action programs)
I. Title. II. Series.
H61.T73 1984   300'.1'519536   84-1969
ISBN 0-8039-2037-7

FIRST PRINTING

Contents

Acknowledgments 13

Foreword by Donald T. Campbell 15

1. Introduction to Regression-Discontinuity 45
The Basic Regression-Discontinuity Design 47
Some Assumptions of Regression-Discontinuity 53
Social Policy and Research Design 57

2. A Short History of Regression-Discontinuity 67
The Academic Tradition 69
The Compensatory Education Tradition 73
Frequency and Location of Use 77
Reasons Cited for Not Using Model C 77
Reasons Cited in Favor of Using Model C 84
Summary of Use Issues 86

3. Design Variations 87
Assignment Variations 88
Measurement Variations 94
Program Variations 95
Postprogram Measure Variations 96
Aggregation Variations 100
Post Hoc Analysis 104
Summary 104

4. Regression-Discontinuity and Allocation Formulas 107
Types of Federal Grants 108
Examples of Allocation Formula Designs 112
Problems in Allocation Formula Designs 115

5. The Statistical Analysis of the Regression-Discontinuity Design   **121**
  A Statistical Model for Regression-Discontinuity   122
  Model Specification   128
  Design Variations and Analytic Implications   133
    Multiple Cutoff Points   134
    Random Assignment in Regression-Discontinuity Designs   135
    The Use of Covariates   137
    Composite Pretest Measures   137
    Pretest Homogeneity in the Program Group   138
    Separate Within–Group Distributions   138
  Illustrative Analyses   139
    Second Grade Reading Program   140
    Fourth Grade Math Program   145
  Summary of Regression-Discontinuity Analysis   148
  The Analysis of the "Fuzzy" Regression-Discontinuity Design   153
    The Relative Assignment Approach   156
    Illustrative Simulations   162
    Illustrative Real Data Analysis   166
    Conclusions   172

6. The "Negative Gain" Controversy   **175**
  Background   175
  The Pattern of Results   177
  Some Likely Sources of the Discrepancy in Results   179
    Three Potentially Biasing Factors in Model A   181
    Residual Regression Artifacts in Model A   181
    Attrition Bias in Model A   187
    Time-of-Testing Bias in Model A   191
    Three Potentially Biasing Factors in Model C   195
    Misassignment Bias in Model C   195
    Measurement-Related Bias in Model C   202
    Data Preparation Problems in Model C   205
  Summary of the Negative Gain Issue   209

7. The Implementation of Regression-Discontinuity   **211**
  Assignment Issues   212
    Placement of the Cutoff Value   212

Selection of the Cutoff Value   213
Measures Used for Assignment   214
Adherence to the Cutoff   216
Assignment Problems and the Estimate of Gain   219
Measurement Issues   220
  Test Administration   221
  Test Characteristics   223
  Test Problems   225
  Data Maintenance and Access   227
Program Issues   231
  Identifying Recipients of the Program   232
  Amount of Service Received   233
  Type of Program Received   234
Data Preparation Issues   236
  Background and Prevalence of Exclusions   237
  Common Exclusions   240
  Data Processing Issues   244
Summary of Research Implementation Issues   245

Appendix A: Computer Analysis of Regression-Discontinuity
Data   249
  MINITAB Analysis of Regression-Discontinuity Data   250
  SPSS Analysis of Regression-Discontinuity Data   251
  Conclusion   253

Appendix B: Regression-Discontinuity Simulation Exercises   255
  The Regression-Discontinuity Design: Part I   255
  The Regression-Discontinuity Design: Part II   261

References   267

About the Author   272

To my parents,
Eugene and Marian

List of Tables and Figures

Figure 1.1   The Regression-Discontinuity Null Case   49

Figure 1.2   The Regression-Discontinuity Design with a Program Effect   50

Figure 1.3   Regression Lines for Regression-Discontinuity Design of Figure 1.2   52

Figure 1.4   Hypothetical Regression Line Outcomes for a Compensatory Regression-Discontinuity Design   54

Figure 1.5   Classification of Causal Hypothesis Testing Research Designs   62

Figure 1.6   Probability of Assignment to Program for the True Experiment   63

Figure 1.7   Probability of Assignment to Program for Regression-Discontinuity   64

Figure 1.8   Probability of Assignment to Program for Fuzzy Regression-Discontinuity and the Nonequivalent Group Design   64

Figure 2.1   The Regression-Discontinuity Design as an Extension of a True Experiment   71

Figure 2.2   Regression-Discontinuity When the Pretest and Posttest Are Uncorrelated   83

Table 3.1   Descriptive Statistics for Posttest Subscales in Providence, RI   97

Figure 3.1   Regression-Discontinuity with a Reading Pretest and Vocabulary Posttest   98

Figure 3.2   Regression-Discontinuity with a Reading Pretest and Comprehension Posttest   99

Figure 3.3   Regression-Discontinuity with a Math Pretest and Computation Posttest   100

Figure 3.4   Regression-Discontinuity with a Math Pretest and a Concepts Posttest   101

Figure 3.5   Regression-Discontinuity with a Math Pretest and Applications Posttest   102

Table 3.2   Estimates of Gain and Standard Errors, Posttest Subscales, Providence, RI   103

Figure 5.1   Pseudo-Effects Resulting from Fitting a True Quadratic Function with a Linear Model   130

Figure 5.2   Bivariate Distribution, Providence, RI, Second Grade Reading Program   141

Figure 5.3   Posttest Means, Providence, RI, Second Grade Reading Program   142

Figure 5.4   R-Squared Value Across Regression Analysis Steps, Providence, RI, Second Grade Reading Program   143

Figure 5.5   Residual Mean Square Values Across Regression Analysis Steps, Providence, RI, Second Grade Reading Program   144

Figure 5.6   Estimate of Gain Across Regression Analysis Steps, Providence, RI, Second Grade Reading Program   145

Figure 5.7   Step Two Model Regression Line, Providence, RI, Second Grade Reading Program   146

Figure 5.8   Step Nine Model Regression Line, Providence, RI, Second Grade Reading Program   147

Figure 5.9   Bivariate Distribution, Providence, RI, Fourth Grade Math Program   148

Figure 5.10   Posttest Means, Providence, RI, Fourth Grade Math Program   149

Figure 5.11   R-Squared Values, Providence, RI, Fourth Grade Math Program   150

Figure 5.12   Residual Mean Square Values Across Regression Analysis Steps, Providence, RI, Fourth Grade Math Program   151

Figure 5.13   Estimate of Gain Across Regression Analysis teps, Providence, RI, Fourth Grade Math Program   152

Figure 5.14   Step Two Model Regression Line, Providence, RI, Fourth Grade Math Program   153

Figure 5.15   Step Five Model Regression Line, Providence, RI, Fourth Grade Math Program   154

Figure 5.16   Relative Assignment Variable Function for the True Experiment   158

Figure 5.17	Relative Assignment Variable Function for Regression-Discontinuity	159
Figure 5.18	Relative Assignment Variable Functions for Fuzzy Regression-Discontinuity and the Nonequivalent Group Design	160
Table 5.1	Fuzzy Regression-Discontinuity Simulation Results ($b_0 = 0$, error variances = 1)	166
Table 5.2	Fuzzy Regression-Discontinuity Simulation Results ($b_0 = 0$, error variances = 4)	167
Table 5.3	Fuzzy Regression-Discontinuity Simulation Results ($b_0 = 3$, error variances = 1)	168
Table 5.4	Fuzzy Regression-Discontinuity Simulation Results ($b_0 = 3$, error variances = 4)	169
Figure 5.19	Fuzzy Regression-Discontinuity with a Vocabulary Pretest and Reading Posttest	170
Figure 5.20	Fuzzy Regression-Discontinuity with a Reading Pretest and Reading Posttest	171
Figure 6.1	Distribution of Gains by Model for Title I Compensatory Education Programs in Florida, 1980	178
Figure 6.2	Regression Artifact with Two Variables	183
Figure 6.3	"Residual Regression Artifact" in Model A	184
Figure 6.4	Hypothetical Correlation Erosion Pattern	186
Table 6.1	Average NCE Gain for Projects Grouped by Pretest Mean NCE	187
Figure 6.5	Average Posttest NCE for Projects Grouped by Pretest Mean NCE	188
Figure 6.6	Time-of-Testing Bias	193
Figure 6.7	The Effect of Challenges on Within-Group Slopes	197
Table 6.2	Estimates of Gain (β_2) and Standard Errors for Simulations of Several Challenge Procedures	201
Figure 6.8	Effects of Cutoff Placement and Chance Levels or Floor Effects on Estimates of Effect	204
Figure 6.9	Effect of Excluding Title I Repeaters	206
Figure 6.10	Hypothetical Pretest-Posttest Relationships for Floor or Ceiling Effect on Either Measure	207

Acknowledgments

There are many people who have contributed to the construction of this work. First, I wish to thank Donald T. Campbell who for two summers (and thereafter) patiently tried to impress upon me the importance of the regression-discontinuity design in social research. He is the initial developer of the design and because of his enthusiasm for the technical issues involved, I found myself intrigued and, finally, captivated. My dissertation advisor, Robert F. Boruch, supported my efforts unconditionally and is spiritually behind this entire volume through his careful critiques of earlier versions. Thomas D. Cook also had a key role as a member of my graduate committee, a patient reviewer, and the first person to suggest that this work might make a worthy book. I am grateful to these advisors and other friends and colleagues from my graduate school days at Northwestern University—especially Charles S. Reichardt and David S. Cordray—for the honesty of their reactions and the strength of their encouragement.

The work presented in this volume has led me to new contacts and collaborations. Richard Berk is largely responsible for encouraging me to set pen to paper and for bolstering my confidence throughout this project. Ronald Visco has become a friend and collaborator and has provided me with a corridor to the real world applications of regression-discontinuity through his own rich experience in the Providence, Rhode Island School District. Cliff Spiegelman provided the statistical framework for the description of analytic approaches to the "fuzzy" regression-discontinuity case. Gary Echternacht was my major contact on the national and regional workings of Title I evaluation.

This work would have been impossible without the financial resources to carry it out. Portions of this work were conducted with funding from NSF Grant DAR 7820374 (Robert Boruch, Principal Investigator), NIE Grant G–79–0128 (Robert Boruch and David Cordray, Principal Investigators), NSF Grant BNS 7826810 (Donald Campbell, Principal Investigator), and NIE Grant G–81–0086 (William Trochim, Principal Investigator).

The production of this volume was expertly accomplished with the assistance of Karen Adams, Maureen Conklin, and, most of all, Leslie Smith who patiently dealt with the vagaries of computerized word processing and my own often erratic habits.

Finally, I wish to thank Mary (and Nora) for tolerating my frequent mental absence while I worked on this volume and for the encouragement and motivation that results from having them in my life.

—William M. K. Trochim

Foreword

DONALD T. CAMPBELL

Lehigh University

It is a great pleasure to be allowed to introduce Bill Trochim's book. It is the first complete (to say nothing of book-length) presentation of the regression-discontinuity quasi-experimental design. Bill and the Sage editors have invited me to use this occasion to present an anecdotal history of the development of the method in Evanston, Illinois. (No doubt it has been independently hit upon several times. I will report later on the cases which we know about.)

Some background: In the period 1958-1968, the National Merit Scholarship Corporation, headquartered in Evanston, supported an impressive research commitment under the direction of John M. Stalnaker, with scholars such as Donald L. Thistlethwaite, Alexander Astin, Robert Nichols, and John L. Holland on the staff at various times. This group, and a similar group at the Association of American Medical Colleges (Helen H. Gee and Edwin B. Hutchins, among others), combined with the faculty of Northwestern University to produce a truly outstanding applied social research community with a special focus on quasi-experimental designs. For example, the cross-lagged panel correlation technique also grew out of this environment.

On some winter day in 1958, I met with Donald Thistlethwaite and others from National Merit in the Faculty Lounge, 304 Kresge Centennial Hall, Northwestern University, whose windows at the time looked out right over Lake Michigan. Our agenda was to discuss how to measure the career effects of receiving a special new Merit Scholarship designated for minority students, under the direction of Hugh Lane. Whereas the regular Merit Scholarships went to students so promising and well supported that the Merit award could do little to augment their level of eventual achievement, these minority awards were expected to make profound career changes in many cases.

Our discussion quickly rejected any broad spectrum use of random assignment, even for a small experimental sample. We spent most of the day trying to convince the program administrators to employ a "tie-breaking" randomization: that is, for those applicants whose scores or ranks were on the borderline between award and no award, one would define a class interval of measurement, within which all who fell would be designated as tied in eligibility, with more numerous such cases than there were awards to cover. Among these, one would break the ties by random assignment. For this narrow band of eligibility, one would have a random-assignment experiment.

But by the end of the afternoon, Don Thistlethwaite and I had become convinced that if awards were made entirely on the basis of a quantified eligibility score or a complete ranking of a substantial pool of applicants in a range that included borderline and less eligible cases, and if one had outcome scores for this full range, one should be able to extrapolate from above and below the cutting point to what a tie-breaking random-assignment experiment would have shown. This double extrapolation produces the "regression-discontinuity" design.

The hypothetical tie-breaking experiment has been both the expository and interpretative key in all of the presentations of the method in which I have participated (Thistlethwaite & Campbell,

1960; Campbell & Stanley, 1963; Campbell, 1969a, 1976; Riecken et al., 1974; Cook & Campbell, 1976, 1979), leading me to reject effects such as change of slope when not accompanied by a change of cutting-point intercept. If a tie-breaking randomized assignment would not have shown the effect, I am unwilling to credit a causal inference based upon an other-than-intercept discontinuity.

The idea of randomization at the margin (tie-breaking) can be regarded as a special case of Boruch's (1975b) "Experiments Nested Within Quasi-Experiments," that is, using multiple designs that are put together to achieve both greater statistical power and more methodologically independent cross-validation. The statistical properties of estimates that we get out of coupling designs can be better than those we get out of single approach designs. To put this more concretely, even had a tie-breaking randomization been permitted, a supplementary regression-discontinuity analysis would also have been desirable. In addition, a tie-breaking randomization no matter how few its cases will always add inferential strength to a regression-discontinuity analysis.

It turned out that in its scholarship awards of any type, National Merit could not implement either the tie-breaking randomization or the regression-discontinuity design due to its commitment to the many funding groups it coordinated, each of which designated a panel to make the final decisions on the few scholarships it was funding. These panels looked over the quantitative and qualitative evidence and produced a 3-category decision (award, alternates, and unconditional rejectees) with no metricizing within categories. Had they been asked to first rank-order the entire pool, and then to use these ranks to decide awards and priority order of alternates, then a subsequent regression-discontinuity analysis using ranks above and below the cutting point would have been possible, but the administrative staff judged this to be too demanding. Post hoc ranking within categories (which might have been done later by a research staff) would have produced a discontinuity in the quality of measurement at each category boundary, undermining the fundamental assumption of measurement homogeneity within and across cutting points.

For a nonmonetary commendation, the Certificate of Merit, the requisites were available in National Merit procedures and records: award based upon a sharp cutting point on a quantitative measure of eligibility, a record of the eligibility scores of persons above and below the cutting point, and follow-up data for all, appropriate to possible effects of the award. Donald Thistlethwaite had already used these data in a more traditional ex post facto impact study. He did regression-discontinuity reanalysis that we published (Thistlethwaite & Campbell, 1960), illustrating its clear superiority over the ex post facto method for causal inference.

My next Northwestern colleague in work on the method was Joyce A. Sween, whose 1971 Ph.D. dissertation "The Experimental Regression Design: An Inquiry into the Feasibility of Non Random Treatment Allocation" (see also Sween, 1977), probed and expanded the method by extensive computer simulation, with special attention to appropriate tests of significance once one has abandoned the usually inappropriate assumption of linear regression. She declared that the regression-discontinuity design produced a *true* rather than *quasi*-experiment, in agreement with later publications by Goldberger (1972), Cronbach, Regosa, Floden, and Price (1977), and Reichardt (1979) who also argue that the magic of randomization is that it enables one to model accurately the exposure to treatment, and that other explicit assignment rules can achieve this same result. (While I admire the brilliance of this perspective, the choosing of an appropriate estimate of the regression lines involves such great difficulties and strong assumptions that I still would emphasize the quasi-ness.)

Sween explored the use of higher-order polynomials to achieve curvilinear regression, and ended up recommending essentially the same procedures Trochim presents in this volume. In the normal curve-fitting strategy one uses the lowest order curve not statistically significantly demonstrated to be too simple. This results in a parsimonious bias toward underfitting. For the double-extrapolation t-test analysis developed by Sween, underfitting (e.g., using a linear model where the true form is quadratic) can lead to pseudo-effects, whereas the reverse error, overfitting, or using too high a polynomial, should not. Thus Sween recommended starting with a cubic or higher order model and working down.

Two anecdotes illustrate the sensitivity of the analysis to slight degrees of curvilinearity. For a long time, the most extensive presentation of the design was in my "Reforms as Experiments," which first appeared in the *American Psychologist* in 1969. In that first presentation there was a profoundly mistaken Footnote 8, deleted in all subsequent presentations (e.g., Streuning & Brewer, 1983). Within a week or so of its appearance, both William Kruskal and Harry Roberts of the University of Chicago Department of Statistics had independently contacted me to tell me I was wrong. There ensued a series of meetings in which Kruskal, Roberts, James Landwehr, Myron Straf, and others from the University of Chicago met with Joyce Sween, Edward Kepka, Donald Morrison, and me from Northwestern, working to discover the source of the problem. In the end, this turned out to be a subtle mistake in our simulation. Since I never got around to publishing the planned errata in the *American Psychologist*, I will take space to do that now.

(The exposition will be clearer if I use the very same illustrations employed in that article. For convenience, I will keep the captions and figure numbers the same, even though I have always regretted the labels of the abscissa and ordinate, a regret which increased with each of the many reprintings of that article. Using the terms "pretest" and "posttest," instead of "eligibility score" as I should have, encouraged the misunderstanding that the design was only appropriate where the same or highly comparable measures were used for both eligibility and outcome. Instead, while this is a limitation for many quasi-experimental designs, including the two most frequently usable, the interrupted time series and the pretest-posttest nonrandomized comparison group design, it is not at all a limitation on the regression-discontinuity design. Indeed, in the original Thistlethwaite and Campbell (1960) paper, the eligibility measure was an achievement test score, and one outcome measure was the distance from the home of the university attended.)

Figure 14 and 15 of Campbell (1969) show simulated regression-discontinuity studies, with no true effect (Figure 14) and with a true effect of some two points (Figure 15). When Joyce Sween and I extended no-effect runs such as Figure 14 to 1000 or more cases, we regularly obtained a significant pseudo-effects in the direction of a beneficial impact of a treatment given to those with the higher eligibility scores. Footnote 8 was a misguided effort to explain this apparent bias.

The correct explanation was as follows: The simulation involved 20 discrete whole-unit true scores (ranging from 0 to 20). To these true scores were added errors of a "continuous" nature, that is, normal random numbers with five significant figures. Separate independent errors were added to the true scores to achieve the eligibility and the outcome scores. Thus all of the obtained scores lower than the lowest true score of zero, and all scores higher than the highest true score of 20, were due purely to error, and hence had a perfectly horizontal regression line, adding a slight curvilinearity, which when fitted with a straight line tilted the two regression lines apart at the cutting point. All of this can be now seen if one looks carefully at Figure 14. Needless to say, in Sween's dissertation, done later, "continuous" normal true scores were employed, and this subtle source of curvilinearity avoided in the intended linear cases.

Here is another example of the subtle effects of overlooking slight degrees of curvilinearity. In the Cook and Campbell (1976) chapter in Dunnette's Handbook, Seaver and Quarton's (1976) study of the impact of being on the Dean's List on subsequent grade point average was used to illustrate the regression-discontinuity design. By the time this material was revised as a separate publication (Cook & Campbell, 1979), Seaver and

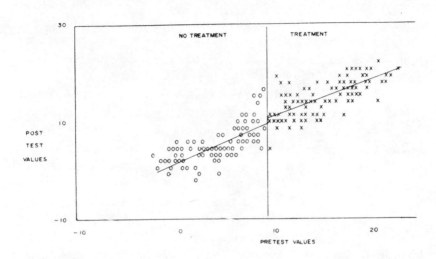

SOURCE: Campbell, D. T. Reforms as experiments. *American Psychologist*, 1969a, 24(4), 409-429. Copyright 1969 by the American Psychological Association. Reprinted by permission of the publisher and author.

Figure 14   Regression-Discontinuity Design: No Effect

Quarton's data had been reanalyzed by Sween allowing for a curvilinear fit, totally removing all indications of any effect.

Sween's and my work as reflected in "Reforms as Experiments" (1969) and her dissertation (1971) were supported by the National Science Foundation continuation grant GS1309X, initiated in September, 1966. Since then I have had continuous NSF support for work on quasi-experimental methodology. For the second 5-year continuation grant, beginning in 1971, Robert F. Boruch was coprincipal investigator, and with his arrival at Northwestern University, new phases of exploration of the regression-discontinuity design began. Boruch and I were both involved in the Social Science Research Council committee that produced Riecken et al.'s *Social Experimentation: A Method for Planning and Evaluating Social Intervention* (1974). While that

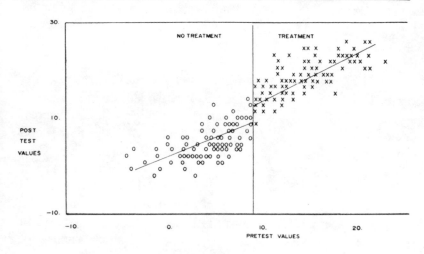

SOURCE: Campbell, D. T. Reforms as experiments. *American Psychologist*, 1969a, 24(4), 409-429. Copyright 1969 by the American Psychological Association. Reprinted by permission of the publisher and author.

Figure 15   Regression-Discontinuity Design: Genuine Effect

volume focused upon randomized assignment to treatment, its one chapter on quasi-experimental designs gave regression-discontinuity pride of place. The most dramatic graph in the whole book for illustrating results from a social program (medicare made available only to the lowest income group) can be interpreted as a regression-discontinuity analysis, although we did not do so in the text. I refer to Figure 4.19, p. 115, data provided by William Lohr of the National Center for Health Services Research.

The economist Arthur Goldberger consulted with the committee, and through this we became aware of his independent discovery of the method (1972a, 1972b; see also Cain, 1975), in papers focused on the problem of error in variables. His conclusion was that bias (in my language "regression artifacts" or "packaging underadjusted selection bias as treatment effects") occurred when assignment to treatment was based on a latent true score, but could be avoided by assignment on the basis of a known variable, even if fallible, as well as by random assignment to treatment. The illustrations were based on linear models and covariance analysis, and were the same as the linear regression-discontinuity analysis.

The independent rediscovery of the central idea of the regression-discontinuity design also occurred in the "special regression" model for compensatory education evaluation presented by Tallmadge and Horst (1976) and Tallmadge and Wood (1978). Although I was critical of several aspects of their variation on the design, such as the estimate of treatment effect at the treatment group pretest mean rather than cutoff and the absence of any attempt to address curvilinear relationships, the frequent use of their version in Title I compensatory education evaluations has provided us with the richest data base of applications yet produced much of which Trochim has reanalyzed according to our tradition.

The addition of Boruch at the faculty level and Charles Reichardt as a graduate student greatly augmented our Psychology Department group's formal statistical training. Meyer Dwass and Jerome Sacks, statisticians in Northwestern's Mathematics Department, had already been giving us occasional advice, but the presence of Boruch and Reichardt greatly increased the level of this interaction. Jerome Sacks decided that the problem of appropriate estimates of effects and tests of significance had a fundamental enough challenge to merit his professional attention. There emerged a seven-year period of close collaboration, most of it devoted to this problem.

The ultra-statistics they brought to the task are discontinuous with the statistical concepts social science methodologists are exposed to, and certainly beyond my mastery, as the least trained of our team. But I will make an effort to indicate some of the issues that motivated our high morale collective search. First of all, curve fitting by composite higher-order polynomials is a very unsatisfactory procedure. Bill Trochim, who joined our team for the last several years, introduced a procedure I recommend to others as a routine aid to inference. He plotted extrapolations of the resultant curve beyond the data it was designed to fit. These extensions were almost always wildly incredible. Since regression-discontinuity analysis, more than other uses of curve fitting, depends upon extrapolation, this is at least a significant conceptual weakness. (Sween emphasizes the minimal extrapolation involved and doubts that any practical liability ensues.)

Second, data points far removed from the cutting point contribute to the determination of the curve fully as much as do data points adjacent to the cutting point, and hence to the extrapolation generating the results of a hypothetical tie-breaking experiment. This weakness is shown in the "Footnote 8" episode above. On many grounds, one would prefer to have the data nearer the cutting point weighted more heavily than remote values in the determination of the curves and extrapolations. In the somewhat analogous problem in the interrupted time-series quasi-experimental design, the methods of Box and Tiao (1979, 1975) weight periods adjacent to the time of impact much more heavily than data from remote periods in generating the predicted values as to what would have been observed in the absence of the impact. While I have never understood how their differential weighting parameters were derived, they are consistent with assuming a positively proximally autocorrelated true score, where time points closer in time are more similar. I cannot now remember whether or not we ever tried out the Box-Tiao transfer function approach as though it were appropriate to regression-discontinuity data. In vision research, "spatial" autocorrelation concepts are now being used, and perhaps they could be rationalized for the regression-discontinuity setting on the basis of assuming a proximally autocorrelated structure in *attribute* space. This would be consistent with a presupposition of induction which I believe most of us share: In place of the assumption that nature is orderly, we assume that nature is "sticky" or "viscous" and that more adjacent regions in space, time, and attribute values are more similar than are remote ones, and can be generalized to with greater confidence (Campbell,

1966; Raser, Campbell, & Chadwick, 1970, pp. 197-199). As an illustration of what I mean a little closer to the present setting, suppose one did an analysis of variance experiment using as one of its classification criteria three levels of our eligibility dimension. We would expect disordinal interactions involving this dimension to occur more frequently if the three levels were far apart than if they were chosen from adjacent values.

I interrupt here to provide more details on the working context. This introductory essay is intended not only as a history of the ideas, not only as a partial agenda of unfinished problems, but also as evidence for a sociology and psychology of interdisciplinary collaboration. The period of collaboration that I am about to describe I regard as ideal, even though it did not promptly produce the practical new methods we hoped for. Myer Dwass's organization in 1972 of a Center for Statistics and Probability at Northwestern University created a faculty community in which Bob Boruch and I were invited to make a series of presen tations on unsolved problems in tests of significance for quasi- experimental designs. In the summer of 1973 and for two following summers, Clifford Spiegelman, a Ph.D. candidate in mathematical statistics under Sacks and Dwass, was employed by our NSF Grant. He spent most of his first summer going over Joyce Sween's Ph.D. dissertation, arguing vigorously with her (by then at nearby DePaul) and the rest of us about it. While in the end he approved of her procedures, it was a very time-consuming process, primarily because of the differences in statistical traditions employed. This experience greatly facilitated future communication. Out of this grew an ad hoc seminar on the problem, led by Jerome Sacks and another math department faculty member, Rose Ray. Such ad hoc seminars characterized our summertime interaction for a number of years. Sacks and Ray devoted great effort to the regression- discontinuity problem, their efforts supported by their own NSF Grants—only their students (Spiegelman and later George Knafl) and them only during summers were supported by the Campbell and Boruch NSF Grant. As a general strategy, I do strongly recommend such summer cross-disciplinary employment. A one-summer commitment permits cross-disciplinary collaboration on a tentative basis. These "shared" graduate students greatly facilitate faculty communication.

Sacks, with Rose Ray for the first year or so, took a general line of approach that I can only crudely characterize. In continuity with Sween's and my approach, the focus was on the sharp cutting point model, and the double-extrapolation technique—that is, extrapolating an estimated value at the cutting point from points below the cutting point, and comparing this with a similar independent estimate based upon the observations above the cutting point. All of the several approaches Sacks and Ray explored had the feature that observations nearer the cutting point (nearer the to-be-predicted value) were weighted more heavily than more remote observations. They also had the characteristic that no specific curve had to be estimated or assumed. (It helped me feel that I had a glimmer of their approaches to note that in extrapolating just one unit beyond the observed data, one will probably get very similar predicted values no matter what curve is employed.) They began first with linear and higher order splines, and then moved to still more complex techniques. Sacks's second approach (Sacks & Ylvisaker, 1978) was to estimate something like a mean prediction from all possible curves within a large class, without ever specifying any one of the curves. While the method is classified as "nonparametric," it produces a predicted value in the metric of the original measures. While costly in degrees of freedom or power, in many situations of application, there would be sufficient numbers of observations so that this cost could be met. George Knafl worked for two summers developing a computer program based upon this analysis. Again and again, computer simulations revealed flaws requiring fundamental changes in the model. Knafl's "Implementing Approximately Linear Models" (1978) reports on this stage.

In 1978, Sacks moved to Rutgers University for a two and a half years. In 1979, I moved to Syracuse University, and our close collaboration was interrupted. A comment in my progress report of August 31, 1978, has a misleading note of finality: "We have recognized from the very beginning that nothing useful might come of this approach, but have felt it very important to take advantage of the opportunity to get such advanced mathematical-statistical thinking turned to our tough applied social science problems." The importance of this exploration I want to heartily reassert from the perspective of 1984, but the note of finality was premature. With Sacks back at Northwestern and Knafl at nearby DePaul, they now have a workable program which can estimate the difference between the two regressions at the cutting point, provide a test of significance, and compare the slopes on either side of the cutting point. The method and program have been successfully applied to an engineering experiment (with the help of Spiegelman and Ylvisaker), and has been tried on some Educational Testing Service data sets. (See also Sacks, Knafl, & Ylvisaker, 1982a, 1982b.)

The Sacks, Ray, Ylvisaker, and Knafl approaches are only half of the story of this interdisciplinary collaboration. Clifford Spiegelman explored two still different approaches, devoting his Ph.D. dissertation to one of them, and continuing these developments subsequently (Spiegelman, 1976, 1977, 1979a, 1979b). Trochim has used his preferred approach in research on compensatory education (1980, 1982; Trochim & Spiegelman, 1980) and expounds it in this volume in his section on "The Analysis of the Fuzzy Regression-Discontinuity Design." Almost immediately Spiegelman abandoned dependence upon the fact of assignment-by-known-rule-or-measure, characterizing the "sharp" or "true" regression-discontinuity analysis, and his methods became a general procedure for assignment by latent unmeasured variables, purporting to avoid selection bias (regression artifacts) in the pretest-posttest nonequivalent control group design (Campbell & Stanley, 1963; Cook & Campbell, 1979), as well as in the "fuzzy" regression-discontinuity setting.

Our Northwestern Psychology Department group was simultaneously active in work on the method all through this period.

Bob Boruch, in addition to being our major participant in the recurrent series of ad hoc meetings with Dwass, Sacks, and their students, was active in both methodological developments and applications (Boruch, 1973, 1974, 1975a, 1975c, 1978). In 1973, Boruch and James S. Degracie, a statistician and Director of Evaluation for the Mesa Arizona School District, began collaboration or field tests of the design in eleven schools. The context was Title I reading programs in which children were supposed to be assigned to programs on the basis of pretest scores. Their findings on first, third, and fifth graders anticipated some of the problems in application of the design during the late 1970s: programs are not delivered uniformly (some children spend only a few weeks in a "nominally" year-long program); children are assigned to special services despite high scores on pretests; and difficulty in fitting curves to the R data due to floor and ceiling effects (Boruch & DeGracie, 1975, 1977; DeGracie & Boruch, 1977).

Especially important was Boruch's 1973 unpublished paper "Regression-Discontinuity Design Revisited," which recommended the comparison of a single overall regression model with the two separate regressions above and below the cutting point. This paper became the "in-house" reference on statistical analysis of the regression-discontinuity design, and provides the underlying model that Trochim developes in this volume.

Boruch was also the director of Trochim's dissertation, and through the heroic Holtzman project (Boruch et al., 1981) provided much of Trochim's funding, and, more important, access to those real-world data, available as a part of that enormous restudy of educational program evaluations. Developing such opportunities is no mean task, and they generally go unrecognized. The data themselves were available because of the efforts of John Evans and others at the U.S. Department of Education to incorporate higher scientific standards into federal regulations governing the evaluation of federally supported compensatory education programs.

Most underreported is the important role of Charles S. Reichardt in our ad hoc seminars and in guiding my own thinking. His Chapter 4 in Cook & Campbell (1979) on "The Statistical Analysis of Data from Nonequivalent Group Designs" is the best published exemplar of his influence, and includes an extension to the analysis of regression- discontinuity designs. For my third NSF five-year Continuation Grant (BNS76-23920, initiated January 1, 1977), he became my de facto codirector, my main statistical superego and intermediary for the continuing explorations in the interrupted time-series design, the cross-lagged panel correlation, the cross-lagged time series, and the regression-discontinuity design. Regarding the latter, I believe it will be helpful to future investigators to give a brief report on our explorations of the "fuzzy" case, joined at an early stage by Trochim, but unreported by him in this volume. To make these intelligible, I will start back again with the earlier presentations.

The concept of a "fuzzy" alternative to the regression-discontinuity design was born on the same day in 1958 as the "sharp" or "true" design. The National Merit decision panels were supplied with quantified examination data and quantified school grades, integrated into a single composite eligibility score. Had the panels been lazy, they could have merely ratified the division into winners, alternates, and also-rans that these scores dictated. Instead, while they made decisions highly related to these scores, they added unquantified evidence such as letters of recommendation and interviews by some panel member with each of the finalists. This evidence was used to change the rankings provided by the quantitative measures in some cases. Were one to have plotted the data organized by the quantified decision scores and the outcome measures, the outcome would be more or less as shown in either Figure 16 or 17 of "Reforms as Experiments" (1969). Figure 16 was based upon a no-effect simulation.

The presence in some cases of the award has made no effect on the relationship between the eligibility score and the outcome measure. This can be seen by comparing the envelope of the

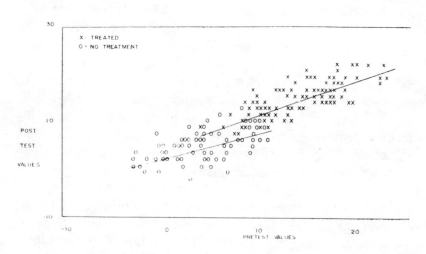

SOURCE: Campbell, D. T. Reforms as experiments. *American Psychologist*, 1969a, 24(4), 409-429. Copyright 1969 by the American Psychological Association. Reprinted by permission of the publisher and author.

Figure 16 Regression-Discontinuity Design: Fuzzy Cutting Point, Pseudo Treatment Effect Only

scatter diagram with that of Figure 14 shown above. Yet in Figure 16, the regression line for the award recipients lies significantly higher than that for the nonrecipients. This significant effect is due to underadjusted selection biases, is a "regression artifact," a pseudo-effect if misinterpreted as an effect of the award. My major emphasis then, and now, is that almost all modes of analyses of "fuzzy" regression-discontinuity data (with the possible exception of those of Spiegelman, Trochim; Barnow, Cain, & Goldberger, 1980) will produce this artifact, this "packaging of underadjusted selection differences as though they were treatment effects." This effect follows if some of the rank reversals made by the decision panel are "valid," either through picking up some current symptom of promise reflected in the later outcome but not present in the eligibility score, or more generally and less easily comprehended, by tapping the same factor or factors as did the quantitative decision score, but

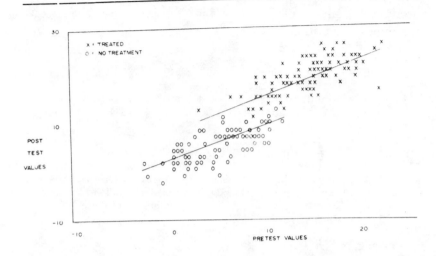

SOURCE: Campbell, D. T. Reforms as experiments. *American Psychologist*, 1969a, 24(4), 409-429. Copyright 1969 by the American Psychological Association. Reprinted by permission of the publisher and author.

Figure 17 Regression-Discontinuity Design: Fuzzy Cutting Point, with Real Treatment plus Pseudo Treatment Effects

through a partially different route, partially independent of the error component in the eligibility score. This need not at all imply that the award panel's decisions were *more* valid than the quantified eligibility score that the staff prepared. They could have been substantially less valid, considered as one single metric compared with another, and this regression artifact pseudo-impact would still occur if the large error component in the fallible award decision did not include all of the error of the eligibility score with which they had been provided. This being so, then for a given eligibility score, the award winners with that score would average higher than the nonwinners on the latent true score, and hence higher on the outcome score for that reason, even in the absence of any genuine award effect.

It will make these conditions and assumptions clearer to specify two alternative models for simulation of the fuzzy regression-discontinuity design.

Let E = Eligibility score
O = Outcome measure
A = Award, 1 if award, O if no award
I = Impact of award (zero in Figures 14 and 16, 2 in Figures 15 and 17)
e = Error component (in Figures 14-17, a normal random number)
T = Latent ability "True Score" (in Figures 14-17, a whole number between O and 20, selected at random, in later simulations, a normal random number multiplied by a constant.)

In these simulations, E and O are measures of parallel structure, sharing for each individual the same true score, but with independent error.

$$E = T + e_E$$

$$O = T + e_O + I$$

For the Sharp case, as in Figure 14,

$$A = 1 \text{ if } E < 10, 0 \text{ if } E > 10$$

For the fuzzy case of Figures 16 and 17, A^* is a third variable constructed is paralled with E and O, then dichotomized,

$$A^* = T + e_A$$

$$A = 1 \text{ if } A^* < 10, 0 \text{ if } A^* > 10$$

For Figures 15 and 17, the I, the impact of the award, $= 2$.

While I believe that the case of Figure 16 is the ubiquitous one, and the one appropriate for the National Merit award process, I feel the need to make explicit another possibility: It could have been that, merely to demonstrate their authority, the award panel deviated from the quantitative scores available in a purely haphazard, irrelevant way, adding error to the Eligibility score by an essentially random process, using no independent channels to the True Score. In such a case, the formula for the award would have been

$$A^* = E + e_A$$

$$\text{i.e., } A^* = T + e_E + e_A$$

$$A = 1 \text{ if } A^* < 10, \ 0 \text{ if } A^* > 10$$

In this event, for the null case of Figure 16, the regression lines for the awardees would have been the same as for the nonawardees. The whole scatter diagram envelope relating E to O would not have changed had this been the case, for Figures 16 and 17, but the regression lines would have. If one could be sure that the awards were based on a $T + e_E + e_A$ basis rather than a $T + e_A$ basis, then an ordinary covariance analysis would be appropriate in the "fuzzy" case too. (Most of the complications one would like to add to make the assignment processes more like reality, and Outcome measures factorially complex in ways not exactly paralleled in the Eligibility measure, will have implications making no-impact outcomes look like Figure 16.)

Reichardt, Trochim, and I initiated explorations of possible analyses of the fuzzy case seeking to find a way of distinguishing between null cases such as Figure 16 and true-effect cases such as Figure 17, within the tradition of higher-order polynomial curve fitting. These explorations are reported in a 1979 report of 35 pages, actually written by Trochim (Campbell, Reichardt & Trochim, 1979), available from Trochim or me. I would like to convey to future explorers in these areas the nature of our attack and its problems.

Our first attack was in imitation of the old experimental statistician's rule of thumb when not all of the experimental group receive the treatment, and some of the controls get it on their own: "Analyze 'em as you randomize 'em." A conservative test, because the impact estimate is diluted by the untreated and the overtreated, but one unlikely to produce pseudo-effects. Our version of this we called a "pseudo-sharp" analysis. With Figures 16 and 17 in front of one (assuming, however, better simulations involving a continuous true score, as per my earlier discussion of Footnote 8 [1969]), assume a pseudo-sharp cutoff point in the middle of the fuzzy transition region (the value 10 will do) and analyze as though all cases to the right received awards, all to the left did not, assuming linearity. Figure 16 will produce a no-effect outcome as did Figure 14. Figure 17, we thought, would show some effect, underestimated because of the misclassified cases. This degree of underestimation might be estimated and corrected for, if one assumed that the award had a constant effect regardless of eligibility-score level, since one knows how many have been misclassified for each eligibility score. Two considerations lead to the rejection of this approach. First, curvilinear fitting eliminates the effect in Figure 17, and we have many reasons to insist on rejecting a linear fit in most settings. (Floor effects and ceiling effects, differentially present in eligibility and outcome, are among them.) Second, in a simulation involving larger error (or unique) components, the overlap of award and nonaward cases would not be restricted to a central area, but would extend the entire range. In such a case, even a linear pseudo-sharp fit to a Figure 17 would show no effect. Evidence incidental to the Certificate of Merit analysis in Thistlethwaite and Campbell (1960: Table 1) shows that the distribution of scholarship awards may have had this characteristic. Another hope was that the linearity or curvilinearity might be established by analysis of the awardees and nonawardees separately, and then the pseudo-sharp analysis limited to this level of polynomial complexity, excluding higher-order ones. Again, if the fuzzy area were restricted to the central region, this might work, but not if it extended throughout the range of observations. In any event, the composite higher-order polynomials approach came to seem to us so unpredictably fickle as to recommend avoiding extreme dependence upon them which any such method would involve (Divgi's [1979] demonstration of the extreme costs in power of using higher-order polynomials augmented our dissatisfaction). In contrast, for the "pure" genuinely "sharp" regression-discontinuity design, the graphic presentation of scatter and column means, provides nondeceptive visual evidence reducing greatly the blind dependence upon curve-fitting statistics.

We considered one other approach to the fuzzy case that remains unexplored. A visual comparison of Figures 16 and 17 will help communicate the basic insight. One of the clues that indicate that in Figure 17 a substantial effect of the award has been built in, is that for the columns containing a mixture of Xs and Os, the column variance is larger than in the pure X or pure O columns, a feature which is absent in Figure 16. If one assumes homoscedasticity (which would be the case throughout if a normal random true score had been used, as in all later simulations from our group, by Sween and Trochim), then deviations from uniform column variance that correspond to the mixture of treated and untreated cases could be solvable for the treatment effect, by assuming a constant level of effect independent of true score or eligibility score, the impact-augmented variance being greatest in those columns in which half of the cases were treated. In general, homoscedasticity assumptions seem obviously untenable for both dimensions in a curvilinear plot. Perhaps for some such data sets, a limited homoscedasticity might be plausibly assumed, in the form of equal column variances in the absence of treatment effect. Having made this one assumption, no other assumption of curve form nor any estimate of it would be required in this analysis. Probably the lower the correlation between eligibility and outcome (that is, the larger the error components), the more reasonable are both assumptions of linearity and homoscedasticity, although this would not hold for the curvilinearity induced by floors or ceilings in the measures.

With my move to Syracuse in 1979 I became less directly involved in the continuing pursuits of an acceptable analysis for the fuzzy case, but received regular reports from Trochim on his own work and his collaboration with Spiegelman. Trochim began with Goldberger's (1972) observation that in the fuzzy case, the true regression lines in each group will be nonlinear. When joined, the overall regression line in the null case will approximate an s-shaped curve. Trochim concluded that a fuzzy case analysis would only work if one modeled the s-curve adequately. Trochim's basic insight was that a plot of the probability of assignment to treatment given the pretest score would, in the fuzzy case, typically yield an s-shaped curve of the type described by Goldberger. He tested this idea out in simulations that involved dividing the pretest scores into columns and, for each column, computing the percentage of cases assigned to treatments. This "assignment percentage" is a rough estimate of probability of assignment to treatment and is used in place of the dummy-coded assignment variable in the analysis. These simulations convinced him that the approach had promise and, through Bob Boruch, he contacted Cliff Spiegelman to obtain some statistical consultation on the feasibility of this analysis. It turned out that Spiegelman (1976, 1977, 1979) had recommended an approach that was mathematically related but more exact, although his recommendation had largely gone unnoticed. Spiegelman's version involved computing a moving average of the dummy-coded assignment variable across the range of the pretest and substituting this estimate of probability of assignment to treatment in the analysis. Trochim and Spiegelman (1980) then collaborated on a paper that presented the statistical argument and computer simulations (this work is described in Chapter 5 of this text). This "probability of assignment to treatment" approach to the fuzzy case (or, in Trochim's terms, the "relative assignment" approach) was independently suggested by Barnow, Cain, and Goldberger (1978) who recommended the fitting of a probit function to the relationship between the dummy-coded assignment variable and the pretest. The central difference between their approach and the Trochim and Spiegelman version is their selection of a profit function to model the s-shaped curvilinearity (Trochim and Spiegelman used essentially distribution-free strategy). While further work is needed to explore the appropriateness of these fuzzy regression-discontinuity analysis strategies, they appear to have great promise for offering a potential solution to one of the most critical problems besetting the design.

I will close this personalized history of the regression-discontinuity design with a report on some efforts to find analyzable instances already implemented in public administrative decision processes. As with randomized experiments, the design is best used prospectively, with quantified decision processes, recorded eligibility scores, and individual identification records permitting follow-up on outcomes at a later time. Usually its implementation will require a much effort and change of customary admission processes as would a randomized assignment to treatment. But with both methods, we should also be alert for retrospective applications, due to administrative arrangements designed for other purposes, such as fairness in the distribution of scarce resources. With regard to randomized assignment experiments, I think of the heroic efforts of Lee Sechrest to try to make use of the land-redistribution lotteries in Pakistan as well as lotteries elsewhere, and of Tom Cook's efforts, also failed, with the British lotteries (Cook & Campbell, 1979, pp. 372-373). A heroic retrospective application has been performed by Sween (1984). Using the applicants to the National Science Foundations's fellowship program between 1952 and 1972 with eleven measures of scientific achievement as outcome, up to twenty years beyond the application time for some cohorts, Sween found that the narrow range in which many of the variables were reported limited the usefulness of a regression-discontinuity design. She found, for example, that the final fellowship eligibility scores were limited to a 6-point ranking scale and that some of the outcome measures were dichotomous (e.g., whether or not the NSF applicant received a Ph.D. degree).

Sween suggests that one way of dealing with such data is to try to replicate treatment effects with other quasi-experimental approaches.

My Fulbright year at Oxford, 1968-1969, with the introductions provided by my host, Michael Argyle, was a great one for quasi-experimental explorations at the national level. I visited the Ministry of Transport and brought back the data on the British Breathalyser crackdown of 1967 (Ross, Campbell, & Glass, 1970; see also Ross, 1973). I spent still more time trying to find out if British Eleven-Plus Exams (which at age 11 tracked pupils into college preparatory or technical curricula) would provide an exemplar of the regression-discontinuity design (Campbell, 1969b). I visited the Education Ministry's research headquarters at Slough and learned that most regions in England had administered the Eleven-Plus Exams in conformity to a fuzzy rather than sharp model. For borderline pupils, decisions were modified by individual interviews, teachers' reports, opportunities to retake the exams, and so on. However, there were a few districts in which the total score on the one examination was decisive. In one of these, H. G. Armstrong, Educational Psychologist for the County Education Department, West Riding of Yorkshire, conducted at our grant's expense a sample follow-up of 1956 examinees. This follow-up showed that none of the pupils near the university track cutoff point were getting into any university. The 1946 change in the British educational system had greatly increased the number of pupils being trained for university education, and the Eleven-Plus examination system had democratized to some extent the choice of those trained, but the number of university openings had not been proportionally increased. Thus the upward mobility "opportunity effect" or passing the exam could not be measured for those near the cutting point, where the regression-discontinuity technique could have been used. It is quite conceivable that for this range of pupils their eventual economic well-being had been harmed rather than helped by being placed in the university track rather than in the technical training track. For such a study, the West

Riding of Yorkshire records would have made possible an excellent regression-discontinuity study. This was never explored.

Through George Madaus of Boston College, I later became acquainted with Professor Thomas Kellaghan of the Educational Research Centre, St. Patrick College, Dublin, and from them learned of the Irish Learning Certificate, given to students around 16 years of age, the passing of which had diverse beneficial effects upon careers including entry to civil service jobs and universities. Our project supported Vincent Greeney in collecting test score records of the 1955 examination, and exploring the possibility of follow-ups. The records gave names in Gaelic spelling. For these, there are often several options in English spellings. Telephone books and other tools for following up individuals fifteen years later usually used English spelling. The judgment was made that usefully dependable follow-up was unfeasible. The structure of the examination system was very complex, with several patterns of passing various numbers of the dozen or so separate exams qualifying an examinee for an overall pass. George Tanaka and I made several analyses trying to tease out regression-discontinuity design possibilities, and in the process encountered one of those understandable irregularities of scoring that threatens the homogeneity-of-metric assumptions upon which the method depends. The physics exam was scored quantitatively, with a fixed-in-advance score for passing. The distribution of scores approximated a normal bell shape except for the near total absence of scores just one step below the passing score, with a corresponding anamolous peak one and two points above. The test graders were reluctant to leave unrevised an item scoring that left examinees just one point below passing. (Appropriate assumptions about this process would still have permitted a very plausible regression-discontinuity analysis.)

The regression-discontinuity design has received its greatest use to date in the evaluation of compensatory education programs. Trochim has investigated over 200 such regression-discontinuity analyses, has illustrated extensively the difficulties involved in implementing the design and the implications of these problems for estimates of treatment effect. His work is particularly valuable for its description of the interaction of social and political issues with the use and validity of the regression-discontinuity design. But this history is best told by Trochim himself and at this point I turn the reader over to his fine extended presentation.

References

Barnow, B. S., Cain, G. C., & Goldberger, A. S. Issues in the analysis of selectivity bias. Pp. 42-59 in E. W. Stormsdorfer & G. Farkas (Eds.), *Evaluation Studies Review Annual, Vol. 5.* Beverly Hills, CA: Sage, 1980.

Boruch, R. F. *Regression-discontinuity designs revisited.* Unpublished manuscript, Northwestern University, 1973.

Boruch, R. F. *Regression-discontinuity designs: A summary.* Paper presented at the annual meeting of the American Educational Research Association, Chicago, May, 1974.

Boruch, R. F. *Executive Summary: Issues in the analysis of regression discontinuity data.* Psychology Department, Northwestern University, January 5, 1975a.

Boruch, R. F. Coupling randomized experiments and approximations to experiments in social program evaluation. *Sociological Methods and Research,* 1975b, 4(1), 31-53.

Boruch, R. F. *Regression-discontinuity evaluation of the Mesa Reading Program: Background and technical report.* Unpublished report, NIE Project on Secondary Analysis. Psychology Department, Northwestern University, November, 1975c.

Boruch, R. F. *Double pretests for checking certain threats to the validity of some conventional evaluation designs or, stalking the null hypothesis.* Unpublished manuscript, Northwestern University, 1978.

Boruch, R. F., Cordray, D. S., Pion, G. M., & Leviton, L. A mandated appraisal of evaluation practices: Digest of recommendations to the Congress and the Department of Education. *Educational Researcher,* 1981, 10, 10-13.

Boruch, R. F., & DeGracie, J. S. *Regression-discontinuity evaluation of the Mesa reading program: Background and technical report.* Unpublished manuscript, Northwestern University, November, 1975.

Boruch, R. F., & DeGracie, J. S. *The use of regression-discontinuity models with criterion referenced testing in the evaluation of compensatory education.* Paper presented at the annual meeting of the American Educational Research Association, April, 1977.

Box, G. E. P., & Tiao, G. C. A change in level of a non-stationary time series. *Biometrika*, 1965, 52, 181-192.

Box, G. E. P., & Tiao, G. C. Intervention analysis with applications to economic and environmental problems. *Journal of the American Statistical Association*, 1975, 70, 70-92.

Cain, G. G. Regression and selection models to improve nonexperimental comparisons. Pp. 297-317 in Carl A. Bennett & Arthur A. Lumsdaine, *Evaluation and experiment*. New York: Academic Press, 1975.

Campbell, D. T. *The principle of proximal similarity in the application of science.* Duplicated manuscript, Northwestern University, 1966.

Campbell, D. T. Reforms as experiments. *American Psychologist*, 1969a, 24(4), 409-429.

Campbell, D. T. *Measuring the "opportunity effects" of university tracking by means of past "Eleven Plus" decisions.* Duplicated manuscript, Department of Psychology, Northwestern University, 1969b.

Campbell, D. T. Focal local indicators for social program evaluation. *Social Indicators Research*, 1976, 3, 237-256.

Campbell, D. T., Reichardt, C. S., & Trochim, W. *The analysis of the "fuzzy" regression-discontinuity design: Pilot simulations.* Unpublished manuscript, Northwestern University, 1979.

Campbell, D. T., & Stanley, J. C. Experimental and quasi-experimental designs for research. In N. L. Gage (Ed.), *Handbook of research on teaching.* Chicago: Rand McNally, 1963.

Cook, T. D., & Campbell, D. T. The design and conduct of quasi-experiments and true experiments in field settings. In Marvin D. Dunnette (Ed.), *Handbook of industrial and organizational psychology.* Chicago: Rand McNally, 1976.

Cook, T. D., & Campbell, D. T. *Quasi-experimentation: Design and analysis issues for field settings.* Chicago: Rand McNally, 1979.

Cronbach, L. J., Rogosa, D. R., Floden, R. E., & Price, G. G. *Analysis of covariance in nonrandomized experiments: Parameters affecting bias. Occasional paper, Stanford University, Stanford Evaluation Consortium, 1977.*

DeGracie, J. S., & Boruch, R. F. *Regression-discontinuity analysis of the Mesa reading compensatory programs.* Presentation at the annual meeting of the Educational Research Association, New York, 1977.

Divgi, D. R. *Choosing polynomials in the regression-discontinuity design.* Duplicated research report, Syracuse University, December 7, 1979.

Goldberger, A. S. Selection bias in evaluation treatment effects: Some formal illustrations. *Discussion Papers*, 123-72. Madison: Institute for Research on Poverty, University of Wisconsin, 1972.

Knafl, G. J. *Implementing approximately linear models.* Duplicated research report, Northwestern University, 1978.

Raser, J. R., Campbell, D. T., & Chadwick, R. W. Gaming and simulation for developing theory relevant to international relations. *General Systems*, XV, 1970.

Reichardt, C. S. The statistical analysis of data from nonequivalent group designs. In T. D. Cook and D. T. Campbell (Eds.), *Quasi-experimentation: Design and analysis issues for field settings.* Chicago: Rand McNally, 1979.

Riecken, H. W., Boruch, R. F., Campbell, D. T., Caplan, N., Glennan, T. K., Pratt, J. W., Rees, A., & Williams, W. *Social experimentation: A method for planning and evaluating social intervention.* New York: Academic Press, 1974.

Ross, H. L. Law, science, and accidents: The British Road Safety Act of 1967. *Journal of Legal Studies,* 1973, 2, 1-78.

Ross, H. L., Campbell, D. T., & Glass, G. V. Determining the social effects of a legal reform: The British "breathalyser" crackdown of 1967. *American Behavioral Scientist,* 1970, 13, 493-509.

Sacks, J., & Ylvisaker, D. Linear estimates for approximately linear models. *Annals of Statistics,* 1978, 6, 1122-1138.

Sacks, J., Knafl, G., & Ylvisaker, D. Model robust confidence intervals, *Journal for Statistical Planning and Inference,* 1982a, 6, 319-334.

Sacks, J., Knafl, G., & Ylvisaker, D. Model robust confidence intervals II. Pp. 87-102 in S. Gupta & J. Berger (Eds.), *Statistical decision theory and related topics,* Vol. 2. New York: Academic Press, 1982b.

Seaver, W. B., & Quarton, R. J. Regression-discontinuity analysis of Dean's List effects. *Journal of Educational Psychology,* 1976, 68, 459-465.

Spiegelman, C. H. *Two methods of analyzing a nonrandomized experiment "adaptive" regression and a solution to Reiersol's problem.* Unpublished Ph.D. dissertation, Northwestern University, 1976.

Spiegelman, C. H. *A technique for analyzing a pretest-posttest nonrandomized field experiment.* Florida State University, Statistics Report M435, 1977.

Spiegelman, C. H. A technique for analyzing an educational program with Monte-Carlo results. *Journal of Educational Statistics,* 1979.

Spiegelman, C. H. Estimating the effect of a large scale pretest-posttest social program. *Proceedings of the Social Statistics Section,* American Statistical Association, 1979, 370-373.

Spiegelman, C. H. On estimating the slope of a straight line when both variables are subject to error. *The Annals of Statistics,* 1979, 7(1), 201-206.

Stradhaus, A. M. *A comparison of the subsequent achievement of marginal selectees and rejectees for the Cincinnati public schools' special college preparatory program: An application of Campbell's regression-discontinuity design.* D.Ed. Dissertation, University of Cincinnati, 1972.

Struening, E. L., & Brewer, M. B. (Eds.), *Handbook of evaluation research: university edition.* Beverly Hills, CA: Sage, 1983.

Sween, J. A. *The experimental regression design: An inquiry into the feasibility of nonrandom treatment allocation.* Ph.D. Dissertation, Northwestern University, 1971.

Sween, J. A. *Regression discontinuity: Statistical tests of significance when units are allocated to treatments on the basis of quantitative eligibility.* Unpublished draft, Department of Sociology, DePaul University, April, 1977.

Sween, J. A. *Academic career achievements of U.S. scientists: The contribution of the National Science Foundation Graduate Fellowship Program.* Report to the National Science Foundation, Department of Sociology, DePaul University, 1984.

Thistlethwaite, D. L., & Campbell, D. T. Regression-discontinuity analysis: An alternative to the ex post facto experiment. *Journal of Educational Psychology,* 1960, 51, 309-317.

Trochim, W. *The regression-discontinuity design in Title I evaluation: Implementation, analysis, and variations.* Ph.D. dissertation, Department of Psychology, Northwestern University, 1980.

Trochim, W. Methodologically based discrepancies in compensatory education evaluations. *Evaluation Review,* August, 1982.

Trochim, N., & Spiegelman, C. H. The relative assignment variable approach to selection bias in pretest-posttest group designs. *Proceedings of the Social Statistics Section,* American Statistical Association, 1980.

1

Introduction to
Regression-Discontinuity

The term "regression-discontinuity" is a formidable one. Both of its parts have negative connotations in their common meaning—the notion of "regression" implying a move backward or a reversion to some prior state; the term "discontinuity" implying some type of interruption or disruption of a process. In fact, the negative connotations are inaccurate from a methodological perspective—the design is one of the strongest methodological alternatives to randomized experiments when one is interested in studying social programs.

Despite the methodological advantages of the regression-discontinuity design, it has received little use in modern social research. There are several reasons for this. First, the design is probably not well understood. Until recently, few introductory methodology texts discussed it in any detail. This is most likely because the design is inherently counter-intuitive. In other multiple group designs, comparison groups are chosen because they are similar or comparable to the groups receiving the program under study. In the regression-discontinuity design, the program and comparison groups are deliberately and specifically different in preprogram ability. If the program group consists of low pretest scorers, the comparison group will, by the structure of the design, be higher scorers, and vice versa. Because of this, the regression-discontinuity design appears, at first glance, to be in flagrant violation of at least two major threats to internal validity: regression to the mean and selection biases. In fact, closer inspection of the logic of the design shows that these threats are not prominant, but undiscriminating interpretation of these issues can make the design a difficult one to defend when facing audiences that are only briefly schooled in the theory of validity.

Second, the design is not easy to implement. While all research strategies are susceptible to poor implementation, in some ways the regression-discontinuity design may be more sensitive than most. In this sense, the strength of the design may also be its greatest weakness. Its specific pattern of intervention into social reality must be followed strictly. The correct execution of the regression-discontinuity design is threatened by social, political, and logistical problems in much the same way as in randomized experiments, and in some cases the difficulties are more serious. For example, assumptions about the functional form of the pre-post distribution are far more critical in regression-discontinuity than randomized designs.

Third, the statistical analysis of the regression-discontinuity design is not trivial. In typical circumstances, a good deal of judgment is required to accomplish the statistical modeling. The nature of the design makes it particularly susceptible to the influences of outliers, floor and ceiling effects, test "chance" levels, and similar factors that may be less salient in other strategies. In the end, one must rely heavily on assumptions of the statistical model used and on the ability to discern visually whether a program effect is plausible.

Fourth, the range of applicability of the design is not fully appreciated. Typical presentations stress the pre-post program-comparison group version of regression-discontinuity, but the design is far more flexible than that. Especially neglected is the potential for using the regression-discontinuity design coupled with quantitative resource or program allocation formulas common to many social programs.

Finally, there are few good instances of the use of this design to guide researchers. Outside of its use in evaluating the effects of compensatory education programs, few published examples can be found.

Despite its very real limitations, there are two major reasons that the design needs to be understood better by the applied social research community. First, it is important as an applied research technique. It is conceptually compatible with the political and social goal of allocating scarce resources to those persons or entities that need or deserve them most. The alternatives to regression-discontinuity typically require that persons who might otherwise be eligible for a program be denied it, either arbitrarily or for the sake of a rigorous test of the effectiveness of the intervention. Second, regression-discontinuity is important for theoretical reasons alone. It occupies a critical position in the taxonomy of research designs and, because of this, increases our understanding of other designs and suggests solutions to generic technical problems, most notably the difficulties associated with selection biases.

THE BASIC REGRESSION-DISCONTINUITY DESIGN

Before discussing the relationship of regression-discontinuity to other research designs and its place in the context of social policy evaluation, it is important for the reader to have an initial understanding of the mechanics of the design. In the next two sections, a simple example of the design is presented along with an introductory discussion of some of the major issues of relevance.

The regression-discontinuity design is one member of a larger class of quasi-experimental methods that can be termed pretest-posttest group designs. In their most basic form, they require a preprogram measure (e.g., the pretest), a postprogram measure that can reflect the effect of the program being studied (e.g., the posttest), and a measure that describes the assignment status of the persons in the study (assignment variable), usually whether they received the program (program group) or did not (comparison or "control" group).

The regression-discontinuity design can be distinguished from the other pretest-posttest group designs by the nature of its assignment strategy. In regression-discontinuity all persons are assigned to program or comparison group *solely* on the basis of a cutoff score on the preprogram measure. Thus, once a cutoff score has been established, all persons scoring on one side of this score are assigned to one group (e.g., program) while those scoring on the other side are assigned to the other (e.g., comparison). The design is useful whenever one wishes to study a program or procedure that is given out on the basis of need or merit. This is the case in compensatory education where children in greatest need of additional instruction (as reflected in a pre-instruction measure) are targeted to receive the services; or, in medicine, where those who most require a new surgical procedure (as reflected in a presurgery measure of severity of illness) are selected for surgery; or, in the awarding of scholarships where those who exceed a certain cutoff criteria (as measured in a test of skill or intelligence) are given the award. In all cases, the postprogram measure is presumed to reflect the effect of the program or procedure.

Perhaps the best way to understand the idea of the regression-discontinuity design is through graphs. First, consider what happens when persons are measured "pre" and "post" but no program is administered (i.e., the null case). This situation is depicted in Figure 1.1. The figure shows the relationship between the pre and post measures for each person in the study. The horizontal scale indicates the range of pretest values while the vertical depicts the posttest. Each point on the graph reflects a pretest and posttest score for a given individual. A continuous straight regression line with positive slope would describe the entire distribution well.

Next, let us consider how the data might look when using the regression-discontinuity design. In Figure 1.2, hypothetical data is presented for the case of regression-discontinuity applied to the study of a compensatory education program. In this hypothetical example, the cutoff score is zero and all students achieving a

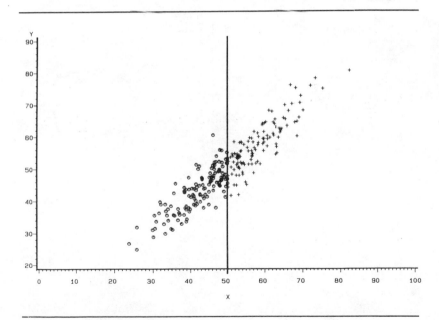

Figure 1.1   The Regression-Discontinuity Null Case

preprogram score that is less than or equal to zero receive the special instruction (program group). In the graph, program group scores are indicated by an "X" while comparison scores are signified by an "O."

We can understand how the regression-discontinuity design works by considering first just the comparison group scores. The portion of the graph to the right of zero on the preprogram measure shows the pretest and posttest scores for those students who did not receive the special instruction being studied. A

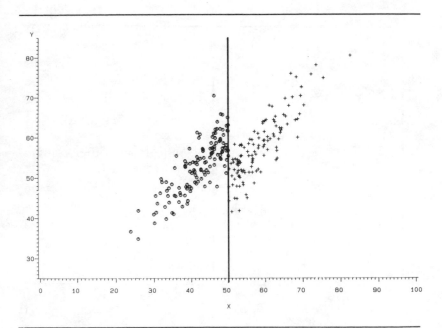

Figure 1.2   The Regression-Discontinuity Design with a Program Effect

regression line could be fit to these scores to describe the pre-post relationship. If this regression line were extended into the region of the program group scores (i.e., to the left of zero on the preprogram measure) the extension would represent the pre-post relationship that would be expected in the program group if they, like the comparison group, had not received the instruction (as shown in Figure 1.1). This situation is shown in Figure 1.3 where the comparison group regression line is indicated by the solid line to the right of zero on the pretest and the expected program group line is indicated by the dashed line.

The essential idea in regression-discontinuity analysis is to determine whether the observed pre-post relationship in the program group differs from the expected relationship as derived from the comparison group scores. For reasons that will be discussed in Chapter 5 this is typically most appropriately reflected in the difference between the program and comparison group regression lines *at the cutoff point.* In Figure 1.3, the obtained program group regression line is indicated by the solid line to the left of zero on the pretest. For any pretest value the obtained line has a higher posttest score than does the line projected from the comparison group scores (in this example, the difference is a constant amount). This indicates that the program group students scored higher on the posttest than was "expected" and one can infer that the instruction had a positive effect on posttest scores. Similarly, if the observed program group regression line had been displaced below the expected line, one could assume that the instruction affected students negatively.

The vertical difference between regression lines at the cutoff point corresponds to what is typically called a "main effect." The design can also be used to examine "interaction effects", that is, the degree to which program gain is related to the pre-program measure. Figure 1.4 shows only the regression lines for a number

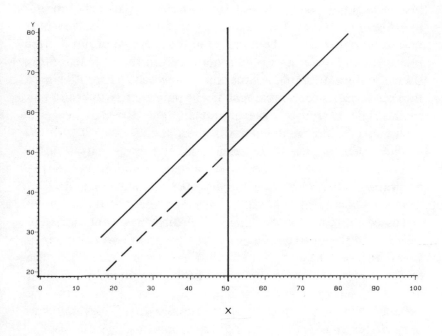

Figure 1.3   Regression Lines for Regression-Discontinuity Design of Figure 1.2

of possible outcomes from a regression-discontinuity design.[1] Figure 1.4a shows the null case—there is no discontinuity in the overall regression lines at the cutoff. Figure 1.4b shows the case just discussed—an additive positive program effect. A negative effect, or program group loss is depicted in Figure 1.4c. Notice that the program group scored *lower* on the posttest than would be predicted from extension of the comparison group line. Figure 1.4d shows an interaction effect without a main effect. While not everyone in the program group appeared to benefit (those nearest the cutoff did not gain), the lower the preprogram score, the greater the posttest gain. Thus, an interaction effect is defined as a discontinuity in the slope of the regression lines at the cutoff. Figure 1.4e shows both a main and interaction effect—discontinuities in both the level and slope between the two groups.

It should be recognized that the above examples illustrate only a simple version of the design. For instance, the preprogram measure can be a pretest (i.e., the same test as the posttest or an alternate form of the same test) or it can be a different measure or composite of several measures. The program group need not be the persons scoring below the cutoff score. If the program is given out on the basis of merit, those scoring above the cutoff might receive it. It is not necessary that the pre-post relationship be linear—any shape that can be modeled with a regression line would be appropriate. The design is not only appropriate for what is traditionally termed "outcome" evaluation. If suitable measures are taken (of all participants, not just the program group) while the program is in action (e.g., measures of change in attitude over the course of the program), the design can be used to study process issues. Similarly, as long as a cutoff assignment rule was followed and persons on both side of the cutoff were measured, the design can be used in a post hoc analysis of archival data. Variations of the design are discussed more fully in Chapter 3.

SOME ASSUMPTIONS OF REGRESSION-DISCONTINUITY

All research designs are based on assumptions. Some are common to almost every design—sufficient quality of measurement, statistical power, correct implementation of the program, and so on. Others are peculiar to a given design and serve to set it apart. The regression-discontinuity design can be characterized by three central assumptions: perfect assignment relative to the cutoff, correct specification of the statistical model, and the absence of "coincidental" functional discontinuities. All three are related to the most distinctive feature of the design, the assignment to condition solely on the basis of a cutoff score on a preprogram measure.

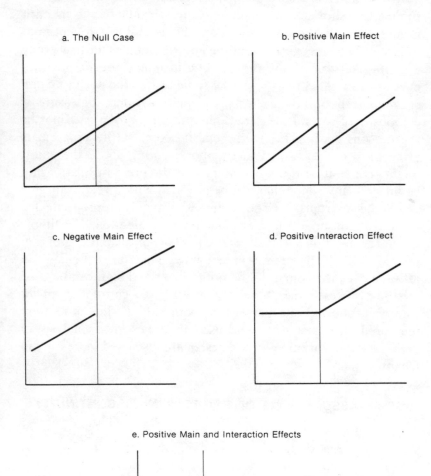

Figure 1.4   Hypothetical Regression Line Outcomes for a Compensatory Regression-Discontinuity Design

The first assumption of the regression-discontinuity design has to do with adherence to the cutoff criterion. The design assumes that there is no misassignment in terms of this cutoff—persons who by their preprogram score should be placed in one group must not be placed in the other. Misassignment can occur for a variety of reasons. If potential participants have political "pull," they may be able to prevail upon administrators to misassign them into a desirable program or out of an undesirable one. Sometimes, misassignment can arise because a well-intentioned administrator does not wish to deny a potentially beneficial program to certain persons, especially those narrowly missing inclusion. Another cause of misassignment is administrative error, that is, insufficient vigilance in assuming that the cutoff criterion is adhered to. Some misassignment will be easily detected by noting cases that did not fall into the appropriate groups, while at other times it will be impossible to detect as when persons are given the program but their participation is not recorded.

Misassignment relative to the cutoff score has been termed "fuzzy" regression-discontinuity by Campbell (1969). When the cutoff is strictly adhered to, we can term the design "sharp" regression-discontinuity. With certain types of "fuzzy" assignment (e.g., random misassignment around the cutoff) the traditional analytic strategy discussed later will yield unbiased estimates of program effect. Other types of misassignment are known to yield biased estimates (Goldberger, 1972). The basic regression-discontinuity design requires sharp assignment. However, the design would be far more flexible if this assumption could be relaxed and fuzzy assignment allowed, thus making it possible for administrators to use more discretion in the assignment of special cases. There has been a good deal of theoretical work on analytic strategies appropriate for "fuzzy" regression-discontinuity (Campbell, Reichardt, & Trochim, 1979; Trochim, 1980; Barnow, Cain, & Goldberger, 1978; Spiegelman, 1976) that will be discussed in greater detail later.

A second major assumption of regression-discontinuity is that the analytical model used to estimate program effect accurately describes the true pretest functional relationship. For example, if the true relationship is in fact linear, but the analysis uses only quadratic, cubic, logarithmic, or other functions, biased estimates of effect are likely. Since the true model is seldom known, one usually chooses a model either a priori, based upon experience with similar data, or through testing likely alternative models. An analyst might, for example, state a priori that the pre-post relationship in the absence of a program is linear, infer from previous experience with the same test and subjects that it is so, or test this hypothesis against likely alternatives such as quadratic, logarithmic, and so on. The problem with models selected in this way is that one is never sure that the chosen model is correct. One approach to model specification is outlined in Chapter 5. It is appropriate only for a certain class of functions (i.e., when the true pre-post relationship can be expressed as a finite and low-order polynomial) and is designed to reduce the possibility of selecting estimates of effect that are biased due to model misspecification.

The third assumption is that there are no other factors that, even in the absence of the program, would result in a discontinuity in the pre-post relationship at the cutoff point. This can be conceptualized in two ways. First, if an effect is observed, it may be due to something other than the program. Second, the effect could be partially due to the program and partially to some other factor. The latter implies that the size of the program effect may be incorrectly estimated and that, even if no effect is observed, this may be due to either an ineffective program or to counteracting factors that disguise the effect.

Any factor that affects the scores in one group and not the other can lead to a discontinuity that is mistaken for a program effect. For example, if the program participants are put in one setting while the controls are in another, any factor associated with the setting (and not the program) that affects the posttest will look like a program effect. Therefore, the regression-discontinuity design assumes that all group factors that differentially affect the posttest, other than the program itself, are accounted for in either the design or analysis.

This brief look at the assumptions that underlie the regression-discontinuity design illustrates the importance of investigating the application of the design in various contexts. While methodologists can outline potential violations of assumptions, a study of research implementation can determine which assumptions are violated most often and why. The final two chapters of this work involve an investigation of the appropriateness of the assumptions of regression-discontinuity within the context of compensatory education where the design has been almost exclusively used.

SOCIAL POLICY AND RESEARCH DESIGN

The regression-discontinuity design is not the only strategy available in social research, nor is it necessarily the best in any specific setting. Put simply, there is more than one way to evaluate any social intervention. In order to understand when regression-discontinuity might be appropriate it is important to look at its relationship to other designs and to consider some of the factors that affect design choice in social policy evaluation contexts. This section discusses the ways in which society allocates resources (e.g., social programs and their goods) and how this is related to the selection of research designs.

Over the past few decades, applied social scientists have aggressively sought strategies for evaluating the effectiveness of social programs and interventions. A major question is whether these programs "help" or "make a difference" in some problem area. The question is by definition a relative one—we typically want to know whether a particular policy works better than some other one or better than no active policy at all. In order to assess this, we often want to look not only at those who receive the program being evaluated, but also at a similar group of persons who do not, because they provide a standard of comparison against which the program in question can be weighed. The issue of who receives the program and who does not is therefore critical not only from a programatic perspective, but also from an evaluative one. Often these two points of view operate at cross-purposes. The policymaker addresses a political and economic context, allocating resources and programs where they might have the greatest impact. The evaluator is primarily concerned with determining that impact and is often willing to deny the resources (even if only temporarily) from some of the target population so that a good comparison group might be attained and the program might be "fairly" tested. If the two perspectives are to be linked, the policymaker must recognize the evaluator's need for a comparative standard that is fair and the evaluator must seek research strategies that are consistent with the political and economic realities of resource allocation.

All societies follow certain procedures or rules for allocating resources. In this context, "resources" can be viewed in a broad sense and can consist of wealth, material goods, status, and such negative entities as penalties and taxes. In a social policy sense, goods are often allocated through definable programs that are constructed to assure better health, education, financial security, and so on.

Most allocation procedures can be classified broadly into three types (or some combination of these). The first of these can be termed a *lottery* allocation. Here, all potentially eligible persons are placed in a "pool" and each is given an equal chance of being selected to receive the resource in question. The notion goes back to the ancient practice of "drawing lots" to allocate scarce resources. Sometimes the practice is used to allocate risk levels, as when soldiers draw lots to determine who will undertake a dangerous mission. This strategy was used to determine which young men in this country would be drafted for military service during the Vietnam war and is also the basis for the awarding of financial prizes to those who participate in state-organized gambling. In social program arenas, it has been used to determine who should be selected to test new drugs or surgical techniques, novel sentences for criminal offences, new approaches to taxation and welfare, and a variety of other innovations.

A second and probably more common form of resource disbursement can be termed *political* allocation. Here, resources are only partially (if at all) given to those who need or deserve them according to some rational criterion. Instead, the process is either haphazard and marginally specifiable or is heavily influenced by political and economic power (often in ways that are difficult to detect). In fact, it is often the unspecifiability of the process that makes it so desirable. The allocation of careers through "old boy" or "old girl" networks or of military expenditures on the basis of geographically based congressional power are examples of this type of allocation.

The final strategy for allocation can be termed *meritorious*. In this case, persons are given resources because according to some specific criteria they "deserve" or "need" them. The strategy is more clearly specifiable than a political one and, therefore, more inherently accountable. It occurs when awards are given to those who perform well or show promise or when special assistance is given to those who perform poorly or are most needy. For example, risky new surgical techniques may be tried only for those who are most desperate or special financial grants given only to those who are most poverty stricken.

Distinctions between allocation strategies are critical when trying to evaluate the effects that resources have on peoples' lives. Typically, the evaluator will have little control over the manner in which resources are disbursed and will have to devise research designs that can be used for various allocation procedures that might be followed. It is important to bear in mind that from an evaluative point of view it is critical to find a fair comparison group against which the resource in question can be evaluated.

The three allocation procedures just described yield different comparison groups by definition and these will differ in the quality of their comparative value. When one allocates by lottery, there will necessarily be a group of people who do not receive the resource by chance alone. All things being equal, this group will be similar to the recipient group in most ways. With political allocation, groups who don't receive the resource are likely to be deficient in political or economic power (or in some other way) and this deficiency will be difficult to specify because of the partially covert nature of the process. With meritorious allocation, persons who do not receive the resource will differ from those who do, but here the difference will be specifiable especially if the criteria for allocation are clear. From an evaluation perspective, lottery allocation yields the most similar comparison group while meritorious allocation generates the least similar. With political allocation it is generally difficult to know how similar the recipient and nonrecipient groups might be. When the degree of similarity can be specified accurately, the evaluator will usually be able to make fairer comparisons (lottery or meritorious allocation), but when it is not (political allocation) the comparisons will be tenuous and assumption-laden.

It is not surprising that the three major types of research designs that can be used to test the effects of social programs correspond to the three allocation strategies outlined above. The designs are distinguishable on the basis of the procedures that are used to assign persons to receive the program study (i.e., the procedures used to "allocate the program"). When persons are randomly assigned or assigned by lottery, the design is termed "experimental." The groups that are created are probabilistically equivalent on preprogram characteristics, that is, on average the groups will appear similar on any prestudy traits that are measured. Designs that are not based on random assignment are traditionally termed "quasi-experimental." They "look like" experimental designs in that they include comparison groups, but we can question whether the groups are truly similar.

The political and meritorious cases can be distinguished by the degree to which we can specify the assignments procedure and the similarity between the recipients and nonrecipients. Both cases are likely to yield "nonequivalent" or dissimilar groups, and, therefore, both designs are considered "nonequivalent group

designs." But in the case of meritorious allocation, the assignment criteria are specifiable—it is implied that there is some
cutoff value or values on some criterion measure or measures that
determine who receives the resource and who does not. For
instance, persons who fall below some specific income level might
receive a financial grant; students who exceed a specific grade
point level might win a scholarship; patients who exceed some
particular illness level might be given an experimental treatment
or therapy. The term "regression-discontinuity" is used to refer
to research designs that are based on meritorious allocation
where cutoff values on preprogram criterion measures are used to
determine assignment to condition. The distinctions between
research designs and their relationships to allocation procedures
are summarized in Figure 1.5. Note especially that the distinction
between quasi-experimental designs in general and the specific
subgroup known as regression-discontinuity designs depends on
the specifiability of the assignment criteria and, more particularly, on the existence of a cutoff value on some continuous
preprogram criterion measure.

Another way to view the distinctions between designs is
through graphs of their assignment strategies. Figure 1.6 shows
such a graph for a simple two-group pretest-posttest randomized
experiment. The pretest is graphed on the x axis and the
probability of assignment to the program group on the y axis. In
the simple random assignment case, the odds of being assigned to
the program are 50/50 for all pretest scores and therefore the
graph consists of a horizontal line at p = .5. At the other extreme
is the regression-discontinuity design. Figure 1.7 shows the
assignment probabilities when those who score below a certain
pretest value are given the program (i.e., the "compensatory"
case).[2] For those below the cutoff the probability of assignment to
programs is p = 1.0, while for those above the cutoff it is p = 0.0.
All other nonequivalent group designs have assignment functions
that range between the extremes of random and cutoff assignment. Two examples are shown in Figure 1.8. If the groups that

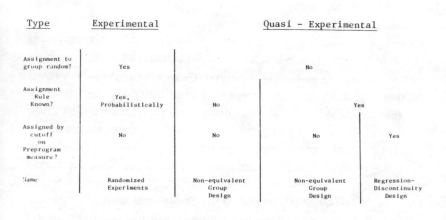

Figure 1.5   Classification of Causal Hypothesis Testing Research Designs

are selected are nearly equivalent, the assignment function will more closely approximate that of the randomized experiment as shown in Figure 1.3. If the groups differ considerably beforehand, the function will be closer to that of the regression-discontinuity design.

These graphs of the probability of assignment for any pretest point out the underlying continuum between experimental and quasi-experimental designs in terms of preprogram equivalence between groups. At one end of the continuum are randomized experiments that guarantee that the groups will be probabilistically equivalent on the pretest. At the other extreme are regression-discontinuity designs that guarantee a maximum nonequivalence. Nonequivalent group designs fall between these two

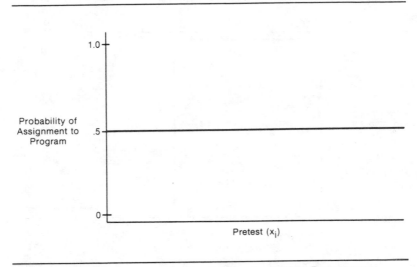

Figure 1.6   Probability of Assignment to Program for the True Experiment

extremes. The implication of this continuum for the statistical analysis of regression-discontinuity will be discussed later.

In general, when internal validity is desired, randomized experiments are to be preferred to quasi-experiments. Boruch (1975a) has argued that random assignment is feasible and ethical across a wide range of social research areas. Nevertheless, there are frequently situations in which random assignment is not practical due to program constraints, ethical considerations (e.g., reluctance to deny the program to "needy" persons) or other logistical factors. In these cases a quasi-experimental strategy may be called for. Quasi-experiments are usually considered inferior to randomized ones because postprogram comparisons between groups are made equivocal by likely preprogram nonequivalence. However, quasi-experimental designs where the assignment strategy is perfectly known (e.g., regression-discontinuity) are generally preferable to designs with unknown assignment. All things being equal, if the assignment strategy is known it can

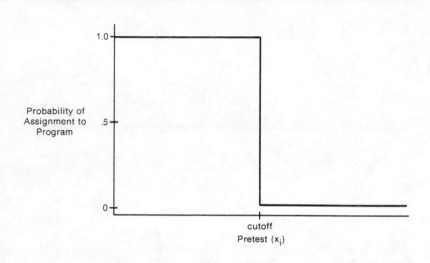

Figure 1.7   Probability of Assignment to Program for Regression-Discontinuity

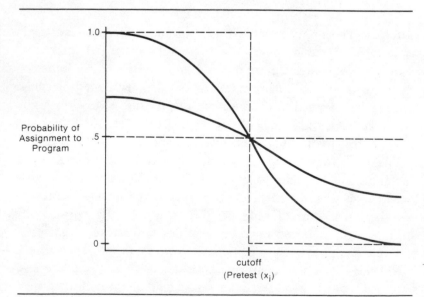

Figure 1.8   Probability of Assignment to Program for Fuzzy Regression-Discontinuity and the Nonequivalent Group Design

be used in the statistical analysis to "adjust" for preprogram nonequivalence and to yield unbiased estimates of postprogram differences.

Thus, regression-discontinuity designs, which are based on known assignment procedures, are among the strongest of the quasi-experimental strategies. When random assignment to groups is not possible, for either research or social policy reasons, regression-discontinuity designs should be a seriously considered alternative.

NOTES

1. In all graphs, it is assumed that the program was given to lower pretest scorers, that is, that this is the compensatory case. In addition, it is assumed that high scores on either measure reflect a more positive performance. It is important to note that the interpretation of program effects as "positive" or "negative" is always dependent on whether the program was given to high or low pretest scorers and the directionality of scale in the posttest.

2. If the regression-discontinuity assignment is "meritorious" in nature, the step function of Figure 1.7 would be revised with low pretest scores having $p = 0$ and those above the cutoff $p = 1$. Similarly, in nonequivalent designs where the program group happens to be superior on the pretest, the assignment function would range between the random one in Figure 1.3 and the regression-discontinuity "meritorious" case.

2

A Short History of Regression-Discontinuity

Why should we look at the history of a research design? Outside of several obvious considerations—the value of documentation, the need for a literature tradition—an historical perspective serves to underscore the fact that research designs are dynamic and evolving entities, not static mechanistic ones. As subsequent chapters will demonstrate, many of the issues in the regression-discontinuity framework remain unsolved or only partially concluded. Good understanding of current issues requires some sense of the contexts that generated them. The story of the regression-discontinuity design encompasses several interesting dramas including the technical disputes of methodologists and statisticians, the political and financial arguments of the evaluation research industry, and the social debate of Congress and the nation regarding the allocation and evaluation of social programs, especially in the educational arena.

A second reason for taking an historical view is that it enables us to learn from previous experience which practices and procedures seem to work in the field and which do not. As will be shown in later chapters, the regression-discontinuity design as presented by theoreticians and methodologists was often difficult to implement, at least within educational settings. An understanding of why this is so will provide the applied researcher who is interested in using the design with some prior warning about difficulties that might arise.

This chapter merely outlines the major historical events, indicates the relevant literature, and discusses some of the factors that influenced the selection or rejection of the regression-discontinuity design for the evaluation of compensatory education programs. Subsequent chapters will provide a more detailed sense of the arguments and controversies involved.

The history of the regression-discontinuity design can be categorized neatly into two major traditions. The first is termed here the "academic" tradition and describes the ongoing technical development of the design. The second is named the "compensatory education" tradition and refers to the use of the design to evaluate programs to that type. The design has almost never been used outside of compensatory education evaluation with the exception of some illustrative examples in the technical literature and a notable evaluation in criminal justice (Berk & Rauma, 1983). This two-fold classification is not meant to imply that the two traditions did not overlap or interact—rather, it is used because it enables us to make better sense of key issues, while at the same time it preserves the integrity of the historical story line.

Because of the important historical role of compensatory education evaluation for the regression-discontinuity design, many of the examples in this volume will be set in the context of compensatory education. This should not imply that the design is useful only in this context for, as will be seen, it has far more general applicability. Rather, the discussion emphasizes the educational tradition because the design can only be understood well within the context in which it is applied and it has almost exclusively been applied to date in compensatory education settings.

THE ACADEMIC TRADITION

The regression-discontinuity design was first suggested in its present form in a paper by Thistlethwaite and Campbell (1960) entitled, "Regression-discontinuity analysis: An alternative to the ex post factor experiment." Initially, regression-discontinuity was not accorded the status of a research "design" but was rather viewed as an analysis. The example that they considered was a study of the effects of winning a scholarship on career plans. Students scoring above a given aptitude level were awarded a scholarship, while those below that score were not.[1] The central post measures reflected the student's desire to undertake graduate study or be a college teacher or researcher. The regression-discontinuity analysis was compared to a randomized experimental procedure. The logic behind this comparison is shown in Figure 2.1. The top graph, Figure 2.1a, shows a hypothetical randomized experimental situation. Students in the study are selected from a relatively small range of the pretest (indicated by two vertical lines). Within that range, students are randomly assigned to either receive a scholarship or not. The "X" in the figure represents the post mean for the no scholarship group. Because the two means differ one might conclude that the scholarship had an effect. Figure 2.1b shows how this logic might be extended. Here, information is also available for students with pretest scores above and below the interval of the random assignment. The high scoring students all receive a scholarship, the low scorers do not. In this case, one might conduct two analyses—one for the cases that were randomly assigned and one for the cases outside that interval. For the latter, regression lines could be fit to each group and projected into the interval. Figure 2.1b shows that the lines would be projected to their respective randomly assigned group means. The effect of the program would be the same for both analyses and is indicated by the vertical distance between the two posttest means. The traditional regression-discontinuity analysis is shown in Figure 2.1c. Here, random assignment is not used at all. The randomization interval is replaced by a single cutoff score. The program is the same as above but is reflected in the vertical distance (jump or discontinuity) in the regression lines at the cutoff. Thus, Thistlethwaite and Campbell (1960) saw regression-discontinuity analysis as a direct extension of or alternative to a randomized experiment. The program effect is estimated at the cutoff because that is where the two groups are most similar or comparable in pretest ability.

The regression-discontinuity design was a frequent topic in the writings of Donald T. Campbell. In 1963, it was included in a monograph on research design by Campbell and Stanley (1963) where it was still cast in the category of an analysis rather than a design. By 1969, however (Campbell, 1969), regression-discontinuity had become a "design":

> But if randomization is not politically feasible or morally justifiable in a given setting, there is a powerful quasi-experimental design available that allows the scarce good to be given to the most needy or the most deserving. This is the regression-discontinuity design. (p. 248)

This paper recognized a number of central issues for the design: the need for adherence to the cutoff criterion; the distinction between "sharp" and "fuzzy" regression-discontinuity; the use of uncorrelated pretest and posttest; the choice of where to estimate the program effect; and the possibility of using a cutoff on a composite measure. The design was recommended for such diverse contexts as the investigation of Job Corps Training or the study of the effects of military conscription.

In the early 1970s, Robert F. Boruch authored and coauthored a number of papers dealing with regression-discontinuity. In "Regression-Discontinuity Revisited," (Boruch, 1973) an un-

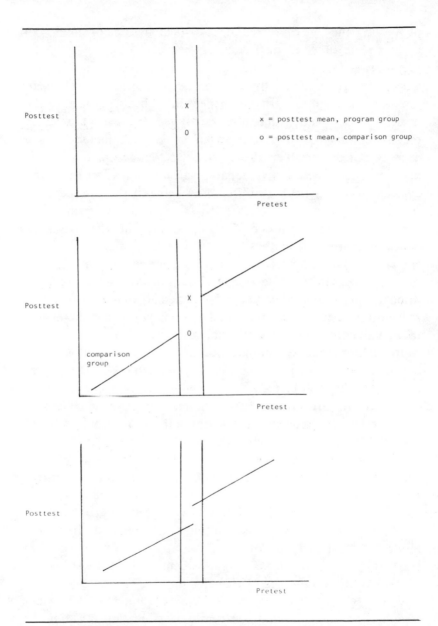

Figure 2.1   The Regression-Discontinuity Design as an Extension of a True
Experiment

published paper, he discusses the statistical analysis of the design in some detail and distinguishes between cases where the preprogram measure can be considered fixed or random, and where the groups come from the same population or represent separate intact groups. In this paper, Boruch also points to the present recommended statistical analysis—the use of a single regression function with the group assignment included as a dummy-coded variable. Prior to this, the accepted analysis involved the calculation of separate group regression lines and construction of a t-test of differences between the intercepts at the cutoff point as discussed by Campbell. A number of applications are suggested for the design in the fields of education, health, mental health, criminal justice, and social welfare. In 1975, Boruch and DeGracie presented an evaluation of a compensatory education program using the regression-discontinuity design. The paper is particularly important for its recognition of the problem of model specification and the effects of curvilinearity on the statistical analysis.

By 1975, the regression-discontinuity design had still received almost no use outside of the illustrative analyses in the papers mentioned above. It had always seemed especially appropriate for evaluation in education where students are often assigned to program on the basis of need as measured on an achievement test. This fact and a desire on the part of Congress to see better evaluations of compensatory education provided the right mixture of ingredients for introduction of the design in that context. Because of its importance, the history of regression-discontinuity in compensatory education is discussed separately below.

More general discussions continued to emanate from the methodological and statistical communities. These ranged from the first dissertation on the design (Sween, 1971) to the statistical theorizing of Goldberger (1972), Rubin (1977), and Sacks and Ylvisaker (1976). The dissertation by Trochim (1980) brought together the academic and compensatory education traditions in a general discussion of regression-discontinuity supplemented with illustrative analyses.

By the late 1970s, the design was being included in both introductory (Kidder, 1981) and advanced (Cook & Campbell, 1979; Judd & Kenny, 1981) methodology texts. However, instances of the use of the design outside compensatory education remained negligible, a study in the criminal justice area by Berk and Rauma (1983) being a notable exception. The purpose of this study was to examine the effects of extending unemployment insurance benefits to ex-offenders from the California prison system. The assignment measure was the reported total number of hours worked for each person in prison jobs or vocational education programs. The legislation set the cutoff for program eligibility at $1500 or 652 hours at the minimum wage paid to prisoners. Eligible ex-offenders could apply for unemployment insurance like anyone else. The amount of payment depended on the hours worked in prison with benefits ranging from $30 to $70 per week for up to 26 weeks. The outcome measure was a reflection of recidivism, specifically, a parole revocation that meant, in effect, a return to prison. Because this outcome is dichotomous, the pre-post functional form was assumed to be logistic. The results indicated that program participants were about 13% less likely to return to prison than they would have been without the program.

Despite the absence of use of regression-discontinuity, the academic history of the design documents the steady increase in the knowledge of its mechanics and points to likely increased use in the future.

THE COMPENSATORY EDUCATION TRADITION

In 1965, the U.S. Congress passed Public Law 89–10, the Elementary and Secondary Education Act (ESEA), of which Title I is most relevant here.[2] It was the first major piece of legislation in the Great Society program of Lyndon Johnson and the largest single federal education grant of its scope. Title I was a singular domestic achievement that required a balancing of several divergent interest groups and not a little political straight-arming (Eidenberg & Morey, 1969). The Statement of Purpose (Section 201) holds that Title I is to

> provide financial assistance . . . to local educational agencies serving areas of concentrations of children from educational programs by various means . . . which contribute particularly to meeting the special educational needs of educationally deprived children.

Each local school district or LEA (Local Education Agency) develops a proposal describing the programs for which it requests funds and submits this to the state department of education, or SEA, for approval. The programs are usually (but not necessarily) confined to basic skill areas such as mathematics, reading, and language arts. In 1979, over $5.5 billion was authorized by Congress for Title I, and nearly $3.4 billion was finally appropriated. Approximately 9 million low-income children were served, and between 5 and 6 million of these were of elementary school age. Nearly 87% of all school districts received some Title I funds (NCES, 1979) that accounted for between 3% and 4% of all national elementary and secondary education expenses (U.S. Office of Education, 1979). Only those aspects of Title I that are relevant to the application of the regression-discontinuity design are discussed here. The reader is referred to documents of the Office of Education and Wick (1978) for a more general description of Title I.

Title I was the first major social legislation that specifically required routine evaluation of its programs. Section 205(a)(5) reads

> effective procedures, including provision for appropriate objective measurements of education achievement will be adopted for evaluation at least annually, the effectiveness of the programs in meeting the special educational needs of educationally deprived children.

In the Amendments of 1974 (Public Law 93–380), Congress attempted to improve and standardize the evaluation procedures at the federal, state, and local levels with the development of research models that

> specify objective criteria which shall be utilized in the evaluation of all programs and shall outline techniques (such as longitudinal studies of children involved in such programs) and methodology (such as the use of tests which yield comparable results) for providing data which are comparable on a statewide and nationwide basis. (Section 151(f))

In doing so, Congress moved away from an approach emphasizing demonstration-type studies by instead attempting to combine the evaluation and reporting functions. The research methods were to be clearly specified and results could be aggregated by district, state, and nation. In 1974, a contract was awarded by the Office of Education to the RMC Research Corporation for the development of such models. The system that they generated is characterized by a common measurement metric and by three alternative research designs that were presumed to yield comparable results (Tallmadge & Horst, 1976; Tallmadge & Wood, 1978). The metric, termed the Normal Curve Equivalent score (NCE), is simply a standard score with a mean of 50 and a standard deviation of 21.06. Estimates of program effect were reported on this scale to enable aggregation of gains at higher levels.

In order to understand the methodological and contextual issues of regression-discontinuity, it is essential to become familiar with the design choices which school districts were given. The three research designs layed out by RMC differed in the manner in which they generated the null case expectation for the program and can be described briefly as follows:

> Model A: The Norm Referenced Model. With this model only the program group students are pre and posttested. In an attempt to avoid regression artifacts it is required that program students be selected by some measure (or measures) other than the pretest. Thus, all students are given a "selection" test (usually, the annual spring achievement test) and only the selected program students are

pre and posttested. The average test scale score is calculated for
the pretest and posttest and these can then be converted to
percentiles or NCE scores. Because the average test scale scores are
used and these are based on test scores obtained from norming
samples the program effect consists of any gain over and above
that which would be expected in the norming sample group. The
comparison group consists of the national norming sample for the
test and for that reason is labelled a "pseudo" comparison group
here.

Model B: The Comparison Group Model. Both program and
comparison group students are pre and posttested with this model.
Ideally, students are randomly assigned to group, thus yielding a
true experimental design. In practice, this is not often possible, and
presumably "comparable" groups are used as program and
comparison, yielding a non-equivalent group design. The program
effect consists of any gain in the average of the program group
over and above the gain in the average of the comparison group.

Model C: The Special Regression Design. This is the regression-
discontinuity design as described here (the term "Model C" will be
applied to refer to the Title I implementation of the design). Two
separate estimates of program effect are computed. The "regression-
discontinuity estimate" is the difference between the program and
comparison group regression lines at the cutoff point. The
"regression-projection estimate" is the difference between the lines
at the program group pretest mean.

All three models can be used with either standardized or
locally developed tests and are distinguished in the model names
with a "1" for the former and a "2" for the latter. For example,
Model A1 is the norm referenced model with a standardized test;
Model A2 is the same model with a locally devised exam.

A system of technical assistance was set up to aid LEAs and
SEAs in the design and execution of the evaluations. In each of
the ten national Department of Health, Education and Welfare
regions a Technical Assistance Center (TAC), upon request, was
allowed to provide advice, training, and sometimes, assistance
with statistical analysis. A good summary of the Title I system in
general and the models in particular can be found in U.S. Office
of Education (1976) and Tallmadge and Wood (1978). A useful

bibliography of Title I evaluation issues was compiled by Strand (1979).

FREQUENCY AND LOCATION OF USE

In order to determine where the regression-discontinuity design was used, interviews were conducted primarily with personnel of the TAC Centers in each of the national Office of Education regions. From these interviews, a list of school districts that were mentioned in connection with the design was compiled.

In all, about 60 school districts (out of a total of about 15,000) were mentioned as possible users of the design in the 1979-1980 academic year. Of these, about 40 were confirmed verbally. The majority of users were located in East Coast regions, specifically, in the states of New Jersey, Virginia, and Florida. In the Midwest and Western states use was primarily restricted to a few large school districts and to "special case" districts such as the Trust Territories.[3]

Another source of information on the use of the regression-discontinuity design is a survey conducted by the National Center of Education Statistics (NCES, 1979). Of the districts that responded, 87% had Title I programs in the 1978-1979 school year and 63% had used some type of model. Of these, 86% used Model A, about 2% used Model B, and about 2% used Model C. The remaining 10% of the districts used an alternative or locally devised one. In general then, while the regression-discontinuity design was used, it was not used frequently, especially relative to Model A.

REASONS CITED FOR NOT USING MODEL C

It is important, when examining why the regression-discontinuity design is or is not used, to bear in mind the alternatives that a school district has. While two other models are available, the choice is most often between Model A and Model C (Echternacht, 1980). Consequently, many of the reasons listed as factors in the decision pertain to the perceived advantages of one model over the other.

In interviews and site visits, ten reasons were frequently mentioned as important in the decision not to use the regression-discontinuity design. These reasons often parallel the major factors cited in other papers such as those by Echternacht (1980) and McNeil and Findlay (1979). It is possible that for any given district some of the reasons that were cited were ill-considered or inappropriate. Nevertheless, these reasons are included because they serve to define, at least in part, how the design is perceived. The following discussion delineates the ten reasons.

1. Model C is not chosen because it is likely to yield "negative" program effect estimates. By far, the most frequently given reason for not using regression-discontinuity is the commonly held perception that it tends to yield "negative" gains for estimates of program effect. This reason was cited by representatives from almost every TAC, and by many persons at the state and local level. Because this issue is of central importance in assessing the appropriateness and feasibility of the design, the controversy is considered separately in Chapter 6.

2. Model C is not chosen because Model A is close to what most school districts had already been using for Title I evaluation. Prior to development of the three models, many districts evaluated Title I programs simply by testing program students before and after the program and determining whether their gain exceeded some goal or norm. In many cases, the only change that was needed in order to use Model A correctly was the addition of the separate selection measure. This was often easy to accomplish because many school districts give an annual achievement test to all students, usually in the spring. During any given evaluation cycle this test could be used as the selection test (which must be administered to all students) and, in the following year, could be used to obtain posttest scores for the program students as well as for the selection test for the next evaluation. All that a district needs to add is a pretest of the program students, and this is usually accomplished through a smaller fall testing program.

3. Model C is not chosen because it requires adherence to the cutoff point criterion for assignment. Several administrators at the school district level claimed they want greater discretionary power in assignment both to allow for favoritism and for the possibility that a given test score may be inaccurate. Two administrators stated that they would like to have a "range of cutoffs" rather than a single cutoff point. In the simplest case, one could have two cutoffs. All students scoring below the lowest cutoff would automatically be assigned to the program group, all those scoring above the higher group would automatically be assigned to the comparison group, while all those scoring between the cutoffs would be assigned at the discretion of administrators, teachers, and so on. Although this strategy has not been used in Title I evaluation, it is a useful possibility, as will be discussed in Chapter 3.

4. Model C is not used because of premature release of research results which erroneously showed it yields biased estimates of effect. One frequently cited reason for not using the regression-discontinuity design provides an illustration of the interaction between social contexts and methodological decisions. Subsequent to the original contract for the development of research models awarded to the RMC Research Corporation, the Office of Education awarded a follow-up grant to the same corporation for purposes of investigating the models in more detail. To examine whether Model C might yield biased estimates, the RMC Research Corporation acquired two sets of data used to norm standardized tests. The first consisted largely of scores from the Comprehensive Test of Basic Skills (CTBS), while the second was comprised of the 1977 norming data for the California Achievement Test (CAT) issued by the McGraw-Hill company. For both of these data bases, it was assumed that the tested students did not receive compensatory education services. For Model C, cases were assigned to either program or comparison groups using an arbitrary cutoff point and an estimate of program effect was calculated. Presumably, since no program was administered, the analyses should have yielded an average program effect in the vicinity of zero.

These tests were carried out in two phases, first on the CTBS data base, and second on the CAT data. The initial results for the CTBS data indicated that Model C tended to yield a biased effect in the direction of a positive result. Subsequent to this portion of the study, and before looking at the CAT data, persons from the RMC Research Corporation, in seminars given throughout the country, appropriately suggested that there may have been problems with Model C that had not been previously anticipated. When the data from the CAT data base was examined using the same procedures, all three models yielded estimates of effect in the vicinity of zero NCE units. At this point, several researchers from RMC began to search for reasons for this apparent discrepancy (Wood, 1979). The reexamination of the CTBS data base turned up the existence of nonnormal or skewed distributions. After transforming the data to minimize this skew, the estimates for Model C were recomputed and, while slightly positive, approached the expected zero value. The final conclusion of the study was that Model C estimates are not biased, although they may be affected adversely by floor and ceiling effects and abnormalities in the marginal distributions (Stewart, 1980a, 1980b).

A distinction needs to be made between the actual results from this study and the effect of premature release of the results. A number of persons, especially at the TAC level, stated that to their knowledge RMC had shown that Model C did not work correctly and should be avoided. None of those who mentioned this seemed aware of the subsequent investigation and the change in the overall conclusion. While it is reasonable to expect that eventually this information was passed along, it is hard to gauge the effect that premature partial information had on the initial selection of research models by school districts. It is reasonable to argue that some districts used this information in deciding against Model C, while others who wished to use Model A cited it to enhance the credibility of their decision.

Even granting that a consistent positive program effect may have been detected in this study, one must be careful to distinguish between the conclusion that Model C yields biased estimates or that implementation problems (e.g., testing problems, matching problems, etc.) degrade estimates of effect with this design. Each conclusion has different implications. If Model C yields biased estimates it would have been reasonable to recommend suspension of its use. If, however, with typical Title I implementations there are problems which act to degrade estimates, one can address these problems directly and attempt to improve the validity of the results.

5. Model C is not chosen because it is more difficult technically than Model A. Model C may appear to be more technically difficult to some degree because it is based on notions of regression lines and projections from regression lines, ideas that are not easily understandable to those who are unfamiliar with research and statistical analysis. In addition, several respondents mentioned that in presenting the three research models, the materials used and the explanations provided for Model C were the most difficult to understand. It is not at all clear whether this is a deficiency in the manner of presentation or a problem that stems from inherent differences in the technical difficulty of the models. Nevertheless, it is a commonly held perception that Model C is more difficult than Model A, that it requires a more technically trained staff, and that it is most appropriately used by districts that have ready access to computer facilities capable of computing the necessary regressions (Bridgeman, 1979). Although all of these considerations have some validity, the investigation of where Model C has been used turned up several districts that used the design despite the lack of sophisticated personnel and facilities. In most cases, these districts either pooled their resources with other small districts or hired outside consultants who were able to conduct the analyses.

6. *Model C is not used because it requires testing of comparison students.* Model C requires pre- and posttesting of comparison students. While it is not absolutely necessary that all non-Title I students be tested (e.g., a randomly selected subsample of non-Title I students could be used instead), the model does require more than simply the pre- and posttesting of program students. For those districts that use a district-wide annual standardized achievement test this requirement poses no problems. However, for other usually smaller districts, the increased cost of additional testing is a considerable burden.

7. *Model C is not used because it requires at least 30 students in the program group.* The original Users Guide for Title I Evaluation suggests that Model C should not be used unless there are at least 30 students in each group. The basis of this is that with larger samples one can achieve greater statistical precision and more accurate estimates of regression lines (McNeil, 1977). While this is certainly an important consideration, the requirement of at least 30 students was arbitrary. Estimation of a regression line is more critical for the comparison group where participants are typically more plentiful. A variation of the regression-discontinuity design that tests for differences between a program group posttest mean (rather than a regression line) and the projection from a comparison group line is discussed in Chapter 3.

8. *Model C is not used because it requires that within-group correlations be at least .4.* The original Users Guide suggests that Model C should not be used unless the pretest and posttest correlation is at least .4. While it may be desirable, from a conceptual point of view, to have a strong pretest-posttest correlation (McNeil, 1977), this is not technically necessary (see Echternacht, 1978). In fact, any measure can be used for the preprogram measure whether it is correlated with the posttest or not. Figure 2.2 presents an example of the regression-discontinuity design where the pretest and posttest are uncorrelated. In this case the regression line in each group is flat, that is, the slope is

equal to zero. Here, one has effectively reduced the design to a test between the program and comparison posttest means. In this case, because there is no relationship between the pretest and posttest, one "approximates" random assignment to program. It is difficult to conceive of such a case occurring in Title I evaluation because of the desire to assign students to a program group on the basis of some measure related to achievement. Nevertheless, this example is included to illustrate that a low pretest-posttest correlation, should it occur, will not by itself result in biased estimates of program effect.

9. Model C is not chosen because it can cause individual schools to lose Title I teacher positions. Another problem that occurs in

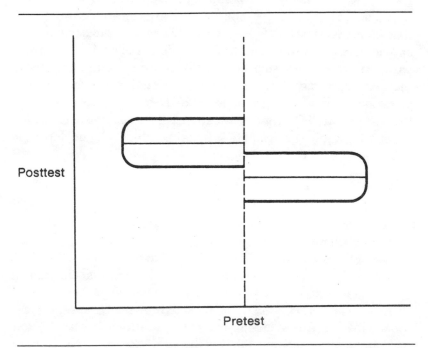

Figure 2.2 Regression-Discontinuity When the Pretest and Posttest Are Uncorrelated

relation to the sharp cutoff point concerns the allocation of Title I teachers to schools. From one year to the next, the number of children within any given school in a district who are eligible for Title I services might change considerably. If Title I teachers are assigned to schools on the basis of the number of children who will be served, there is a possibility that a given school will lose Title I teachers from one year to the next. Few schools are likely to accept unchallenged a reduction in the number of teachers they are allocated. Other types of allocation procedures could be developed as in one case, where a creative approach that capitalized on an already existing busing program equalized teacher allocation by means of moving students from one school to another.

10. Model C is not chosen because the SEA discourages its use. Another reason cited for not using regression-discontinuity is that in many states the SEA strongly recommends the use of another design, most often Model A. While the decision to use a particular research design technically is the option of the LEA, the SEA does have the right to review and approve program proposals. While no respondent stated that the SEA rejected their use of Model C, many mentioned that the existence of an explicit or implied state policy favoring Model A did have an effect on their decision.

REASONS CITED IN FAVOR OF USING MODEL C

Fewer reasons were listed as favoring the use of Model C. They are summarized as follows:

1. Model C is used because it is conceptually closest to the idea of Title I training. Title I programs are supposed to be given to those students who need them most. More than the other two models, Model C provides an explicit quantified measure of such need and a clear decision rule for the allocation of service. There are other ways to exploit the correspondence between the regression-discontinuity design and allocation procedures used for Title I. For example, each school district must designate which schools are eligible for Title I programs on the basis of a quantified measure of poverty. If a cutoff on this measure is used to assign the schools, one can conceive of a regression-discontinuity analysis of the effects of Title I training at the school level. Variations of this type are discussed in Chapter 3.

2. Model C is used because it fits in well with annual district-wide testing programs. Those districts that have annual testing programs find that no additional testing is required for Model C. The test given in each year acts as the posttest for the current year and as the pretest and selection measure for the year to follow. In the typical implementation of Model A, all students in the school district are tested (for example, in the spring), those students selected for Title I service are pretested (for example, in the fall), and all students are posttested the following spring. Thus, in the annual cycle, the spring testing provides both the selection measure for the subsequent year and the posttest for the current year. However, it is necessary to include a separate pretest. Essentially, this issue involves a trade-off between the two models. Model A requires less testing in that only program students are given the pretest and posttest (although all are given the selection test). Model C involves less testing in that a separate selection measure is not needed. Depending on the type of district testing program that exists, a given district might find it less costly to use either Model A or Model C.

3. Model C is used because it is perceived as methodologically stronger than Model A. Another set of reasons cited in favor of using Model C is related to perceptions about the quality of the design. Those districts that employ researchers who have been specifically trained in research methodology are more likely to be aware of the academic history of Model C and of its advantages from a methodological viewpoint. In addition, because of this history and the common perception within Title I evaluation circles that Model C is the most technically difficult of the three models, a degree of higher status might be accorded those districts that use the model. One Title I evaluator from a large metropolitan school district said that he felt his district should "lead the way" in attempting to implement more technically difficult research designs. This is more likely to be the case for districts that have well-trained staffs and sufficient computer facilities.

SUMMARY OF USE ISSUES

The regression-discontinuity design is used under the name of Model C for Title I evaluation, although infrequently. While it is certainly appropriately used in this context, it tends to be judged relative to Model A. From the typical school district's perspective, Model A is easier to understand, easier to use, less costly, and likely to yield "favorable" results. If both models were of similar methodological quality, Model A would clearly be the better choice. In Chapter 6, the issue of the relative quality of these two designs is considered.

To summarize, we can see in the history of Title I the development of an evaluation system of national scope, specifying three presumably "equivalent" (in terms of program effect estimates) research designs, one of which is the regression-discontinuity design of interest here. These conditions make the context of Title I evaluation the richest source that is currently available for information on the application of the regression-discontinuity design.

NOTES

1. The situation is actually more complex. Students may be awarded a scholarship on the basis of several criteria (e.g., high school grades, test scores, recommendations), but only test score assignment was studied here.

2. Under the Reagan administration, the educational legislation has been considerably reorganized. For the most part, what is referred to here as "Title I" now falls under the name of "Chapter I." The Title I evaluation system is no longer formally required in the federal legislation, but nevertheless has been maintained with little or no change by many individual states. While the term "Title I" is used in this volume for historical consistency, the issues considered are applicable under present circumstances.

3. For instance, the design was used in Puerto Rico because there was no suitable achievement test in Spanish that had normative data (thus making Model A untenable).

3

Design Variations

The intent of this chapter is to expand upon the basic definition of the regression-discontinuity design as outlined in Chapter 1 by suggesting alternative variations and applications. It is important to keep in mind that the major distinguishing feature of the design is the assignment to conditions on the basis of a cutoff on some quantified measurement. Any analysis that is based at least in part on such a strategy will be considered here a variation of the design.

The regression-discontinuity design is far more versatile in principle than its present applications might suggest. This chapter is devoted to consideration of some of the major useful variants. Six major areas are considered: different strategies for handling assignment to condition; measurement variations; pro-gram-related variations; alternative postprogram measures; the use of the design on aggregate units; and the use of the design on a post hoc basis.

ASSIGNMENT VARIATIONS

The major distinctive characteristic of the regression-discontinuity design is the assignment to condition on the basis of a sharp cutoff score on a preprogram measure. There are many aspects of this assignment strategy that can be altered to improve the estimates of program effect that are generated.

In theory, the most methodologically sound way to assign units or persons to conditions is through random assignment. In fact, the regression-discontinuity design is recommended primarily when random assignment to conditions is not feasible. A major advantage of random assignment (assuming that the program groups have a sufficient sample size) is that the groups that are assigned will on the average have the same expected value on any characteristic measures prior to the administration of the program. Thus, groups can be considered to be "equivalent" prior to the program and differences that occur can be attributed to either the program or some other event that occurred subsequent to assignment. For a variety of reasons, random assignment to condition is not used as frequently as would be desired (Boruch, 1975a).

Little work has been conducted to compare the regression-discontinuity design directly with the true experiment (i.e., a design based upon random assignment to condition). Goldberger (1972) suggests that all things being equal, one needs at least 2 1/2 times as many program participants for the regression-discontinuity design as for a randomized design in order to attain the same degree of precision in estimating program effect. One of the strongest variations of the regression-discontinuity design, therefore, would be one that incorporates random assignment to condition, at least in part. Much of the following discussion on coupling the regression-discontinuity design with random assignment follows from the suggestions outlined by Boruch (1975b).

Many of the difficulties that occur in the implementation of the regression-continuity design stem from the requirement of adhering to a strict cutoff. While lack of adherence to this requirement may be motivated by a factor like political favoritism, it is often the case that misassignment is due to the reasonable belief that persons closest to the cutoff score may be misassigned simply as a result of random error in the preprogram measure. Thus, an administrator may feel that a test score for a certain individual does not reflect well that person's ability. If the person scored near the cutoff, their assignment could be dependent on whether they had a good or bad day or on factors related to the testing setting. An alternative to the sharp cutoff procedure would be to define a cutoff interval rather than a single cutoff point and to randomly assign persons within this interval to program or comparison group. Within this cutoff interval it would be assumed that all persons have approximately the same true score but differ on the measure primarily due to random measurement errors. Conceptually, it might even be useful to set the width of the interval on the basis of some estimate of measurement error (such as the standard deviation or standard error).

One way to view this modified design is as a true experiment "imbedded" within a regression-discontinuity design. Several analytic strategies would be possible. One could analyze just the data within the cutoff interval as a true experiment of its own. Alternatively one could analyze the data on either side of the cutoff interval by means of a standard regression-discontinuity analysis where the cutoff is the midpoint of the interval. Such a strategy would only be recommended for cases where the cutoff interval is relatively narrow and regression lines could be fairly estimated for the remaining data, especially in the comparison group. Finally, it would be possible to include all the data in a standard regression-discontinuity analysis as outlined in Chapter 5, even though assignment is not sharp relative to the cutoff. This is acceptable as long as random assignment within the cutoff interval has been adhered to because random misassignment around a cutoff will not result in biased program effect estimates.

This design would be especially useful where the possibility of nonlinearity in the data exists. Assuming that there is sufficient sample size for groups within the cutoff interval, one would be most confident in the estimates generated by the true experimental portion because nonlinearities would be equivalent across groups. The analysis of the data for the whole range on the preprogram measure could be conducted to increase the precision and generalizibility of the estimates and as an aid in determining whether there are problems that occur in the tails of the distribution. This design has been discussed as an extension of the "tie-breaking experiment" by Campbell (1969), Riecken et al. (1974), and Boruch (1973).

Random assignment could be incorporated at other points along the preprogram continuum than in the vicinity of the cutoff point. This might be most useful if random assignment is not feasible for all the participants but can be justified for a smaller number of "test" participants. There are three ways in which this could be done. First, one could randomly select points on the preprogram measure at which random assignment to condition would be used. This is superior to randomizing within a small interval because it allows one to generalize across a wider range of scores. Second, one could systematically select values or ranges on the preprogram measure within which participants are randomly assigned (Hansen, 1977). This would be useful especially in evaluation if it could be done at the extremes of the pretest distribution. Here, any floor or ceiling effects would be accounted for by the fact that they would be exhibited equally, on the average, in both the program and comparison groups. Finally, one might be able to randomly assign within certain subgroups or subpopulations. While it might not be possible to randomly assign throughout an entire school district, for instance, it might be feasible to select several schools as test sites and to randomly assign within the schools.

As above, several analyses would be appropriate. In effect, one has imbedded a randomized block design within the regression-discontinuity. One would place greatest confidence (in terms of internal validity) in the analysis of the randomly assigned cases and could include other cases for purposes of increasing precision or for completeness in reporting and generalizability. A major reason cited for not using random assignment in Title I evaluation is because it will result in a situation where students who need and may be eligible for service are denied such service. This criticism makes less sense when one considers that the procedures for allocating Title I services to schools lead to students (who qualify for the program on the basis of their pretest score) being denied service because they come from designated non-Title I schools. It should be noted that random assignment to program or comparison group is advocated within the Title I evaluation system as a version of Model B, but this design is almost never used. Nevertheless, some of the advantages that result from using random assignment can be achieved through coupling such strategies with Model C, the regression-discontinuity design, as mentioned here.

There are several other useful applications of random assignment within the regression-discontinuity design. This includes the random assignment of schools to Title I or non-Title I status, or the use of a cutoff interval in assigning schools with all schools within that interval being randomly assigned. One could easily devise analogous designs at the classroom level or, perhaps, even at the school district level. In general, imbedding random assignment procedures within the regression-discontinuity design will improve the methodological qualities of the study and should be encouraged.

In addition to random assignment to conditions, there are times when random selection from a larger population will improve the design and its analysis. It is, for example, acceptable within the Title I evaluation system to select a comparison group randomly from the population of comparison students in a district. In a district that has a large number of students, it may be more efficient to select randomly a small comparison group for purposes of analysis, although in general it would be preferable to include all such students if that is possible.

Another use for random selection would be possible where programs are administered in two phases with half of the eligible persons receiving service in the first half of a year (or some other appropriate period) and the remaining persons receiving it in the second half. Here, one randomly selects from eligible persons those who will get the program first and those who will get it second. The advantage of such a strategy is that one has a suitable comparison group (namely, those persons who are not serviced in the first half of the year), without the need to ultimately deny service to any eligible persons. If such a strategy proves unworkable it might be possible to modify this by instead randomly selecting those institutions (e.g., schools, social agencies) that will implement the program in the first half of the year and those that will do so in the second. This type of design is a powerful methodological alternative to the three models that are currently used for Title I evaluation, and should be encouraged. Three separate analyses could be used. The first would involve a comparison of students who received Title I service in the first half of the year and those eligible students who did not. The second would involve the comparison of the same two groups after the students have all been served. In the first case, one would expect that if the programs have an effect, such an effect would be detected. If one is found, and if the second phase of the program also has an effect, one would expect that the original difference between the two groups would diminish in the second analysis. Finally, a standard regression-discontinuity analysis could be applied for both program groups separately or the two combined. One can readily conceive of interesting, and at times, even more complicated design variations. For example, students who receive service in the first half of the year could be assigned to either continue service or not for the second half of the year. This assignment could be random or could be by means of the cutoff score. Thus, one could have a regression-discontinuity design imbedded within a true experiment that is in turn imbedded within a larger regression-discontinuity design.

When random assignment is not possible it is often useful to search for other comparable groups of students that can act as comparisons in the analysis. This essentially involves coupling the pretest-posttest nonequivalent group design (Reichardt, 1979) with the regression-discontinuity design. With this design, equivalence between the groups is not assumed, that is, nonequivalence is allowed. Consequently, the potential for biases due to selection is ever present. A strategy of this type is readily available in Title I evaluation because of the existence of schools that are ineligible for Title I and are likely to have students who score below the district cutoff point and, hence, could be used as comparison students. Matching of students from Title I and non-Title I schools is not advisable (Campbell & Stanley, 1963) and no ready strategy for selecting a "comparable" group from the non-Title I schools is available. As a result, an analysis like this should be interpreted cautiously. There may be times when it is possible for a design of this type to be incorporated at school district levels. This might be so if a school district that is not receiving any Title I funds can be located and is comparable to the district receiving funds. This is not likely, however, due to the fact that most school districts in the country receive at least some Title I funding.

Another variation on assignment strategies would involve the use of multiple cutoff points with the group most in need being served first, the next needy group second, and so on. In this case, the first group could stop receiving service when the second group begins or each group could continue receiving service once it has begun. Separate analyses could be conducted comparing the most recently serviced group with all persons not yet receiving service, or a single analysis could be run by including suitable program by order of admission terms into the analysis. It is important to recognize with this design that there will probably be a need for repeated testing of all subjects. Thus, a pretest is administered, a test is administered as a posttest for the first program group and all comparisons, another test is administered as the second posttest, and so on.

A variation of this stagewise design is suggested in Riecken et al. (1974) and is termed a "trickle" design. This design is especially useful for an agency that is continuously processing persons through its program such as a hospital, mental health center, or social agency. It is necessary in this variation that the number of applicants exceed the number of available spots in the program at any given point in time. All applicants are tested when they present themselves to the agency and are put into a pool for the next cycle of the program. For this pool of applicants, a cutoff score on the preprogram measure is selected on the basis of the number of available spots in the program. The problems that occur here are related to the fact that one is likely to have different cutoff points each time the program is run, depending upon the number of applicants who present themselves. Nevertheless, this variation of the design would be a useful method for agencies that are continually processing applicants.

MEASUREMENT VARIATIONS

The assignment to conditions under the regression-discontinuity design is dependent upon the measure or measures used to assign. Technically, the assignment measure need not be statistically related to the posttest, although this may be desirable for conceptual reasons and for statistical power. In addition, it will often be useful to construct a composite variable made up of several measures suitable for assignment. In educational evaluation, such a composite variable might include an achievement test score, a grade point average, a rating of need by a teacher or admissions committee, and the like. Technically, it is not necessary that the variables that go into this composite be continuous ones. One could use dichotomous designations, rankings, or ratings (e.g., 5- or 7-point Likert-type ratings).

It is desirable that the composite measure be close to a normally distributed continuous variable with adequate measurement properties. For example, if a 5-point Likert rating of the acceptability of a person for the program is used, it would be advantageous to have several administrators, or other program personnel complete this rating and to average the scores. As a result, the 5-point scale would be transformed into a scale with finer gradations than the original 5 points. The major problems in developing composite assignment measures are related to how individual variables should be combined and how missing observations on these variables should be handled. The formula for the composite measure could be additive, multiplicative, a combination of these, based on a ratio of several variables, and so on. Each variable could be weighted equally or in accordance with the preferences of the particular agency. Another strategy could be to use multivariate statistical methods such as multiple regression analysis or factor analysis for devising a composite measure. It is not clear how one should proceed in the event that there are missing observations on one or more of the variables that enter the formula. This would be analogous to the univariate case where the pretest value is missing. One might attempt a more complicated assignment model for the case of missing data by utilizing other information to estimate the missing values. Issues related to the development of composite measures have been discussed by the RMC Research Corporation (1979), Campbell (1969), Cordray (1978), and Boruch (1973).

PROGRAM VARIATIONS

Variations of the basic regression-discontinuity design can be developed by altering the usual dichotomous program-control designation. Many of these variations have been mentioned earlier and, as a result, will only be discussed briefly. First, it is possible to have multiple levels of the program or to test different versions of the program. In Title I evaluation, for example, one could test different amounts of the program (e.g., five days versus three days a week versus one day a week), different settings (e.g., in-class versus pull-out), as well as different methods of instruction. The sets of comparisons can be made with or without a comparison group, although they will usually be stronger if "no program" comparison groups are included because in those groups the bivariate distribution will not be affected by the program. When this is not possible, as in the case of federal grants where all potential recipients receive some degree of funding, comparison of different levels of the program, especially if the difference between them is quantifiable, will often provide useful information relevant to the program effect. Again, it is important to recognize that when multiple program conditions are used, persons must be assigned to these using a sharp cutoff criterion in order for the design to be considered a regression-discontinuity design.

POSTPROGRAM MEASURE VARIATIONS

It has been mentioned throughout this work that it is not necessary for the pretest and posttest to be the same measure. In fact, any measure that is relevant to or is likely to be affected by the program may be used as a posttest. In addition, it is not necessary to limit the study to one posttest for each pretest, that is, several measures can be analyzed for the same pretest.

In educational evaluation there are several ways in which alternative post-program measures might be incorporated. Most standardized achievement tests, for example, are comprised of several subscales or subtests. Thus, a reading score might be a composite of scores obtained from tests of spelling, grammar, and punctuation. There is no reason why the analysis of the effects of a reading program should be limited to looking only at effects on the total reading score. Separate analyses could be conducted using each of the subscales as postprogram measures.

To illustrate the use of different measures of postprogram performance, data from the third grade reading and fourth grade math programs in Providence, Rhode Island, were reanalyzed using subtests in place of the posttest. In the analyses using total posttest score, the third grade reading program evidenced no effect, or possibly, a slight positive one, while the fourth grade math program exhibited clear negative gains (see Chapter 5). Analyses of posttest subscales might make the interpretations of the reading program less equivocal or the negative gains of the math program more specific.

Two posttest subscales that measure vocabulary and comprehension were available for the reading analysis. Three subscales measuring computation, concepts, and applications were available for the math data. The sample size, mean, variance, skewness, and kurtosis for all five measures are shown in Table 3.1. A four-step polynomial regression model as described in Chapter 5 was used for the analyses. For the third grade reading program, the bivariate plots are shown for the vocabulary subscale in Figure 3.1 and for the comprehension measure in Figure 3.2. For the fourth grade math program the plots for the computation, concepts, and applications subscales are shown in Figures 3.3, 3.4, and 3.5, respectively.

The estimates of gain and their standard errors are shown for each step in the analysis in Table 3.2. Both reading subscales show a similar pattern of gains across steps. On the basis of the analysis, we would conclude that there is no clear program effect. Although inspection of the graphs provides some evidence for an effect, assuming a true linear relationship, there is some evidence for slight curvilinearity especially at the lower end of the program group scores. This could be due to a floor effect or chance level problem.

TABLE 3.1
Descriptive Statistics for Posttest Subscales in Providence, RI

	N	Mean	Variance	Skew-ness	Kurtosis
Third Grade Reading					
Vocabulary	488	341.15	2905.40	.089	−.129
Comprehension	488	356.37	5078.55	.296	.806
Fourth Grade Mathematics					
Computation	537	386.10	1989.51	−.290	−.391
Concepts	537	386.91	3467.97	.180	−.266
Applications	533	379.29	4801.45	−.073	−.137

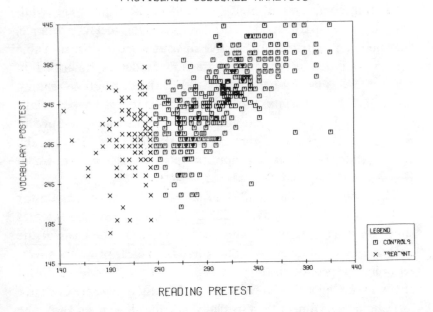

Figure 3.1   Regression-Discontinuity with a Reading Pretest and Vocabulary Posttest

The analyses of the math subscales are more illuminating. The only measure that shows the consistent negative gains across steps is the concept subscale. Since similar gains were detected in the analysis using the total posttest math score, one might conclude that they can be attributed primarily to this subscale. The implication is that Title I students in that program lose the most ground (relative to comparison students) on conceptual mathematical skills and that increased attention to this aspect of instruction may improve future program results.

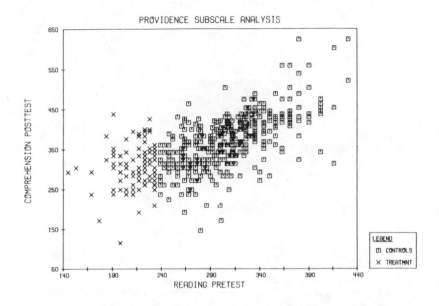

Figure 3.2   Regression-Discontinuity with a Reading Pretest and Comprehension
Posttest

One might wish to look at other postprogram measures such as the self-esteem of students and estimate the effects of the program on these constructs. Other variables useful in "process" evaluation or to examine potential threats to the major analyses could be considered, such as attendance rates, migrancy, and so on. Just as the assignment variable can be a composite, there is no reason why the posttest cannot be comprised of several measures. One might wish to develop indices related to program effect and use these as the postprogram measures.

A major question of interest in evaluation concerns whether the effects of the program are sustained over extended periods. In this regard, it would be useful to look at the posttest 2 or 3 years removed from the program. Generally, it would be beneficial in most evaluations to encourage the use of the regression-disconti-

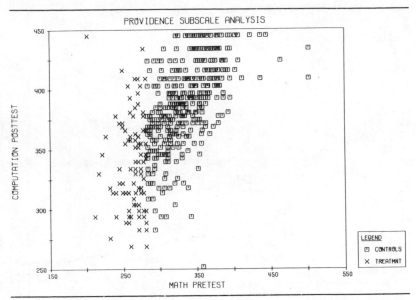

Figure 3.3   Regression-Discontinuity with a Math Pretest and Computation Posttest

nuity design for the estimation of program effects on more than simply a single outcome measure.

AGGREGATION VARIATIONS

Many variations of the regression-discontinuity design for aggregated data are discussed throughout this work. Sometimes the aggregation is in terms of the unit of analysis as when the design is applied to a higher level of allocation formula (e.g., when allocating from the federal government to the states). At other times the analysis can be performed on aggregated data, such as means for various units of analysis. Thus, if one is looking at the effects of Title I instruction at the school level one might use an estimate of the mean reading achievement score for each school. The use of the regression-discontinuity design on aggregated data is discussed in an example given by Boruch (1973) on the effects of medicaid funding on the number of

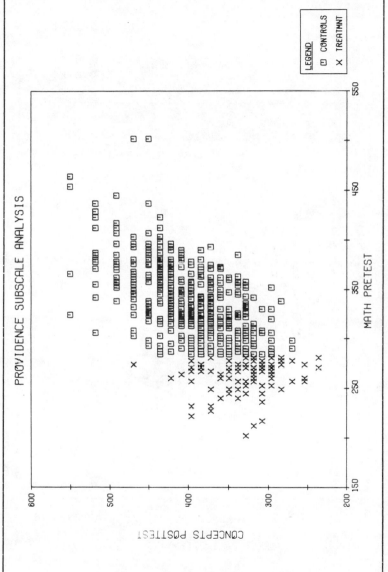

Figure 3.4   Regression-Discontinuity with a Math Pretest and a Concepts Posttest

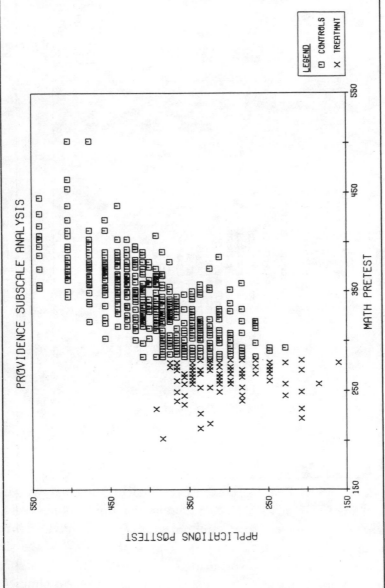

Figure 3.5   Regression-Discontinuity with a Math Pretest and Applications Posttest

TABLE 3.2
Estimates of Gain and Standard Errors, Posttest Subscales,
Providence, RI

Step	$\hat{\beta}_2$	$SE(\hat{\beta}_2)$
Reading Vocabulary Subscale, Grade 3		
1	27.02	5.59
2	14.36	6.32
3	22.66	8.40
4	−1.00	10.52
Reading Comprehension Subscale, Grade 3		
1	31.94	8.21
2	19.95	9.38
3	9.47	12.47
4	−7.48	15.79
Math Computation Subscale, Grade 4		
1	−5.41	5.04
2	−13.65	6.03
3	5.61	7.96
4	−12.03	9.93
Math Concepts Subscale, Grade 4		
1	−8.79	6.78
2	−28.46	8.02
3	−29.98	10.76
4	−38.93	13.48
Math Applications Subscale, Grade 4		
1	.13	7.10
2	−21.08	8.39
3	−4.64	11.17
4	−27.21	13.95

physician visits that are made. The data for this analysis was taken from previously published data on the impact of medicaid. The assignment measure was an indicator of income divided into six family income levels. Only families at the lowest of the six income levels qualified for medicaid. The dependent measure consisted of the mean proportion of physician visits (to families) per year. Thus, the entire database consisted of only six values, one average describing the frequency of physician visits for each income level. While one might expect a loss of statistical power when operating with such small sample sizes, the loss may be offset when working with data that is aggregated across large numbers of individual units (such as nationally aggregated data) by the greater stability or reliability that one generally expects with aggregate information.

POST HOC ANALYSIS

The regression-discontinuity design would appear to have special advantages for conducting analyses "after the fact," that is, on a post hoc basis. There are several reasons why post hoc analysis with this design is promising, especially for social programs that are allocated on the basis of a formula as described later. First, it is often the case that the data for these programs, that is, the pre- and postprogram measures, are routinely collected by government agencies. Even in cases where this data is not collected routinely, it is often possible to construct appropriate indices that can be used. Second, this data is often readily accessible in the form of government documents or computerized magnetic tapes. Often, the major problems that will arise concern locating and accessing this data and determining its quality (Trochim, 1981). Third, it may be possible to conduct a regression-discontinuity analysis even if the allocation formula does not require sharp assignment in terms of a cutoff score. Chapter 5 includes a description of how an analysis of a "fuzzy" regression-discontinuity design might proceed.

SUMMARY

The purpose of this chapter was to demonstrate the versatility of the regression-discontinuity design. If the design is eventually to be used more widely there will have to be a greater recognition on the part of researchers of when a setting is amenable to its use. In the early stages of design selection, one of the first characteristics one should look for is whether the treatment or program of interest is to be given out on the basis of need or merit. If so, then it is important to examine how the allocation decision is to be made, most especially, whether a cutoff point on some indicator (or a cutoff interval, multiple cutoff points, etc.) will be an acceptable criterion. If a cutoff strategy is appropriate for that setting, one next needs to determine whether the assignment variable will be on a continuous scale or whether it will have only a few discrete values. Obviously, one needs sufficient variability on this measure in order to estimate regression lines adequately. Finally, one needs to have at least one dependent measure that has been collected for both program and comparison cases, and that is presumed to reflect the effects of the independent variable under study. Here, restrictions on scale are less critical than with the assignment variable. For instance, regression procedures exist (i.e., logit and probit models) that can accommodate dichotomous measures of the "success-fail" type.

When the circumstances listed above hold for a given setting, there is a strong possibility that some variation of the regression-discontinuity design will be feasible. Greater creativity and recognition of feasibility on the part of the research community should assure wider application of the regression-discontinuity design in the future.

4

Regression-Discontinuity
and Allocation Formulas

The previous chapters show that the regression-discontinuity design is appropriate for the evaluation of social programs that are given out on the basis of need or merit as determined by a cutoff value or values on some quantitative assignment measure. Government agencies, most especially at the federal level, allocate billions of dollars each year for programs that are designed to address social problems in education, health, criminal justice, and other areas. In most cases, program resources are allocated, at least in part, based on some type of formula. Very often, the formula has a cutoff structure that determines the level of allocation to different recipients. For instance, funding for an antipoverty program might be given on the basis of quantitative records indicating the percentage of people below the official poverty level of income or the percentage of people on unemployment. Educational programs might be given to those who fall below some value on national achievement tests. Housing money might be allocated to localities based on housing start rates or levels of real estate taxes collected.

Probably the greatest potential of the regression-discontinuity design lies in the possibility of coupling it with existing procedures for allocating social resources in order to evaluate their effectiveness. A review of the federal grant system may turn up programs that already meet the basic requirements of the regression-discontinuity design. More likely, such a review would indicate a large number of programs that could, with minor modification, be amenable to regression-discontinuity analysis. This chapter is a first step in such a review. A typology of federal grants is presented along with some discussion of the allocation formulas that are typically used. Following this is a discussion of several more detailed examples of programs which use formulas and the issues involved in using the regression-discontinuity design to evaluate them. Finally, the major problems in coupling the regression-discontinuity design with existing allocation formula structures are discussed.

TYPES OF FEDERAL GRANTS

The grant system can be divided generally into three types of grants, the typology primarily dependent on the degree of intended specificity for the use of the funds. The first type of aid, General Revenue Sharing (GRS) has the fewest spending strings attached. Funds from GRS are allocated to local governments by formula and can be spent on whatever the local government considers necessary. Therefore, in some communities, GRS money is used to defray the costs of necessary municipal services like police and fire protection while in others it is directed to services that the community would be hard pressed to provide on its own, like social services and aid to the elderly.

The second general type of grant is known as the block grant. In 1980, there were five major block grants: the Partnership for

Health, the Omnibus Crime Control and Safe Streets Act, Comprehensive Employment and Training Act (CETA), the Housing and Community Development Act, and the Title XX Social Services Act. Funds for these grants can be spent on a wide variety of programs, as long as they can be justified in terms of the intent of the act. Therefore, while they are more specific than GRS, they are not as narrowly defined as the third type of grant—categorical aid.

Over the past decade, the largest number of federal grants (442 in 1975) were categorical, that is, grants where expenditures are confined to a specific category or type of program. Furthermore, the categorical grants can be divided into two categories: formula or project. Generally, with formula grants (146 in 1975) the funds were allocated from the federal government to smaller governmental units by means of a formula. Project grants (296 in 1975) are open for proposal bids. Funds are given out based on some judgment of the acceptability of the proposals received.

Formulas may be used to allocate resources at various steps or levels in the process. First, they are often used to allocate money from the federal government to the major recipient, most often a state. In turn, a second level of allocation may be set up to disperse funds within each state to the local government. There can, in some cases, be additional levels of allocation from local governments to subunits. The procedures used to disperse funds for Title I provide a good illustration of a multilevel allocation system. Here, funds are first allocated to the states and territories, then to school districts (often coterminous with county or parish boundaries), then to individual schools within the district, and finally to the programs that serve the students. At each level of allocation, a variety of formulas incorporating different measures may be used. These can include demographic variables, measures of need such as an index of poverty or socioeconomic status, or measures of achievement.

The use of formulas for allocation is not confined to the formula-based categorical grant. For example, GRS and several of the block grants (e.g., CETA) allocate funds by formula. In addition, many of the categorical project grants, after allocating funds on the basis of proposal awards, require or allow the use of a formula in the next level of allocation.

A useful distinction can be made between allocation formulas and eligibility formulas. An allocation formula is used to disperse funds from one level of government to another. An eligibility formula is used to screen the potential recipients of the program or funds. Medicaid, for example, makes use of both types. Funds are allocated to states on the basis of the formula relating state and national per capita income. Beneficiary eligibility is determined by a separate formula based on age and disability. A similar distinction can be made for the allocation procedures used for Title I. The final stage in the allocation process is to determine eligible participants. Thus, in Title I, the use of a cutoff score on an achievement test can be considered an eligibility formula that forms the last step of the funding allocation process.

In most cases, it is Congress who clearly and specifically states the allocation formula and the factor weightings. Several classifications have been offered of the types of variables used in allocation formulas. One group (ACIR, 1978) suggests three major types of measures: those related to population, financial need, and program need. Specific measures are used in different ways depending upon the grant. Measures related to population, for example, can be used as continuous measures or as "qualifiers." Thus, the allocation of funds could be based on the number of persons residing in each defined geographic area (e.g., county, city, school district), or funds could be dispersed to all areas having greater than a specific percentage of the national population (e.g., urban areas). Measures of financial need are usually related to income. For instance, funds could be dispersed on the basis of the per capita income in a geographical area. Program need is sometimes reflected through a measure of income and at other times is a more direct measure of need. For example, a program for boating safety might use the number of vessels registered while a medical aid program might rely on estimates of the number of available hospital beds. Sometimes population or demographic measures are presumed to reflect program need if only because they tend to define the constituency of interest. Thus, funds for an adult education program might be restricted on the basis of the number of persons over 18 years of age. Another classification of formula variables (U.S. Department of Commerce, 1978), divides the types of measures into the categories of need, capability, and effort. Here, need refers to population and demographic measures as well as more direct indicators. Capability refers to the amount of revenues that a local or state agency might be expected to provide from their own taxes and income. Effort relates to the amount that is already being spent for a given program from nonfederal sources. However, these measures are classified, it is clear that quantified indicators are often used in the allocation process.

The formulas that are used differ considerably in structure. As an example, one can consider the formula that is used to allocate GRS funds. The formula is essentially a ratio of "effort" (the taxes collected) to a measure of "capability" (per capita income) multiplied by total population (that is presumably reflective of need). Generally a given variable will be used either directly in the formula or as a "quantifier" or "constraint." These are used to define the target populations and/or to protect against sudden fluctuations in allotment from one year to the next. One example of this can be seen in what is commonly termed a "hold-harmless" provision. Here, funds are allocated in a given year by means of a formula, but any recipient who does not qualify for the current year and who received funds in the previous year may be allowed to continue receiving funds or to have these phased out gradually over a period of several years. Provisions of this nature are included because of political considerations or a desire to provide continuity in the programs that are offered from one year to the next.

EXAMPLES OF ALLOCATION FORMULA DESIGNS

It is apparent that many of the formulas used to allocate funds meet one or more of the requirements for the regression-discontinuity design. Many rely on continuous quantified measures or combinations of measures to determine the amount of funds that are allocated. Some specify a cutoff value for allocation or eligibility, while others have multiple cutoffs or "cutoff ranges" within which the amount of funds varies continuously.

To illustrate how the regression-discontinuity design could be coupled with allocation formulas consider the allocation of Title I funds from the school district to individual schools. Here, a measure of poverty (presumed also to be reflective of educational disadvantage) is used. This might be a measure like the percentage of free lunches that are served in each school or the number of children in families receiving AFDC. Schools are ranked by this measure and designated as eligible for Title I funds on the basis of a cutoff. Clearly, several of the requirements for the regression-discontinuity design are met here. The preprogram measure can be the estimate of free lunches and schools divided into "program" or "comparison" groups solely on the basis of a cutoff score. The postprogram measure could be an estimate of average achievement test scores for each school.

This example illustrates some of the difficulties that will arise when trying to couple the regression-discontinuity design with allocation formulas. One problem concerns the fact that not all eligible schools receive the same amount of funds and only a small percentage of a school's population will receive services. As a result, a postprogram measure that reflects the average achievement for the school will only be partially reflective of the effect of Title I services. While this might appear to be a serious difficulty, it is simply a variation of the problem that normally occurs in trying to estimate the degree of program implementation. Just as the amount of service given to each student will differ even within the same Title I program and classroom, we expect that the amount of Title I program services differs from school to school. It would be necessary in this hypothetical design to estimate a "weighting" factor that indicates the degree of Title I service provided at each school. This is analogous to estimating the amount of service that a given student receives. For example, one might consider the percentage of students in a given school who are enrolled in a Title I program as a suitable covariate in the analysis.

A second example can be constructed to illustrate how the regression-discontinuity design could be used to evaluate the Airport Development Aid Program (Public Law 91–258). The objectives of this law are "to assist public agencies in the development of a nationwide system of public airports adequate to meet the needs of civil aeronautics" (OMB, 1979). Generally, funds are used for "constructing, improving, or repairing a public airport or portion thereof." All public airports are eligible for funds, but the level of funding differs depending upon a cutoff value on a pre-funding measure. The measure used to determine the amount of funding is the number of enplanements at each airport. The federal government will pay not more than 75% of the cost of a project at an airport that enplanes one-fourth of 1% or more of all passengers enplaned at such airports, and will pay 80% for projects at all other airports. Thus, the cutoff point is "one-fourth of 1%" of all enplanements.

This example illustrates a different set of difficulties than the previous one. Here, one is not testing the difference between a "program" and "control" group, but rather between two levels of funding. In addition, the levels of funding are not all that different and one might not, depending upon the program of interest, predict that a difference of 5% in the funding level will result in differences in post-funding measures. In this example, the preprogram measure is the number of enplanements. The airports are divided into different levels of program by means of a sharp cutoff value on this measure, and the postprogram measure might also be the number of enplanements in a subsequent year or some measure related to airport activity. As in the previous example, it would be useful to search for "weighting" variables that reflect the amount of funding or program implementation at each airport.

Another example can be constructed using the regression-discontinuity design to conduct a post hoc evaluation of the Comprehensive Employment and Training Act (CETA) programs. The objectives of CETA programs are

> to provide job training and employment opportunities for economically disadvantaged, unemployed, and underemployed persons to assure that training and other service lead to increased earnings and enhanced self-sufficiency by establishing a flexible decentralized system of Federal, State and Local programs. (OMB, 1979)

The allocation formulas for the CETA program were extremely complicated due to a large number of qualifiers and exceptions. In addition, the grant was divided into six major parts or "Titles" and each part had its own set of formulas. Of special interest here is Title VI, which provided public service employment in areas of high unemployment. The allocation of funds for Title VI included the following provisions:

> Not less than 85% of the funds appropriated are allotted as follows: (a) 50% in proportion to each area's share of all unemployed persons; (b) 25% in proportion to the area's share of all unemployed persons in excess of 4.5% of the labor force; and (c) 25% among areas of substantial (6.5% for three consecutive months) unemployment as defined in the CETA regulations. (OMB, 1979)

This formula appears to have two cutoff points—one at 4.5% unemployment and the other at 6.5% unemployment. Those areas below 4.5% unemployment received the least amount of funds, those above 6.5% received the most, and those between the two cutoffs were allocated funds on the basis of a separate formula. Here, we have a situation analogous to the airport development grant where we are dealing with different levels of the program or funding. The preprogram measure would be the indicator of unemployment, units are assigned to groups on the basis of the two cutoffs, and postprogram measures of program implementation could be incorporated as covariates.

These three examples serve to illustrate how the regression-discontinuity design could be coupled with allocation formulas. All have in common the existence of a continuous quantified preprogram measure and a specified cutoff value or values that are used, at least in part, to determine program funding or eligibility. Many of the problems of implementation discussed earlier will also tend to occur in these applications. In addition, problems related to the context of federal allocation procedures will also occur and are discussed in the next section.

PROBLEMS IN ALLOCATION FORMULA DESIGNS

Every research context and, in fact, every federal grant, is likely to pose its own set of problems for any methodology. In this section, the context of federal allocation formulas is examined generally for likely potential problems for the application of the regression-discontinuity design. It is important to keep in mind that the grants administered under the federal government cover an impressive range of purpose and form and that the use of the regression-discontinuity design or any other should be examined carefully before it is applied to any particular project.

A major problem in using the regression-discontinuity design coupled with allocation formulas concerns the number of units that are available for analysis. The first level of allocation in many grants is from the federal government directly to the state and trust territories. It would be difficult indeed to have confidence in an analysis based on between 50 and 60 data points, although the generally better measurement properties of state-level aggregated data could allow for a reasonable analysis. In many cases, the state subsequently allocates funds to smaller units of government within their boundaries. This may or may not be done by a predetermined formula. Often, the states are given guidelines for this second level of allocation but are not required to restrict themselves to a predetermined formula. It will sometimes be the case, therefore, that there will be too few units to justify a regression-discontinuity analysis. The possibility of "skipping" an allocation level and doing an analysis on substate units will often be ruled out because of inconsistencies in formulas or data between states.

A second problem that will often occur concerns the distributions of the variables that are available for the analysis. The statistical procedures used to analyze the regression-discontinuity design for the most part assume that the distributions for the variables are normal or that they can be transformed into normally distributed variables. Previous experience indicates that many of these variables, especially those related to income, are not likely to be so distributed. While procedures for analyzing nonnormal distributions are being explored (Sacks & Ylvisaker, 1976), distributional problems may minimize the utility of the design for certain projects at this time.

Federal funds are often dispersed under certain "matching" considerations. In these cases, the state and/or local government is required to provide a certain percentage of the funding. The total amounts of funds which are available are determined in part by these local governments. The most common matching ratio is 50–50, or half federal funds and half funds from other sources. Problems generated by matching provisions may be able to be at least partly accounted for in regression-discontinuity analysis by the inclusion of a variable that measures the level of program funding in each unit.

Another potential difficulty concerns the fact that, at least at certain levels of allocation, there are no comparison groups. Especially when the federal government allocates to the state it is usually the case that few if any states are denied at least some funding. This is probably due in part to political considerations. We are left, in the absence of comparison groups, with a strategy that attempts to test differences between various levels and types of programs rather than between the program and no program at all. This was illustrated in two of the hypothetical examples outlined above.

Numerous constraints or exceptions are often allowed for a given formula. These are dictated by the political necessities involved in order to get the bill through Congress, but nevertheless pose some difficulty for the application of the regression-discontinuity design. Sometimes these take the form of allowing the director of the appropriate federal department to have certain discretionary powers in allocating funds while at other times they are evidenced by the inclusion of specific subgroups who would not necessarily qualify by means of the formula but should be included anyway. These exceptions result in a class of misassignment and exclusion problems similar to those discussed Chapter 7. The same approaches that are advocated there could be applied here. This might include separate analyses for different subgroups of interest to determine whether estimates of program effect differ, as well as exploratory analyses designed to assess the degree of this difference.

Another problem that holds some similarities with problems evidenced in Title I evaluation concerns the existence of competing programs to which a particular governmental unit could apply if they do not get federal funding from the government. Thus, state and local governments may already have their own programs for airport development, compensatory education, or manpower training. It may even be the case that these programs exist primarily to provide funds to governmental units that are denied funds from the federal government because of their placement by the formula. When similar programs exist for purposes of equalizing funding to governmental units, these can act to degrade a comparison between groups or between different levels of the program.

A variety of measurement problems can occur depending upon the program and the variables that are used. A major problem results from the fact that many of the variables used in allocation formulas, especially those related to population and income, are obtained from census data that is collected every 10 years. Sometimes an attempt is made to provide updated estimates, but these are often based upon fallible prediction models and must be considered suspect. Some work has been done on developing continuously measured indices, such as the cost of living index and the unemployment index, and such developments should improve measurement qualities of the regression-discontinuity design.

Another problem stems from the fact that the regression-discontinuity design requires the pre- and postprogram measurement of comparison subjects or units. It will often be the case that the information of greatest interest when determining the effect of a federal program will only be collected for the program group. For example, in the case of medicaid programs, relevant indicators of the effects of medical care may only be collected (or even if collected, may only be aggregated) for the program group because that is the group of prime interest. An analysis may be possible at a higher level of aggregation (e.g., general health indicators), but this may not be the primary issue of interest.

A federal grant is simply an offering from the federal government to other governmental agencies or individuals. Participation in programs or even application for such programs is by no means mandatory. There are many cases in which an eligible unit will not apply for or receive the program. This may occur if the governmental units recognize in advance that they will not qualify, if they are unwilling to submit to federal requirements and paperwork, of if they are simply unaware of the existence of the program. In any event, this self-selection process is likely to have an effect on the constitution of the groups of interest and, subsequently, on the analysis itself.

One of the most difficult problems in applying the regression-discontinuity design to allocation formulas concerns the placement of cutoffs and the assignment to conditions. Given the political factors that it must consider, Congress is hard put to develop formulas that are simply constructed just for the sake of expediency or methodological clarity. In addition, it is not clear that the sharp cutoff for assignment that is a requirement for the basic regression-discontinuity design is always politically desirable or feasible. To get an idea of the difficulty involved in decisions concerning cutoff points, consider a passage from the Report of Statistics for Allocation of Funds (U.S. Department of Commerce, 1978):

> Undesirable discontinuities may be introduced into an allocation system by cutoffs, especially by sharp cutoffs. For example, if an area must have an unemployment rate of 5% before it can receive any funds, a very trivial error in the estimation of the unemployment rate can easily throw an area from under 5% or from over 5% into the other group. Here a very small error can make a tremendous difference and lead to continual complaints about the accuracy of the data on the part of the governmental units which feel the cutoff operates to their disadvantage.
>
> A common solution to controversies over cutoffs is to provide alternative cutoffs and to permit each jurisdiction to select the formula which is most advantageous. While this works moderately well, it has the disadvantage of making it difficult to predict in advance (and budget for) the amount required for the process if no fixed overall sum to be allocated is specified. If no overall sum is specified but each jurisdiction may choose which formula it will use in determining its share (with computed amounts totaled over all competing jurisdictions so that the per cent of the total allocated to each jurisdiction can be determined) one gets a floating cutoff point where the amount one jurisdiction gets depends upon the decisions made by other jurisdictions.
>
> For eligibility cutoffs it is almost always possible to devise a formula such that there is a gradual approach to zero (or to some cutoff point lower than the existing absolute cutoff). Here, small errors in the data lead only to small changes in the allocation and the tendency to prolonged (and insoluble) arguments over minor errors is removed. Of course, major errors will and should continue to be the subject of controversy but one will be spared the waste of time and effort involved in the use of a formula which requires data of unattainable accuracy.

The use of a formula based on a continuous allocation of funds implies, at least for some cases, that there will be multiple cutoff points. All units scoring below the lower cutoff point get one level of the program, those scoring above the highest cutoff point get another level, while all those scoring between these two get a continuously varying level of the program. This was illustrated in the example above for the CETA program. The regression-discontinuity design or a variation thereof could be appropriate for these cases. What must be avoided, if regression-discontinuity is to be used, is the use of a formula that allocates continuously different levels of funding across the entire range of the preprogram measure. As long as there are clear cutoff points that differentiate between the level of funding or program in adjacent groups (as measured on the preprogram variable), one expects that if these levels of treatment or program have an effect this will show up as a discontinuity in the relationship between the pre- and postprogram measures.

We can see from this discussion that there are a large number of potential problems that can act to degrade the analysis of program effect by means of the regression-discontinuity design. Nevertheless, the sheer magnitude of federal domestic aid, the need to evaluate the effectiveness of these programs, and the potential usefulness of the regression-discontinuity design in this regard, warrants a more detailed exploration of the appropriate uses for the design in this type of context.

5

The Statistical Analysis
of the
Regression-Discontinuity
Design

Up to this point, this volume has concentrated on design issues of regression-discontinuity. The present chapter focuses instead on the statistical analysis of data obtained using such design structures. The analytic strategy outlined in the first part of this chapter is not new—it simply involves the application of the General Linear Model to the data at hand. However, there are some issues of importance concerning how to best apply this general model in regression-discontinuity contexts.

Experience with the use of the regression-discontinuity design, especially in compensatory education contexts, indicates that a major problem in the implementation of the design involves adherence to the assignment by a cutoff value. The last section of this chapter outlines an analytic strategy that holds promise for such "fuzzy" regression-discontinuity situations. If further studies of this analytic approach (and related strategies) confirm their appropriateness, the range of applications of the regression-discontinuity design would be greatly enlarged.

A STATISTICAL MODEL
FOR REGRESSION-DISCONTINUITY

A good deal of work has been devoted to the issue of how one should analyze the regression-discontinuity design when the cutoff criterion has been adhered to. Sween (1971), in a dissertation on the topic, advocated the calculation of separate regression lines for the program and comparison groups and the estimation of the program effect by means of a t-test of the difference between the regression lines at the cutoff. In several papers, Boruch (1973, 1974) and Boruch and DeGracie (1975) summarize a variety of potentially useful analytic models and distinguish cases where the pretest variable is random or fixed, assignment is sharp or "fuzzy" (i.e., the cutoff criterion is not followed perfectly) and the groups come from the same normal distribution or comprise separate ones. The recommended model for a commonly expected situation, that is, when assignment is sharp and the groups are thought to represent a single population, is suggested in the work of Chow (1960) and consolidated in a more general model by Gujarti (1970). Reichardt (1979) and Campbell, Reichardt, and Trochim (1979) discuss this general model within the context of regression-discontinuity specifically. A similar approach is outlined more recently in Judd and Kenny (1981). The ESEA Title I evaluation context has resulted in papers by Echternacht (1978) and Echternacht and Swinton (1979) that discuss a number of approaches that might be employed when there is evidence for a curvilinear relationship such as might be caused by floor or ceiling effects. Analytic issues were also considered by Berk and Rauma (1983) who present a regression-discontinuity analysis in the area of criminal justice. Econometricians and statisticians have shown some interest in the design. Related discussions can be found in Spiegelman (1977, 1979), Rubin (1977), and Goldberger (1972). Some work on a general model appropriate for the nonlinear case or when distributions are not normal has been carried out by Sacks and Ylvisaker (1976).

The analytic model presented here is similar to many of the above procedures and has been described in Trochim (1980). Given a pretest, x_i, and posttest, y_i, the model can be stated formally as follows:

$$y_i = \beta_0 + \beta_1 x_i^* + \beta_2 z_i + \beta_3 x_i^* z_i + \ldots$$

$$+ \beta_{n-1} x_i^{*s} + \beta_n x_i^{*s} z_i + e_i$$

Where:

x_i^* = preprogram measure for individual i minus the value of the cutoff, x_0 (i.e., $x_i^* = x_i - x_0$)

y_i = postprogram measure for individual i

z_i = assignment variable (1 if program participant; 0 if comparison participant)

s = the degree of the polynomial for the associated x_i^*

β_0 = parameter for comparison group intercept at cutoff

β_1 = linear slope parameter

β_2 = program effect estimate

β_n = parameter for the sth polynomial or interaction terms if paired with z

e_i = random error

The major hypothesis of interest is:

$$H_0: \beta_2 = 0$$

tested against the alternative:

$$H_1: \beta_2 \neq 0$$

There are several key assumptions that must be met for this model to be appropriate:

1. The cutoff criterion must be followed. There can be no misassignment relative to the cutoff score. The analysis of "fuzzy" regression-discontinuity designs (where a strict cutoff is not followed) is discussed briefly below.

2. The true pre-post distribution must be describable as a polynomial in x. If the true model is instead logarithmic, exponential, or some other function, this model is misspecified and the estimates of program effect are likely to be innacurate. If the data can be transformed to a polynomial distribution prior to analysis, the model above may be appropriate. It should be noted that this assumption is not necessarily restrictive. Any functional relationship in the data can be described sufficiently by a high enough order polynomial function.

3. There must be a sufficient number of points in each group to enable the estimation of regression lines. This is more important for the comparison than the program group because it is the comparison group function that describes the null expectation. The analysis of cases where there are not enough points to estimate a regression line in the program group is discussed below.

4. Both groups must come from a single pretest distribution. The cutoff value divides this original distribution into two groups. The use of groups that come from separate distributions (e.g., in a "post hoc" regression-discontinuity where the two groups are distinct populations such as two classrooms, one of which is for advanced placement students and the other of which is for slow learners, thus resulting in a "naturally occurring cutoff") is considered below.

5. The program conditions must be implemented uniformly within each group. The model assumes that all persons in the program group receive the same "amount" of the program and those in the comparison group receive no program. If the program is not implemented or some comparison persons receive comparable treatment, the model stated above will be misspecified and, consequently, the results may not be valid.

It should be noted that the key to the analysis outlined above is that the correlations between the preprogram variable and all other possible regressors reduce to zero when partialled for the group assignment variable. The reader is referred to discussions by Goldberger (1972) and Judd and Kenny (1981) for more detailed consideration of this issue. One implication of this is that any kind of model that uses the regression equation as an argument (e.g., a logit model) will be appropriate. This is illustrated well in the evaluation conducted by Berk and Rauma (1983) that made use of both logistic regression and proportional hazard analysis.

The general model estimates both main and interaction effects as discontinuities at the cutoff. It is important to recognize that this is accomplished by subtracting the cutoff value from each preprogram score to create x_i^*. This has the effect of moving the cutoff value to the y-intercept point and improves the interpretability of the coefficients. As will be shown below, when this transformation is applied, the β_0 term is both the y-intercept for the comparison group regression line and the predicted y-value for the comparison group at the cutoff. From this, it follows that β_2, the program main effect estimate, is the difference between the two group regression functions at the intercept and at the cutoff. The effect can be estimated at other pretest points (as in Title I evaluation where it is also estimated at the program group pretest mean) by subtracting the value of interest from the preprogram scores to create x_i^*.

It is useful to examine the mechanics of this model to see how it operates. Consider a case where the true function is linear, the slopes in the two groups are equal, and there is a main program effect. The true model can be written as:

$$y_i = \beta_0 + \beta_1 x_i + \beta_2 z_i$$

where the terms are defined as above. Using the general model given earlier, the comparison group line is:

$$y_i = \beta_0 + \beta_1 x_i^*$$

and the estimate of where this line intersects the cutoff is simply:

$$y_c = \beta_0$$

because $x_i^* = 0$ at the cutoff. The program group line for this situation is:

$$y_i = \beta_0 + \beta_1 x_i^* + \beta_2$$

The estimate of where this line intersects with the cutoff is:

$$y_p = \beta_0 + \beta_2$$

The main effect is defined as the vertical difference between the lines at the cutoff. This would again be:

$$y_p - y_c = (\beta_0 + \beta_2) - \beta_0$$

$$= \beta_2$$

Thus, β_2 is the main program effect.

Now consider a case where the true function includes both a main and interaction effect:

$$y_i = \beta_0 + \beta_1 x_i + \beta_2 z_i + \beta_3 x_i z_i$$

Here, the comparison group line would be:

$$y_c = \beta_0 + \beta_1 x_i^*$$

while the program group line is:

$$y_p = \beta_0 + \beta_1 x_i^* + \beta_2 + \beta_3 x_i^*$$

The difference between these lines is:

$$y_p - y_c = (\beta_0 + \beta_1 x_i^* + \beta_2 + \beta_3 x_i^*) - (\beta_0 + \beta_1 x_i^*)$$

$$= \beta_2 + \beta_3 x_i^*$$

Here β_2 is still the main effect of the program—the vertical distance between the two lines at the cutoff. The interaction effect is reflected in β_3 which can be interpreted as the difference in slopes between the lines of the two groups. It is worth noting that β_0 is where the comparison group line hits the cutoff and that β_2 can be interpreted as the amount that must be added to this value in order to find the program group cutoff intercept. Similarly, β_1 is the linear slope of the comparison group, and therefore β_3 can be interpreted as the amount that must be added to this slope in order to determine the slope in the program group.

The explanation extends to any order polynomial. For instance, consider a more complex true function like:

$$y_i = \beta_0 + \beta_1 x_i + \beta_2 z_i + \beta_3 x_i^3 + \beta_4 x_i^3 z_i$$

The comparison group line is:

$$y_c = \beta_0 + \beta_1 x_i^* + \beta_3 x_i^{*3}$$

while the program group line is:

$$y_p = \beta_0 + \beta_1 x_i^* + \beta_2 + \beta_3 x_i^{*3} + \beta_4 x_i^{*3}$$

The difference between the lines is:

$$y_p - y_c = (\beta_0 + \beta_1 x_i^* + \beta_2 + \beta_3 x_i^{*3} + \beta_4 x_i^{*3}) -$$

$$(\beta_0 + \beta_1 x_i^* + \beta_3 x_i^{*3})$$

$$= \beta_2 + \beta_4 x_i^{*3}$$

The main effect is again β_2 but in this example there is no linear interaction. However, there is a cubic interaction (a difference in third-order function between the groups) that is estimated by β_4.

The significance of main and interaction effects can be examined by constructing a confidence interval around the particular β. For instance, a 95% confidence interval for the main effect would be:

$$CI_{95\%} = \beta_2 \pm 2SE(\beta_2)$$

The βs and their standard errors are typical output from most computerized regression analysis packages.

MODEL SPECIFICATION

From the general model described above, one needs to select that subset of variables (i.e., polynomial and interaction terms) that describes the true functional form of the data. If the true model is known, the specification issue is trivial—the correct terms of the general model are simply used in the analysis. However, the true model is seldom known in practice unless extensive previous research or theory consistently point to a specific functional form. Methodological strategies that might help uncover the true model, such as the use of double pretests (Boruch, 1978), are seldom applied. In most settings, the analyst will have to rely on visual and empirical exploration of the data in order to determine what the "likely" true model for the data might be.

Hocking (1976) discusses five computational procedures that are useful for subset selection: all possible regressions; stepwise methods (forward and backward); optimal subset procedures; suboptimal methods; and ridge regression techniques. For most of these procedures, one usually defines selection criteria that are used to determine whether a particular variable will be included in the final model. Among the criteria that are commonly used are the following: change in residual mean square; the squared multiple correlation coefficient; and the total squared error. In addition, if a stepwise procedure is used, one usually needs a stopping criteria to help determine when an acceptable subset of variables has been selected. The reader is referred to Hocking (1976) for an excellent discussion of subset selection.

The choice of computational procedure and criteria for subset selection should be guided by the goals of the analysis. Typically, the primary goal in regression-discontinuity is to obtain an unbiased and statistically efficient estimate of program effect. This is perfectly achieved only if the subset of variables that is selected from the general model exactly describes the true model in the data. In practice, exact specification is hard to accomplish. Hocking (1976) states, "The problem of interpreting the subset information is complex. The question of whether any of the proposed criteria are effective in identifying 'true' variables is difficult to answer" (p. 44).

If the selected model is not exactly specified, then it must be either over or underspecified.[1] A model is overspecified if it includes all variables in the true model along with additional terms that are not in the true model. It is underspecified if it does not include all the terms that are in the true model. Sween (1971) and Hocking (1976) argue that parameter estimates will generally be biased when the true model has been underspecified. Trochim (1980) demonstrated with simulations that this was the case for the regression-discontinuity design. An overspecified model, on the other hand, will yield an unbiased estimate of program effect, but this estimate will be less efficient (i.e., have greater variance) than one obtained from an exactly specified model (Sween, 1971, 1977; Trochim, 1980).

To see this, consider again the data that was presented in Figure 1.3. The model that generated the data included a single linear term across both groups with an additive or main program effect. If the linear and assignment variable terms of the general model are the only ones selected for the analysis, the resulting model will be exactly specified and the estimate of program effect will be unbiased. If higher order terms are added to the model, these new terms should be nonsignificant and the program effect estimate should remain the same. However, because there are more parameters in the model, one has fewer degrees of freedom available for estimating the effect as well as multicolinearity between variables, and the standard error of the effect estimate will be larger. Nevertheless, no pseudo-effect will result from adding in the higher-order terms.

Consider next the null case for a true quadratic model as shown in Figure 5.1. While this function might be unlikely in practice, it provides a useful illustration of the pseudo-effect problem. Here, one expects that first order models will yield pseudo-effects while second order ones will not. If both linear and quadratic terms are included, the model is overspecified. The linear terms should be nonsignificant and the estimate of effect unbiased (although less efficient than with only quadratic terms). If cubic terms are added, these should also be nonsignificant and, again, an unbiased estimate is obtained.

The same logic can be extended to models of any order. If the true function is quintic, analyses that underfit this function are likely to yield biased estimates while analyses that include the quintic term and any other terms will yield unbiased estimates although these will be less efficient than an analysis that only includes the quintic.

With this in mind, the rationale for subset selection in regression-discontinuity is straightforward. If an unbiased estimate of effect is desired, what is needed is an approach that optimally yields a model that is exactly specified and, if not, one which is overspecified. In practice, this will often be difficult to achieve, in large part due to the high multicolinearity between predictor variables as discussed below. Previous analytic recommendations (Judd & Kenny, 1981; Trochim, 1980) rely on

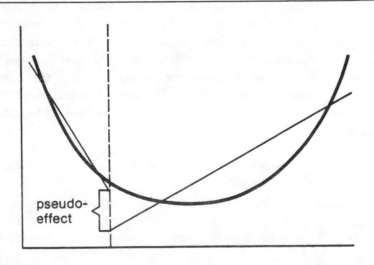

Figure 5.1   Pseudo-Effects Resulting from Fitting a True Quadratic Function with a Linear Model

overfitting of the likely true function and elimination of extraneous terms using various criteria (e.g., r-square, significance of βs). However, no single criterion or regression approach can guarantee that the optimum subset will be selected. What is recommended here is a broad-based multiple-criterion approach to subset selection that requires that the analyst exercise considerable judgment in the model selection process. It should be stressed that the following approach assumes that the analyst is primarily interested in obtaining unbiased estimates of the program effect even if some price is paid in terms of efficiency.

This approach begins, as do others, with a determination of the "likely" pre-post relationship through visual inspection, experience with the data, or other means. This "likely" function is used as an initial guide in the analysis. The general model outlined above is then applied to the data in a series of steps until this likely function is overfitted by several terms. For example, assume that inspection of the bivariate distribution or previous theory indicates that a quadratic or second-order model is likely. In the first step of the analysis, one might only fit the linear term, x_i^*, and the assignment variable, z_i. Theoretically, this model would be underspecified and the estimate of effect would be biased. In the second step, one could add the first-order interaction term. This should also be underspecified. The third step would add the quadratic term, and the fourth its interaction. If the analyst was correct in guessing the true function, the model should at this point be at least overspecified and, perhaps, exactly specified. In subsequent steps, higher-order terms can be added one by one until the analyst is fairly confident that the model is overspecified.

Several indicators can be used to help verify the appropriateness of the likely true function or lead to selection of another. Plots of estimates of gain, r-squares, and residual mean squares across steps should evidence some change at the step where the model becomes exactly or overspecified. In general, estimates of gain should stabilize, r-squares should level off, and residual mean squares should reach their minimum at that step. Plots of regression lines for various models should also be examined. Higher-order models that "explode" outside the pretest data range may fit the data well but be difficult to explain in any substantive sense.

If the evidence is compelling, the analyst can be satisfied to accept the likely function as an appropriate model. In the absence of such evidence, it is generally preferable to report multiple estimates, or, if a single estimate is required, to select one from a reasonable higher-order step in the analysis. In certain cases it may be possible to eliminate some lower-order terms while retaining higher-order ones. Such exclusions should be made with great caution because of the presence of multicolinearity and the possibility of underspecification and consequent bias.

The central tension in this analytic approach is between over and underspecification. As more terms are added to the model the potential for bias is reduced, but so is the precision of the estimates. Furthermore, higher-order models will ultimately fit the data well, but will often yield functions that are clearly absurd in any substantive sense. Typically, models higher than second or third-order will not be theoretically justifiable in most social science arenas. If the analytic evidence supports a higher-order model, one should suspect that the assumptions of the general model may not be met, implementation difficulties may have distorted the true function, or that outliers are disproportionately affecting the analysis.

A major feature of the approach to subset selection outlined here is that it is conservative. Deliberate over-fitting of the "likely" true function will tend to lead to unbiased estimates that are somewhat imprecise. If the true model is a low-order polynomial, the imprecision should not be too great. With higher-order true models the efficiency may decline considerably because of the tendency of this approach to retain polynomials of lower order than in the true model. This feature, however, makes some intuitive sense. In many research contexts there is reason to consider more complex distributions as less likely and often, indicative of measurement problems, poor data quality, poor research implementation, and so on.

The lack of a more definitive analytic strategy that can be mechanically followed may be unsettling to some analysts. This situation reflects inherent uncertainties in the data, not in statistics. Short of divine revelation of the true function, no mechanistic approach can guarantee its detection. As a result, we must rely on statistical indicators and good analytic judgment to help select a model that is efficient and that minimizes the chance of bias.

Finally, a word about graphics is warranted. The quality of a regression-discontinuity analysis is to a great extent dependent on the ability of the analyst to determine the likely true functional form. Plots of the data are obviously essential for accomplishing this well. For example, it is useful to plot regression lines obtained at each step in the stepwise procedure. These plots should not be confined only to the range of the obtained data. Higher-order polynomial models that fit the obtained data well will often be clearly absurd when extended beyond the range of the data. One will also often get a clearer picture of the pre-post relationship by plotting posttest means for various size intervals on the pretest. Outliers that may be distorting the regression analysis might also be examined through plots of influence functions (Hampel, 1974; Thissen, Baker, & Wainer, 1981). Riecken and Boruch (1974) state well the importance of graphics for regression-discontinuity analysis when they say that one should even "distrust the results if visual inspection makes plausible a continuous function with no discontinuity at the cutting point."

DESIGN VARIATIONS AND ANALYTIC IMPLICATIONS

The model outlined above will be suitable for the analysis of most basic regression-discontinuity designs as defined in Chapter 1. When the design is more complex, variations of this model need to be devised. This section discusses a number of design variations and some of their implications for the analysis.

MULTIPLE CUTOFF POINTS

In some situations, one might wish to use more than one cutoff value for assignment. For instance, if one wished to compare two programs and a control condition, two cutoffs would be needed to distinguish the three groups. This might be especially useful if the program that was thought to be most powerful could be applied to those most in need, the comparison condition to those least in need, and the other program to persons falling between these two groups on preprogram indicators. The analysis of such a design follows from the general model outlined above. The major difference stems from the need to indicate the assignment to groups. Unlike, the two-group case, this situation requires two assignment (z) variables. If the true pre-post relationship is linear and there is no interaction effect an appropriate analytic model might be

$$y_i = \beta_0 + \beta_1 x_i + \beta_2 z1_i + \beta_3 z2_i + e_i$$

where all terms are as before except for the two assignment variables, z1 and z2 which could be defined as:

$$z1_i = 1 \text{ if program 1; 0 otherwise}$$

$$z2_i = 1 \text{ if program 2; 0 otherwise}$$

In this model, β_2 would be the estimate of the difference between program 1 and the comparison group; β_3 would be the difference between program 2 and the comparison group; and $\beta_2 - \beta_3$ would be the program 1 − program 2 difference.

In multiple cutoff situations, only one cutoff can be subtracted from the pretest to create the x_i^* term of the general model. As a result, one must be careful when interpreting the regression models. For example, if in the above analysis the cutoff that separates the program 1 and program 2 groups is subtracted from the pretest, then all estimates of effect are computed at that pretest value. Thus, the program 1-comparison group difference, β_2 would estimate the vertical distance between the lines of the two groups at the subtracted cutoff value. If it is desirable to obtain different estimates at different cutoffs within the same analysis, this can be accomplished by substitution in the obtained regression equation.

The model specification issue also becomes more complex in the multiple group situation. In effect, one has the equivalent of several general models that must be specified. For example, considering just first-order terms, it will be necessary to include the interactions between $z1$ and x, and $z2$ and x. Assuming the same number of cases as the two-group design, one will in general have fewer degrees of freedom and greater pretest homogeneity in the multigroup situation.

RANDOM ASSIGNMENT IN
REGRESSION-DISCONTINUITY DESIGNS

As mentioned in Chapter 3, the regression-discontinuity design is usually recommended only if random assignment to condition is not possible. Nevertheless, the two strategies can each be enhanced in various ways by combining them within a single study. Several analytic approaches for coupling the designs are discussed here.

In some settings, reliance on a single inflexible cutoff rule may be impractical or undesirable. For instance, teachers may feel that test unreliability results in deserving students being on the "wrong" side of the cutoff for placement into the program of interest. Given that there may be difficulty in accepting the assignment of cases close to the cutoff, it may be preferable to replace the cutoff point with a cutoff interval and to randomly assign to program within that interval. In the compensatory case, for example, one would select two cutoffs—those scoring below the lower cutoff would receive the program; those scoring above the higher cutoff would be in the comparison group; and those scoring between the two cutoffs would be randomly assigned. In this situation, the randomized part of the design would not be troubled by the functional form and model selection issues mentioned above because, due to the random assignment, the same functional form can be assumed for the two randomized groups and mean differences can be examined. The regression-discontinuity portion of the design, while probably lower in internal validity, enables generalization over a wider range of pretest scores.

The use of random assignment presents no fundamental difficulty in terms of analysis. In fact, three separate analyses are possible. First, one can look only at the cases within the random assignment interval and use Analysis of Covariance to estimate differences between groups. In terms of the general model stated earlier, this would involve inclusion of the linear term and assignment variable. Second, one could exclude the data within the interval and analyze just the regression-discontinuity portion of the design. Here, the interval would be treated as a cutoff. Estimates of effect could be made at the mean or median pretest value of the interval (by subtracting it from all pretest cases in the analysis). Finally, one could analyze all of the data at once using the general model and again estimating effect at the mean or median within the cutoff interval. The redundancy in analysis has some advantages. Model specification problems of regression-discontinuity become less critical, statistical power will generally be greater due to the incorporation of random assignment (Goldberger, 1972), and institutional reluctance to randomly assign all participants is reduced.

Random assignment can also be used effectively across the entire pretest range to reduce the model specification problem. Several intervals for random assignment can be constructed and estimates of effect from these can be compared with overall regression-discontinuity estimates at those points. Similar results add credibility to the interpretation.

Typically, random assignment to two groups implies an equal probability of assignment to program (i.e., p = .5) for any participant, but this need not be the case. Instead of a single cutoff interval, one could use several and have declining probabil-ities of assignment to program as pretest scores move from the program group to the comparison group ranges. For instance, three intervals could be incorporated into the compensatory case with those in the lowest interval having a probability of .75 of assignment to program, those in the middle interval having a probability of .5, and those in the highest interval having a probability of .25. Such a strategy would probably be perceived as "fairer" within many institutional settings than either reliance on a single strict cutoff or a single cutoff interval. The analysis would again follow that of the general model described above.

THE USE OF COVARIATES

In most settings other program measures will be available as covariates in the regression-discontinuity analysis. In educational contexts one might use grade point average, socioeconomic status, attendance records, and so on. The general model can easily be extended to include covariates, as discussed in Judd and Kenny (1981). Essentially, this involves simply adding relevant covariate terms to the model described above. As with any covariance analysis it is important to select the covariates judiciously because inclusion of terms that are highly correlated will act to reduce the efficiency of program effect estimates. This is especially important in regression-discontinuity analysis as outlined above because it is already possible that there may be some loss of efficiency due to overspecification.

COMPOSITE PRETEST MEASURES

The preprogram measure in regression-discontinuity need not be a single test value—assignment to group can be made on the basis of joint consideration of a number of measures. For example, both clinician ratings and psychological test scores could be combined into a single index and persons could be assigned to condition on the basis of a cutoff on the total score. The total score could be obtained in a number of ways—for example, through simple additive or weighted indexes or through factor analysis. The general model would be appropriate for analysis, substituting the total score where the pretest, x_i, occurs. Judd and Kenny (1981) recommend that all of the individual measures that make up the composite except one be included in the analysis.

PRETEST HOMOGENEITY IN THE PROGRAM GROUP

If the program can only be administered to a small percentage of the total sample there may not be sufficient pretest variance in the program group to warrant the estimation of regression lines for the group. This was probably the case in the Seaver and Quarton (1976) study of the effects of being selected for the Dean's list on subsequent grade point averages. The analytic approach for such a case follows from the general model with two major modifications. First, since it is not reasonable to estimate regression functions for the program group, investigations of interaction effects (i.e., changes in slope or regression function between groups) are ruled out. Thus all interaction terms in the general model (e.g., $\beta_3 x_i^* z_i$, $\beta_5 x_i^{*2} z_i$) should be excluded. Second, because it no longer makes sense to speak of the difference between the within-group regression lines at the cutoff, the program effect can more logically be estimated at a central pretest value for the program group (e.g., the pretest mean or median for that group) by subtracting that value from pretest scores.

SEPARATE WITHIN-GROUP DISTRIBUTIONS

Boruch (1974) distinguishes between cases where the entire sample comes from a single pretest distribution and where the groups come from separate and distinct pretest distributions. The general model assumes the former—an original single distribution is dichotomized by the cutoff point. There are two major settings in which separate distributions might arise. First, if the assignment variable is a composite that is constructed using discriminant function analysis, the resulting measure will be bimodal. Second, if two intact groups are selected for study because they are naturally distinct populations, the pretest distribution will also be bimodal. This might occur if one discovers two extreme groups that have a "natural" cutoff as might be the case when selecting for study two intact classrooms, one of which consists of slow learners and the other of which is composed of high achievers.

The key difference between the single and multiple distribution cases stems from the implications of random measurement error and within-group regression to the mean. When groups come from a single pretest distribution, the general model encompasses the entire pretest range. Attenuation of slope due to measurement error will occur across the entire range and will not bias estimates of effect. Similarly, regression will be toward the overall pretest mean and will be offsetting across groups. When groups represent distinct populations, measurement error and regression to the mean can operate separately within the groups. Thus, even in the absence of the program, within-group attenuation of slope will lead to pseudo-effects.

The statistical analysis for the separate pretest distribution case must therefore incorporate a correction for measurement error. Traditionally, corrections of this sort involve adjusting pretest scores in each group using a measure of within-group reliability. The adjusted pretest scores could then be incorporated into the general model in place of the original pretest scores. The reader is referred to Campbell and Boruch (1975) and Cook and Campbell (1979) for more detailed discussion of the issues involved in pretest score adjustment.

ILLUSTRATIVE ANALYSES

The data that is used to illustrate the analytic approaches outlined above is from the Title I compensatory education programs of the Providence, Rhode Island School District. The Comprehensive Test of Basic Skills (CTBS) was administered in March, 1978 (pretest) and March, 1979 (posttest). Analyses are presented for the second grade reading program and the fourth grade mathematics program, both of which began in September of 1978 and continued until the posttest.

SECOND GRADE READING PROGRAM

The bivariate distribution for the second grade program is shown in Figure 5.2. Program participants are those scoring below the cutoff score. Visual inspection of the graph indicates that a discontinuity at the cutoff is plausible. It appears that, on average, program group posttest scores are elevated above a visually extrapolated comparison group regression line. The pre-post relationship in the comparison group appears reasonably linear. The program group is considerably limited in pretest variance, but there is some indication of a possible first-order interaction—low-scoring program students seem to have gained slightly more than high-scoring ones. The pattern in the data is clearer in the plot of posttest means versus pretest scores shown in Figure 5.3. To obtain this plot, all posttest scores for each pretest value were averaged. It is important to recognize that plotted values are based on different n's with fewer cases at pretest extremes. One might also try several plots of this type for intervals on the pretest rather than for individual scores alone. Nevertheless, the comparison group function clearly looks linear, although evidence for an interaction effect remains marginal.

The correlations between predictor variables point to a major difficulty in using polynomial functions—the high degree of multicolinearity that results. For example, the correlation between x^2 and x^3 is .96681 while the correlation between the quadratic and cubic interaction terms is $-.96987$. As more terms are added to the analysis, the covariance matrix approaches singularity, making it difficult to estimate models in a strict hierarchy of terms beyond third or fourth order.

The analysis that was conducted consisted of ten steps. Visual inspection indicated that the likely pre-post function was linear, with perhaps a linear interaction. In the first step the linear term

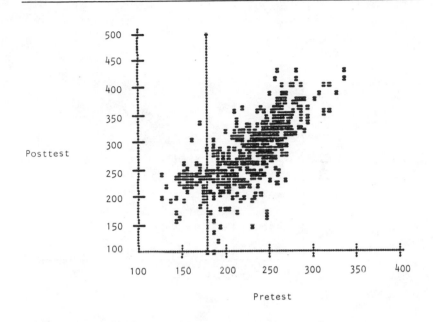

Figure 5.2   Bivariate Distribution, Providence, RI, Second Grade Reading Program

and dichotomous assignment variable were used. In the second step, the linear interaction was added. The third and fourth steps added the quadratic and quadratic interaction terms while the fifth and sixth added the cubic and its interaction. Because of high multicolinearity, the seventh and eighth steps added the fifth-order and its interaction term while the ninth and tenth steps added the eighth-order terms. In the tenth step, the eighth-order interaction term was significant, thus making it difficult to use backward elimination on the basis of the significance of the β as outlined in Judd and Kenny (1981).

R-squared values for all ten steps are shown in Figure 5.4. Recall that r-squared values will never decline as more terms are added to a model. There is a slight jump at step two (linear and linear interaction) and a slightly larger one when eighth-order

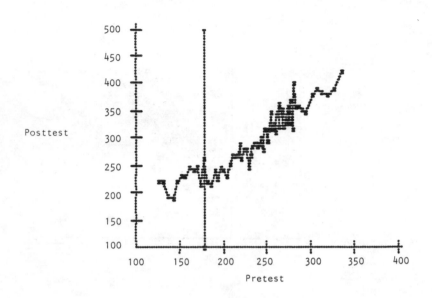

Figure 5.3   Posttest Means, Providence, RI, Second Grade Reading Program

terms are added in steps nine and ten. We expect a "leveling-off" of the r-squared function when the model becomes overspecified and there is some evidence that this occurs at step two but the jump at step nine may indicate some higher-order component. The values for the residual mean square at each step are shown in Figure 5.5. We expect that this value will be at a minimum at the step where the model is closest to exact specification. As with the previous graph, the evidence favors the model at step two or the higher-order model of step nine. Estimates of gain at each step are shown in Figure 5.6. We expect estimates to stabilize when the model becomes overspecified although the increase in standard errors for higher steps may make this function difficult to interpret. There is some evidence for stabilization between steps two and four but the function becomes erratic thereafter.

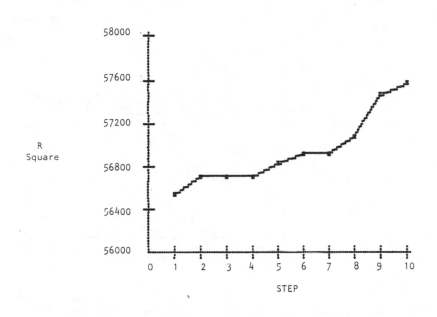

Figure 5.4 R-Squared Value Across Regression Analysis Steps, Providence, RI,
Second Grade Reading Program

It appears from these criteria that there are two major choices. First, the reasonableness of a linear true function is supported to some extent. Second, the possibility that the model may be far more complex is also suggested. To help decide between these we can examine plots of the regression lines for each model. The regression line for the model in step two (linear and interaction) is shown in Figure 5.7. The evidence for an interaction is visually slight and, in fact, the interaction term was not significantly different from zero at this step. The regression line for the model in step nine is shown in Figure 5.8. This function is clearly not substantively plausible although it fits the data well. Probably it is more reflective of idiosyncracies in the sample or of research implementation difficulties than of any true pre-post function. These graphs illustrate well the problems involved in using

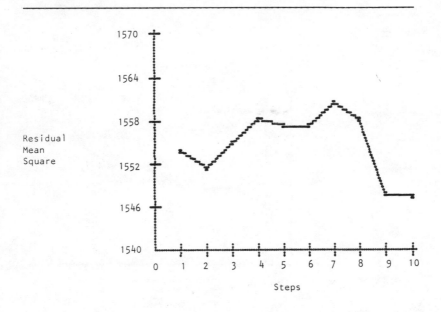

Figure 5.5   Residual Mean Square Values Across Regression Analysis Steps, Providence, RI, Second Grade Reading Program

polynomial regression and the importance of judgment of the part of the analyst. Simple reliance on statistical criteria might make plausible an eighth-order model, but inspection of the function clearly reduces its sensibility.

The pattern that emerges from the analysis is clear. Either a linear (step one) or linear plus interaction model (step two) appears to be the best model for the data. The estimate of gain for step one is 44.61 (s.e. = 7.50) while for step two it is 35.84 (s.e. = 10.07). Visual inspection confirms the presence of a discontinuity. On this basis, it is reasonable to conclude that the program group improved in reading ability relative to the comparison group.

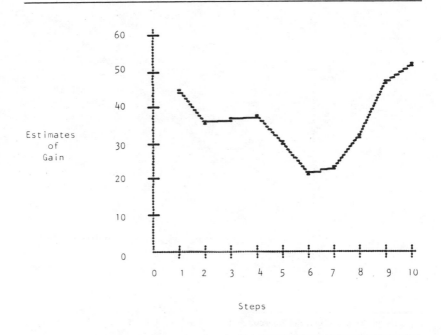

Figure 5.6   Estimate of Gain Across Regression Analysis Steps, Providence, RI, Second Grade Reading Program

FOURTH GRADE MATH PROGRAM

The bivariate distribution for the fourth grade math program is shown in Figure 5.9 and the graph of posttest means in Figure 5.10. There appears to be some curvilinearity although this is somewhat exaggerated by the presence of several apparent "outliers" at either end of the pretest distribution. Except for these cases, the comparison group distribution could be plausibly linear. As with the second grade data, there is little pretest variability in the program group and, therefore, it will be difficult to detect interaction effects. There appears to be some slight visual evidence for a discontinuity with a considerable number of program cases near the cutoff who obtained a relatively low

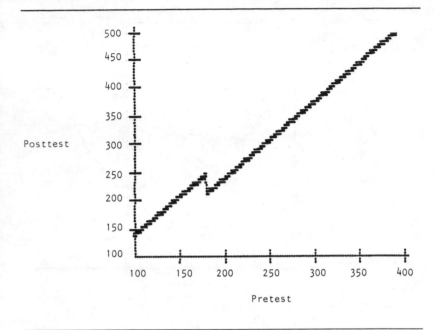

Figure 5.7   Step Two Model Regression Line, Providence, RI, Second Grade Reading
Program

posttest score. The distribution suggests that the "likely" function may be second or third order.

The analysis consisted of ten steps. Steps one through eight
involved adding in from first through fourth-order terms and
their interactions. Because of the high multicolinearity, steps nine
and ten added in the seventh-order term and its interaction. The
plot of r-square values across steps is shown in Figure 5.11. There
appears to be a clear jump at step two (linear interaction) and
step five (cubic) with a leveling-off at higher steps. Figure 5.12,
the plot of residual mean squares across steps, shows a similar
pattern reaching a minimum level at step five. Estimates of gain
are shown in Figure 5.13. Again, these appear to level off at step
five or six.

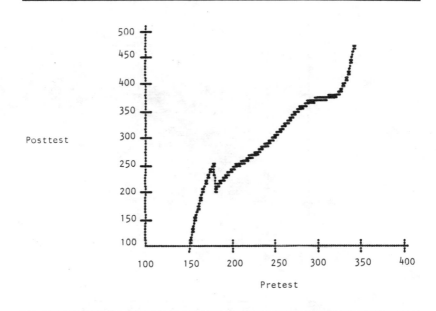

Figure 5.8   Step Nine Model Regression Line, Providence, RI, Second Grade Reading
Program

The pattern that emerges suggests two possibilities—the model at step two (linear plus interaction) or the model at step five (cubic). Regression lines are shown for these two in Figures 5.14 and 5.15 respectively. The cubic model shown in Figure 5.15 fits the data well but appears to be strongly influenced at the extremes by the presence of a few cases. The model makes little substantive sense—it seems unlikely that multiple repetitions of the study would yield similarly complex functions. It is worth noting that the estimates for the step two model ($\beta_2 = -19.04$; s.e. $= 5.31$) and the step five one ($\beta_2 = -21.82$; s.e. $= 7.65$) do not differ considerably. In both cases, the estimate is significantly negative at a .05 level and one could reasonably conclude that program students on average performed relatively worse than comparison students on the posttest. One should be hesitant in

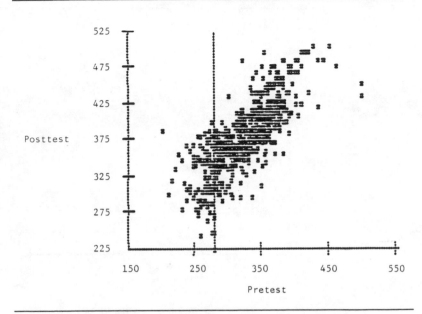

Figure 5.9   Bivariate Distribution, Providence, RI, Fourth Grade Math Program

this case about selecting one of these models over the other and probably reporting both estimates is the most sensible course.

SUMMARY OF REGRESSION-DISCONTINUITY ANALYSIS

The analyses above clearly show that the central problem in regression-discontinuity analysis is model specification. There is no simple or mechanical way to determine definitively the appropriate model for the data. As a result, judgment and discretion on the part of the analyst are warranted. In addition, more experience in interpreting regression output across a series of steps is needed. As a first step, this could be examined with simulations to verify that reasonable models would be selected.

The model selection problem calls to mind the inherent conflict in regression analysis between its uses for prediction and

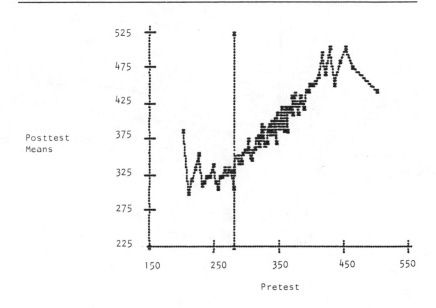

Figure 5.10   Posttest Means, Providence, RI, Fourth Grade Math Program

for model building. When one wishes to predict with accuracy there is some advantage in using a large number of predictors and accepting that there will be some amount of multicolinearity. In general, more complex models are acceptable for predictive purposes. When the goal of regression analysis is to build a theory or model there is usually a desire for parsimony—a search for the most generalizeable model given the given the smallest reasonable subset of predictors. Regression-discontinuity analysis falls somewhere between these two goals. Prediction of the jump at the cutoff point is critical, but it is not desirable to accomplish this by generating complex models that make no substantive sense for the data. This chapter argues that the model selection process should seek out a model that, if anything, slightly overspecifies the likely true function (rather than underspecify-

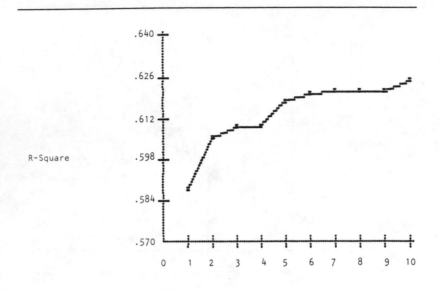

Figure 5.11   R-Squared Values, Providence, RI, Fourth Grade Math Program

ing), but not to the extent that the selected model is inappropriate substantively. Statistical considerations alone are not sufficient—analytic discretion is required.

Another way to view the differences between traditional regression analysis and regression-discontinuity analysis centers on the role of the predictor variables included in the model. In typical regresion analyses, we need to be concerned about which specific variables should be included, as well as about the nature of the functional form. In regression-discontinuity analysis, the central emphasis is almost exclusively on the functional form specification because the measures that are included are determined by the design (i.e., the dummy-coded program indicator, the preprogram assignment measure, polynomials of the assignment measure and interaction terms).

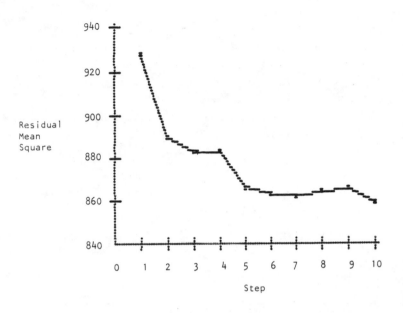

Figure 5.12   Residual Mean Square Values Across Regression Analysis Steps, Providence, RI, Fourth Grade Math Program

Methodological approaches to reducing the model specification problem seem especially promising and deserve further attention. One possibility is to couple randomized strategies with regression-discontinuity as discussed earlier. Boruch (1978) has also suggested that double pretests might be useful for determining what the pre-post function is. If double pretesting is done, the model that best fits the pretest 1 – pretest 2 distribution could be directly applied to the pretest 2 – posttest analysis. Of course, one still faces the problem of specifying the model for the double pretests, but such an analysis would be valuable, especially for distinguishing between real interaction effects and pseudo-effects that result from test floors, ceilings, and chance levels.

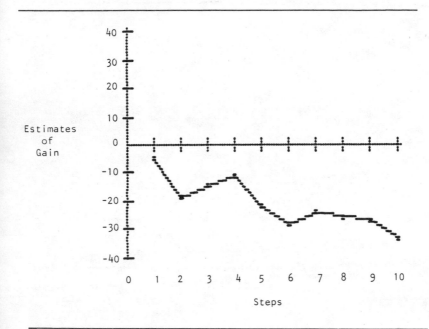

Figure 5.13   Estimate of Gain Across Regression Analysis Steps, Providence, RI, Fourth Grade Math Program

Another problem has to do with implementation of the design. Although poor research implementation is a threat to any research effort, regression-discontinuity may be particularly sensitive to it because of the need to determine the functional form rather than the mean level of the data. Chapter 6 argues that the most common implementation errors that occur when using regression-discontinuity in compensatory education evaluation tend to lead to consistent *underestimates* of program effect.

Finally, the analytic approach offered here will often lead to choices between several reasonable models, and, therefore, program effect estimates. While this is reasonable given statistical and methodological limitations, it may be unpalatable politically when single estimates are desired for program decision making. It

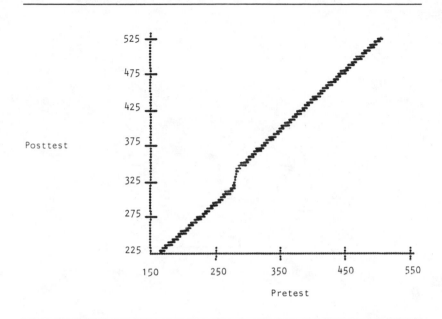

Figure 5.14   **Step Two Model Regression Line, Providence, RI, Fourth Grade Math Program**

is certainly possible that different analysts could reach different conclusions given the same data. This state of affairs points to the importance of secondary analysis of data from multiple perspectives (Boruch et al.,1981) and to the need for better strategies for resolving conflicting results.

THE ANALYSIS OF THE "FUZZY" REGRESSION-DISCONTINUITY DESIGN

A great deal of work has been devoted to analytic possibilities for the case where there is misassignment in terms of the cutoff criterion because adherence to this standard appears to be a major implementation problem for the design (Trochim, 1980, 1982).[2] Goldberger (1972) showed that under typical assump-

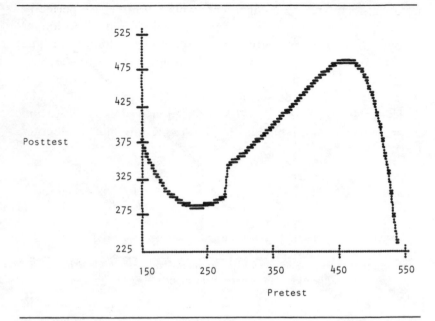

Figure 5.15   Step Five Model Regression Line, Providence, RI, Fourth Grade Math
Program

tions misassignment will result in artificially induced within-group curvilinearity that can lead to biased estimates of effect. Campbell, Reichart, and Trochim (1979) showed through simulations that none of the traditional regression analysis approaches (analysis by actual assignment; analysis by original cutoff assignment; exclusion of misassigned cases; exclusion of all cases in the interval of misassignment) eliminated the pseudo-effect.

The central problem in such fuzzy regression-discontinuity designs can be restated in terms of selection bias threats to internal validity (Cook & Campbell, 1979). In the sharp assignment case, the groups are deliberately nonequivalent, but the source of this nonequivalence is perfectly known because it is generated by the cutoff on the preprogram measure. When misassignment occurs (except in the unusual cases of random misassignment or misassignment whose source is perfectly known), inclusion of the pretest in the analytic model no longer accounts for group nonequivalence. Some methodologists argue that if the degree of misassignment is not great (i.e., if fewer than 5% of the cases are misassigned) the sharp regression-discontinuity analysis will not be seriously biased (Judd & Kenny, 1981).

The problem of selection bias has been viewed as specification error or omitted-variable bias by Barnow, Cain, and Goldberger (1978) who state:

> Selectivity bias addresses the question of whether there is some characteristic of the treatment (or control) group that is both associated with receipt of the treatment and associated with the outcome so as to lead to a false attribution of causality regarding treatment and outcome. So stated, selectivity bias is a version of omitted-variable bias, which is commonly analyzed under the rubric of specification error in econometric models. (p. 4)

Selection bias may affect program estimates when a variable related to z_i and y_i is not included in the analytic model.

In Chapter 1, three pretest-posttest group designs were presented as varying along a continuum based on their assignment functions. Randomized experiments have perfectly known assignment (probabilistically) with a probability of assignment to program of .5 for any given pretest value. Regression-discontinuity designs also have perfectly known assignment functions where the probability of assignment is 0 on one side of the cutoff (comparison cases) and 1.0 on the other side (program cases). Because the assignment functions are known, neither of these cases is susceptible to selection bias. All nonequivalent designs fall between these two extremes in terms of their assignment function and, because the assignment rule is unlikely to be known, these designs are susceptible to selection bias. The fuzzy regression-discontinuity design represents a degradation of the true regression-discontinuity design where the assignment function is no longer clear because misassignment was allowed. Thus, it also falls somewhere between true experiments and true regression-discontinuity designs and is susceptible to selection bias.

The potential for selection bias is a major factor preventing the development of a general analytic scheme that would be appropriate for all four of these conceptually similar pretest-posttest group designs. The need for an analytic solution to the selection bias problem in the fuzzy regression-discontinuity and nonequivalent group designs is especially apparent when one considers the frequency with which these two designs occur in practice. While both can occur in their own right, they also represent the degraded versions of the true regression-discontinuity and randomized experiment (i.e., versions where the assignment strategies for either are incorrectly implemented). Conner (1977) for example, points out the difficulties of adhering to random assignment in practice, while Chapter 7 describes the almost universal occurrence of misassignment relative to the cutoff value in implementations of the regression-discontinuity design within the context of compensatory education evaluation.

To summarize, in the true experiment and regression-discontinuity designs, the assignment procedure is known and is perfectly accounted for by the inclusion of the prestest, x_i, and the assignment variable, z_i, in the analytic model. With the fuzzy regression-discontinuity and nonequivalent group designs, assignment is not perfectly accounted for by regressing y_i on x_i and z_i and an analytic model based on these is likely to exhibit selection bias. The development of an analytic solution to the selection bias problem is seen here as a step toward unifying analytically this set of conceptually similar designs.

THE RELATIVE ASSIGNMENT APPROACH

Suppose as in Spiegelman (1976, 1977, 1979) that x_i, v_i, and q_i are unobserved variables where x_i denotes true ability, v_i denotes pretest random measurement error, and q_i denotes posttest random measurement error. The data analyst and program evaluator observe x_i, y_i, and z_i that are related to the unobservables (for simplicity of exposition) by the equations

$$x_i = x_i^! + v_i$$

and

$$y_i = \beta_0 + \beta_1 x_i^! + \beta_2 z_i + q_i$$

where $z_i = 1$ if the research participant has received the program and 0 otherwise. In general terms, the approach to selection bias recommended here relies on an estimate of $E(z_i | x_i)$, which is termed the relative assignment variable, z_i°, in place of z_i in the analytic model. Spiegelman (1976, 1977, 1979) has shown that an appropriate estimate of b_2 based on the estimate of $E(z_i | x_i)$ is asymptotically unbiased under rather general conditions. Specifically, it is argued here that the regression of y_i on x_i and z_i° (instead of z_i) will yield unbiased estimates for common selection bias situations. The estimate, z_i° is not assumed to be related in any way to x_i or $x_i^!$ except that it may not be perfectly colinear with x_i (i.e., $z_i^\circ \neq a_1 + a_2 x_i$).

It is useful to picture what z_i° is estimating. First, consider assignment in the true experiment. Here, $E(z_i | x_i) = .5$ for any given x_i, which is to say that for any given pretest value, one expects on average about half the cases will be assigned to the program and half to the comparison group. In this case, the relative assignment variable can be described in relation to x_i by a horizontal straight line at $z_i^\circ = .5$ as shown in Figure 5.16.[3] In these graphs, z_i° is on the vertical axis and can take values from 0 to 1 (i.e., none or all in the program group). The pretest values, x_i, are shown on the horizontal axis. Second, consider the regression-discontinuity design when assignment is "sharp" relative to a pretest cutoff value. Here, it might be that $E(z_i | x_i) = 1$ if x_i is less than or equal to the selected cutoff and 0 if it is greater. This step-function is shown in Figure 5.17. Finally, for fuzzy regression-discontinuity or the nonequivalent group design, the relative assignment can be described by a function that ranges between the horizontal line of the true experiment and the step-function of the sharp regression-discontinuity design. Several functions of this type are sketched in Figure 5.18. It is clear that z_i° can be viewed as the *estimated* probability of assignment or as an estimate of the proportion of cases assigned to the program for any given pretest value.

Two methods for estimating relative assignment are offered here. The simplest and most straightforward can be termed the assignment percentage method and is presented primarily for heuristic reasons. It can be calculated in two ways. With the first procedure, cases are ordered by their pretest values and divided into equal size pretest intervals. In the second procedure, cases are similarly ordered by the pretest but are divided into intervals having an equal number of cases. For both procedures, the percentage of cases assigned to the program is calculated within each defined interval and then divided by 100 to yield values that range from 0 to 1. These values are then assigned to each individual case within the intervals. Spiegelman (1976) has shown that for extremely large n, estimates from both procedures will on average be equivalent.

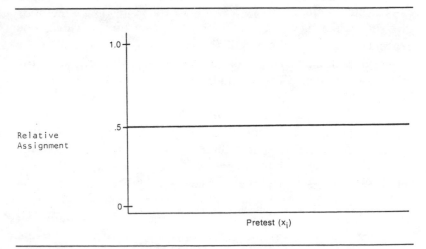

Figure 5.16   Relative Assignment Variable Function for the True Experiment

in terms of fuzzy regression-discontinuity rather than the nonequivalent group design.

Five models of misassignment are used to generate data for the simulations and are indicated by the symbols $z1_i$ to $z5_i$. To begin with, we generate a true score, $x_i^!$ normally distributed with a mean of zero and variance of nine units. In addition, we generate three error terms, v_i, q_i, and w_i, such that each is normally distributed with zero mean and variances of one or four units depending on the simulation. Here, w_i can be considered assignment error and v_i and q_i are pretest and posttest error respectively. We can now construct a pretest, x_i, such that:

$$x_i = x_i^! + v_1$$

Once we generate z_i using one of the five models described below, we can construct a posttest, y_i, such that:

$$y_i = gz_i + x_i^! + q_i$$

where "g," the program effect, is either zero or three (i.e., the null case or a gain of three units). The five models used to generate z_i are

(1) Assignment by pretest plus independent assignment error:
$$z1_i = 1 \text{ iff } (x_i^! + v_i + w_i) \leq 0$$
$$= 0 \text{ otherwise}$$

(2) Assignment by true score:
$$z2_i = 1 \text{ iff } (x_i^!) \leq 0$$
$$= 0 \text{ otherwise}$$

(3) Assignment by true score plus independent assignment error:
$$z3_i = 1 \text{ iff } (x_i^! + w_i) \leq 0$$
$$= 0 \text{ otherwise}$$

(4) Assignment by true score and pretest
$$z4_i = i \text{ iff } x_i^! \leq 0 \text{ and } x_i \leq 0$$
$$= 0 \text{ otherwise}$$

(5) Assignment by true score intervals:
$$z5_i = 1 \text{ iff } x_i^! \leq -1.0 \text{ or } (\ .5 < x_i^! \leq 0)$$
$$= 0 \text{ otherwise}$$

For each of the five models of misassignment, we use relatively low or high error variances (i.e., equal to 1 or 4) and a gain, g, of either 0 or 3 units. Thus, we have 5 (assignment models) X 2 (gain) X 2 (error variance) = 20 separate conditions. For each condition twenty independent simulations were carried out yielding a total of 20 X 20 = 400 runs, each based on 1000 individual cases (i.e., n = 1000).

For each run the following general linear regression model was used to estimate the effect:

$$y_i = \beta_0 z_i + \beta_1 + \beta_2 x_i + e_i$$

Where

      y = posttest for individual i

      x_i = pretest for individual i

      β_0 = parameter for program effect estimate

      β_1 = parameter for intercept

      β_2 = parameter for linear slope

      e_i = random error

      $z_i^\prime$ = assignment (i.e., $z1_i...z5_i$) or estimate of z_i° as described below

For each run, five analyses were conducted:

(1) Analysis using real assignment (i.e., $z1_i ... z5_i$, depending on the simulation) in place of z_i.

(2) Analysis using moving average estimate of z_i°.

(3) Analysis using assignment percentage estimate of z_i°.

(4) Weighted analysis using moving average estimate.

(5) Weighted analysis using assignment percentage estimate.

With the analysis based on real assignment, we expect treatment estimates to be biased for all assignment models except for $z1_i$, assignment by pretest plus independent assignment error. In this case, misassignment occurs randomly with respect to the pretest and will be reflected equally on the average in both groups. If the relative assignment variable approach successfully removes selection bias, the four analyses based on z_i° should yield unbiased estimates for all five assignment models.

The results are presented in Table 5.1 (g = 0; low error variances) Table 5.2 (g = 0; high error variances), Table 5.3 (g = 3; low error variances), and Table 5.4 (g = 3; high error variances). Each table presents, for all five assignment models and all five analyses, the average gain, the standard error of the average gain and the minimum and maximum obtained gain for twenty runs. Results will be considered biased if the true gain, β_0, lies outside the interval $\beta_0 \pm 3SE(\beta_0)$.

Several conclusions can be drawn from the tables. First, as expected, estimates from the analyses based on real assignment are biased except when misassignment is random. Second, the moving average estimates of relative assignment appear to yield unbiased estimates of gain for most of the models and conditions that were studied. Even for the three (out of twenty) sets of conditions where bias is detected, two of these had average estimates that were not greatly biased, especially when considered relative to estimates from the analyses by real assignment. Third, it appears that estimates from the moving average analyses are in general less biased than the ones from the assignment percentage ones. This may be in part because the assignment percentage functions in these simulations are based on only 50 intervals of only 20 z_i values each. Thus, the estimate of z_i° can only take on twenty values between 0 and 1 (i.e., 0, .05, .10... .95, 1.0), whereas the moving average estimate is more finely differentiated. Finally, the estimates yielded by relative assignment variable analyses appear to be less biased when error variances are low. It may be that with large sample sizes (i.e., larger than n = 1000) and correspondingly greater statistical power, estimates would in general be unbiased. In fact, Spiegelman (1976, 1977, 1979) has been careful to point out that the method is efficient only for large sample sizes.

TABLE 5.1
Fuzzy Regression-Discontinuity Simulation Results
(b_0 = 0, error variances = 1)

Model	Analysis[*]	$\hat{\bar{b}}_0$	$SE(\hat{\bar{b}}_0)$	$min(\hat{b}_0)$	$max(\hat{b}_0)$
$z1_i$	Real	.007	.027	−.293	.210
	MA	.k023	.050	−.375	.545
	AP	.037	.043	−.306	.482
	MA(w)	.040	.055	−.394	.553
	AP(w)	.050	.051	−.342	.514
$z2_i$	Real	−1.171	.026	−1.356	−.918
	MA	−.051	.056	−.540	.283
	AP	−.185	.058	−.745	.251
	MA(w)	−.086	.058	−.552	.290
	AP(w)	−.167	.057	−.613	.288
$z3_i$	Real	−.922	.022	−1.105	−.728
	MA	−.178	.054	−.701	.316
	AP	−.350	.047	−.686	.067
	MA(w)	−.143	.058	−.685	.328
	AP(w)	−.265	.049	−.744	.129
$z4_i$	Real	−.623	.033	−.843	−.361
	MA	−.003	.033	−.248	.423
	AP	−.054	.032	−.283	.341
	MA(w)	.009	.038	−.239	.491
	AP(w)	−.032	.036	−.272	.431
$z5_i$	Real	−.979	.024	−1.177	−.771
	MA	.040	.059	−.316	.641
	AP	−.129	.055	−.437	.385
	MA(w)	.078	.065	−.405	.648
	AP(w)	−.054	.057	−.409	.429

[*]Real = real assignment; MA = moving average; AP = assignment percentage;
MA(w) = weighted moving average; AP(w) = weighted assignment percentage

ILLUSTRATIVE REAL DATA ANALYSIS

Two sets of fuzzy regression-discontinuity data were constructed from the third grade reading scores for a Title I compensatory education reading program in Providence, Rhode Island (Trochim, 1980). It is useful to apply the relative assignment variable approach to such data to see how the assignment functions differ from the simulations and to detect

TABLE 5.2
Fuzzy Regression-Discontinuity Simulation Results
($b_0 = 0$, error variances $= 4$)

Model	Analysis*	$\hat{\bar{b}}_0$	$SE(\hat{\bar{b}}_0)$	$min(\hat{b}_0)$	$max(\hat{b}_0)$
$z1_i$	Real	.001	.054	−.422	.606
	MA	−.019	.187	−1.253	1.794
	AP	−.060	.148	−.969	1.664
	MA(w)	−.049	.184	−1.246	1.931
	AP(w)	−.074	.150	−.914	1.695
$z2_i$	Real	−2.715	.034	−2.979	−2.418
	MA	−.398	.183	−1.518	.946
	AP	−1.113	.142	−2.154	.131
	MA(w)	−.371	.183	−1.586	.866
	AP(w)	−1.031	.148	−2.143	.191
$z3_i$	Real	−1.685	.038	−1.985	−1.350
	MA	−.231	.266	−2.486	1.823
	AP	−1.020	.207	−2.654	.685
	MA(w)	−.163	.246	−2.563	1.751
	AP(w)	−.922	.207	−2.703	.620
$z4_i$	Real	−1.706	.045	−2.268	−1.423
	MA	.039	.080	−.722	.791
	AP	−.141	.081	−.954	.530
	MA(w)	.45	.083	−.631	.935
	AP(w)	−.137	.083	−.864	.677
$z5_i$	Real	−2.490	.054	−2.939	−2.157
	MA	−.143	.173	−1.335	.929
	AP	−1.020	.153	−2.331	.321
	MA(w)	−.110	.167	−1.356	.892
	AP(w)	−.945	.148	−2.220	.163

* Real = real assignment; MA = moving average; AP = assignment percentage; MA(w) = weighted moving average; AP(w) = weighted assignment percentage

any unforeseen difficulties in application. The linear model used in the simulations is applied here because visual inspection of the data indicates that a linear model may be appropriate and because there are relatively few program participant cases available for estimating changes in slope or function. Only the weighted and unweighted moving average analyses were carried out (in addition to analysis by real assignment) because the illustrative simulations indicate that they were less likely to

TABLE 5.3
Fuzzy Regression-Discontinuity Simulation Results
(b_0 = 3, error variances = 1)

Model	Analysis*	$\hat{\bar{b}}_0$	$SE(\hat{\bar{b}}_0)$	$min(\hat{b}_0)$	$max(\hat{b}_0)$
$z1_i$	Real	2.992	.025	2.808	3.135
	MA	3.141	.048	2.747	3.535
	AP	3.025	.043	2.679	3.442
	MA(w)	3.126	.053	2.646	3.510
	AP(w)	3.017	.048	2.593	3.425
$z2_i$	Real	1.860	.021	1.686	2.079
	MA	2.995	.047	2.659	3.380
	AP	2.804	.049	2.393	3.209
	MA(w)	2.830	.048	2.435	3.199
$z3_i$	Real	2.086	.027	1.785	2.225
	MA	2.976	.066	2.316	3.485
	AP	2.785	.053	2.257	3.160
	MA(w)	2.976	.062	2.365	3.532
	Ap(w)	2.783	.048	2.277	3.055
$z4_i$	Real	2.425	.034	2.012	2.705
	MA	3.184	.041	2.812	3.564
	AP	2.969	.039	2.616	3.278
	MA(w)	3.158	.040	2.790	3.572
	AP(w)	2.975	.038	2.626	3.323
$z5_i$	Real	1.992	.023	1.862	2.231
	MA	3.098	.058	2.599	3.431
	AP	2.908	.049	2.479	3.199
	MA(w)	3.117	.063	2.588	3.648
	AP(w)	2.960	.056	2.553	3.431

* Real = real assignment; MA = moving average; AP = assignment percentage; MA(w) = weighted moving average; AP(w) = weighted assignment percentage

exhibit bias than the assignment percentage estimates. In a previous analysis of data from this program where sharp regression-discontinuity data were used, the estimate of gain for the same linear model was β_0 = 29.73 with a standard error of 6.12 (Trochim, 1980).

The first set of fuzzy data results from the use of the vocabulary subscale of the reading pretest rather than the total score. Assignment is sharp relative to the total score, but is fuzzy

TABLE 5.4
Fuzzy Regression-Discontinuity Simulation Results
($b_0 = 3$, error variances $= 4$)

Model	Analysis*	$\hat{b}_0$	$SE(\hat{b}_0)$	$min(\hat{b}_0)$	$max(\hat{b}_0)$
$z1_i$	Real	2.908	.056	2.203	3.356
	MA	2.944	.148	1.844	4.146
	AP	2.874	.122	1.867	3.855
	MA(w)	2.951	.157	1.851	4.273
	AP(w)	2.876	.127	1.889	3.936
$z2_i$	Real	.401	.047	−.134	.785
	MA	2.969	.130	1.930	4.131
	AP	2.007	.102	1.304	2.956
	MA(w)	3.017	.125	2.047	4.261
	MA(w)	2.134	.098	1.437	3.047
$z3_i$	Real	1.277	.043	.894	1.508
	MA	2.001	.271	.039	4.764
	AP	1.553	.168	.363	3.016
	MA(w)	2.038	.266	.047	4.697
	AP(w)	1.596	.176	.351	3.335
$z4_i$	Real	1.343	.051	.869	1.821
	MA	3.139	.081	2.248	3.869
	AP	2.841	.081	1.814	3.627
	MA(w)	3.164	.084	2.242	3.936
	AP(w)	2.892	.083	1.847	3.713
$z5_i$	Real	.524	.038	.235	.900
	MA	2.568	.165	1.001	3.895
	AP	1.901	.126	.908	2.806
	MA(w)	2.650	.183	1.094	4.229
	AP(w)	2.019	.141	1.032	3.161

* Real = real assignment; MA = moving average; AP = assignment percentage;
MA(w) = weighted moving average; AP = weighted assignment percentage

relative to the subscale. The bivariate plot of the data is shown in Figure 5.19. Here, the analysis by real assignment, z_i, showed no significant gain ($\beta_0 = 11.13$, $SE(\beta_0) = 6.22$), whereas the relative assignment variable analyses showed gains similar to the one found in the sharp regression-discontinuity case ($\beta_0 = 30.05$, $SE(\beta_0) = 10.13$ for the unweighted moving average analysis and $\beta_0 = 29.43$, $SE(\beta_0) = .56$ for the weighted moving average analysis).

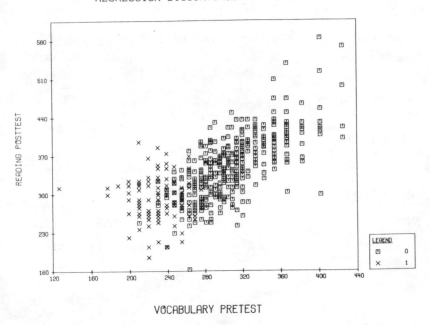

Figure 5.19   Fuzzy Regression-Discontinuity with a Vocabulary Pretest and Reading Posttest

The second set of fuzzy data is from the same program and results from the inclusion of the scores of children who come from schools in the district that were ineligible for service. Some of these students qualify for the program on the basis of their pretest score. The total reading score is used for the pretest and posttest and the bivariate distribution is shown in Figure 5.20 Here, all estimates of program effect are significant at the .05 level, although the estimate from the analysis by real assignment appears smaller than the relative assignment estimates ($\beta_0 = 23.32$, $SE(\beta_0) = 5.60$ for real assignment analysis, $\beta_0 = 47.82$, $SE(\beta_0) = 7.37$ for unweighted moving average analysis and $\beta_0 = 48.77$, $SE(\beta_0) = .41$ for the weighted moving average analysis).

Clearly, the results of analyses based on real assignment tend to differ from those based on relative assignment. Given that the former are likely to be biased and the latter are not (at least under the conditions specified here), one might place greater faith in the

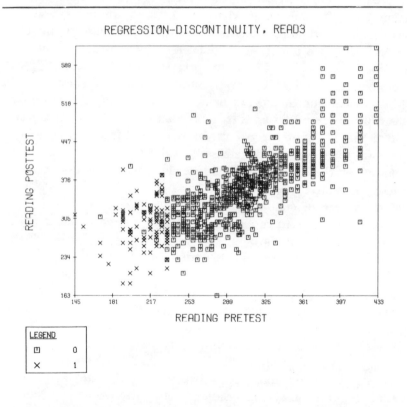

REGRESSION-DISCONTINUITY, READ3

Figure 5.20 Fuzzy Regression-Discontinuity with a Reading Pretest and Reading Posttest

relative assignment analyses and conclude that this reading program had a positive effect.

CONCLUSIONS

While the relative assignment variable approach, especially using a weighted moving average analysis, appears in general to yield unbiased estimates in several models where selection bias is expected, there are still important unanswered questions. For example, it is not clear whether unbiased estimates will be obtained under more realistic or complex assignment models. Specifically, it is important to determine by simulatons whether estimates are biased when the pretest-posttest relationship is nonlinear, when a wider variety of sample sizes are tested, and when misassignment occurs nearer the extremes of the pretest distribution. In addition, it is not yet clear whether the analysis yields biased results in general or whether the biases obtained here are related to sample size, interval size or other conditions chosen for these simulations. More definitive simulations than these illustrative ones require a greater number of runs for a wider variety of conditions.

It is reasonable to conclude that appropriate estimates of the relative assignment variable can be used to produce realistic estimates of program effect under many conditions where selection bias is expected. On this basis we might tentatively advance the outline of a more general analytic approach for pretest-postest group designs. First, if the true randomized experiment or regression-discontinuity design are used and assignment has been implemented correctly the analysis may be based on the regression of y_i on x_i, z_i polynomials in x_i, interactions of x_i and z_i, and other appropriate covariates. Second, if the fuzzy regression-discontinuity or nonequivalent group designs are used or if the assignment procedures of a true regression-discontinuity or randomized design are not correctly implemented, an estimate of z_i°, the relative assignment variable, can be used in place of z_i in the analytic model, at least as one part of a multiple analysis scheme (as described in Trochim, 1980) for estimating program effect.

NOTES

1. The use of the terms "overspecified" and "underspecified" in this text are not standard in the regression literature. They are distinguished here because each condition has different implications for the analysis even though both can be considered specification errors.

2. The discussion in this section is adapted from Trochim and Spiegelman (1980).

3. Note that these figures are the same as in Chapter 1 except that these refer to empirical estimates (relative assignment) of the probability of assignment function discussed there.

6

The "Negative Gain" Controversy

This chapter describes a controversy that directly involves the regression-discontinuity design and it's potential applicability.[1] While the debate is set in the context of compensatory education, the reader should not assume that the issues involved are peculiar to that arena. A firm understanding of the regression-discontinuity design requires more than just knowledge of how the design works in principle. The controversy that is discussed in some detail here illuminates some of the more subtle issues that arise when one attempts to implement the design in some real context.

BACKGROUND

Chapter 2 described the Title I evaluation system and the three research models that are used in it. These models represent three major traditions in social science research methodology. Model A, the Norm Referenced Design, and similar strategies represent a tradition in educational research that relies on normative information from standardized tests for an estimate of the growth that would be expected in the absence of special training (Tallmadge, 1980). Model B, the Comparison Group Model, is either a randomized or "true" experiment in the Fisherian tradition or, if random assignment is not used, is a pretest-posttest nonequivalent group design in the tradition of quasi-experimental designs outlined by Campbell and Stanley (1963) and Cook and Campbell (1979). Model C, the Special Regression Model, described here as the regression-discontinuity design, is also in this quasi-experimental tradition.[2] The Title I evaluation system makes it possible to compare these traditions directly because the designs are used in multiple evaluations of similar types of programs.

When the three Title I models were first presented, it was assumed that they were in some way equivalent—evaluations of the same programs by different models were expected to yield similar results. However, the initial pattern of results does not support this notion of model equivalence. Instead, the pattern that emerges suggests that Model A tends to yield positive estimates of the program effect while Model C estimates are near zero or even slightly negative on average.[3] Because of these results, the possibility of inherent bias in the estimates of one or both of the models has become an important issue. One implication of this controversy is that, regardless of the truth of the matter, the discussion itself has affected the perception of the models, especially regression-discontinuity, and consequently affected the degree to which it has been used.

Aside from the technical issues involved, the controversy is an intriguing and well-documented example of the interplay between technical methodological matters and the social-political context that encompasses them. The following discussion presents the issue in some detail primarily to document a conflict between two important research traditions, but also to illustrate the importance of considering contextual factors and relative design features when examining the history and implementation of a design.

THE PATTERN OF RESULTS

Three major sources of information provide evidence for a discrepancy in the average gains obtained when using Models A and C: interviews of Title I evaluators at the local and regional levels; review of relevant Title I literature; and the distributions of gain estimates obtained from Title I programs.

Trochim (1980) reports the results of interviews conducted with at least one representative of each of the ten Title I regional Technical Assistance Centers (TACs) and many local Title I evaluators. Interviewees who were aware of instances of both designs indicated virtually unanimously that the designs appeared to yield different results on the average. It was also generally agreed that the average results from Model A tended to be higher than those from Model C. Furthermore, persons who were most familiar with the results from many evaluations corroborated the notion that, in general, Model A yielded positive gains while Model C yielded gains that were near zero or even negative.

This discrepancy has been acknowledged in the Title I literature. Hardy (1978) and Echternacht (1978, 1980) cite results obtained in Florida where sufficient instances of both designs permitted the determination of a pattern of results. Others who have attempted to compare the two designs directly on the same program (Murray, 1978; House 1979; Long et al., 1979) obtained results that are not inconsistent with the general pattern cited here, although these studies are based on too few instances to permit confident generalizations.

The most convincing evidence for the pattern of gains for the two designs initially came from the State of Florida, largely because there were sufficient instances of the application of both designs to permit meaningful comparisons. All estimates of program effect in Florida for Model A for the 1978-1979 school

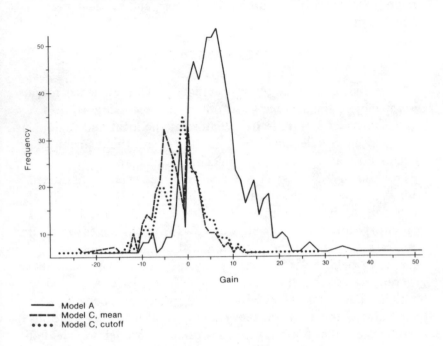

— Model A
—■—■— Model C, mean
●●●● Model C, cutoff

Figure 6.1 Distribution of Gains by Model for Title I Compensatory Education Programs in Florida, 1980

year (n = 614) and all estimates for Model C for the 1977-1978 and 1978-1979 school years (n = 273) were obtained. The average gains were 6.595 NCE units (SE = .302) for Model A, −.799 NCE units (SE = .398) for the Model C estimate at the program group pretest mean, and −2.371 NCE units (SE = .377) for the Model C estimate at the cutoff. The distributions of gains for these three estimates are depicted in Figure 6.1. Clearly, the evidence indicates that, on the average, Model A yields significantly positive estimates, while Model C appears to yield a zero or perhaps slightly negative gain.

Other studies of compensatory education provide little guidance concerning which of these two designs yields estimates that are closer to the truth. On the basis of what is known about the effects of compensatory education in general, it is difficult to say what the 'expected' gain might be. Many previous studies have been criticized on methodological, measurement, or analytic grounds (Wick, 1978; Campbell & Erlebacher, 1970; Campbell & Boruch, 1975). Even granting that biases in analysis have been against finding effects, programs of this nature have not been found to be conspicuously effective when more appropriate modes of analysis have been used (Magidson, 1977; Bentler & Woodward, 1978). In spite of this, significantly harmful effects have so far primarily been explainable as mistaken methodology. Thus, in order to determine the likely source of the discrepancy in results reported here, it is necessary to examine the designs in question within the context of Title I evaluation.

SOME LIKELY SOURCES OF THE DISCREPANCY IN RESULTS

It is possible, although hardly plausible, that both designs could be yielding accurate estimates of effect even though they disagree. For example, it may be that since Model A tends to require less cost and effort than Model C, districts that use it have more time, money, or energy to devote to programmatic efforts. The discrepancy in gains might then be attributable to differential implementation of the programs rather than to the designs themselves. However, explanations of this type are not likely and it is reasonable to hypothesize that one or both of the designs yields biased estimates of effect.

It is useful to begin an investigation of bias by considering how the methodological community views the strengths and weaknesses of each of the designs. Judgments about the relative strengths of research designs are often made in the methodological literature and, in general, Model C is usually depicted as "theoretically" stronger (at least in internal validity) than Model A (Tallmadge & Wood, 1978; Murray et al., 1979; Echternacht, 1979). Typical of such distinctions is a statement by Linn (1979):

> If viewed as research designs, the three RMC models are ranked easily in terms of their relative internal validity. In its idealized form Model B is a classic experimental design and ranks highest in terms of internal validity. Model A ranks third, with Model C somewhere in between. This ranking agrees with the stated order of preference provided by developers of the models. (p. 25)

The quality of Model A has been questioned in several key areas (Hansen, 1978)—the appropriateness of using the norming sample for comparison, especially when many norm students also receive compensatory education; the viability of the equipercentile (or, more properly, equi-NCE) assumption that holds that in the null case, the program group pre- and post-average NCEs should be equal; the use of out-of-level testing; and the testing of students at different times during the academic year from those at which the norm group was tested.

While Model C is generally perceived as methodologically stronger than Model A, it is also usually seen as more difficult to implement. This is at least in part due to the requirement of strict adherence to the cutoff value in assignment, to the need to compile data for both program and comparison students, and to the relatively more complex statistical analysis that must be conducted.

The remainder of this chapter involves a consideration of several major issues that affect each of the designs and that may contribute to the discrepancy between their results. No claim is made that these are the only relevant issues, or even the most important. The discussion of these factors simply indicates that the discrepancy is likely to be resolvable by careful consideration of the implementation of the designs. The reader should note again that many of these issues are likely to be operative in settings other than just compensatory education.

THREE POTENTIALLY BIASING FACTORS IN MODEL A

The three issues considered here in relation to Model A concern the potential for regression artifacts, the effects of various attrition patterns, and the pattern of measurement over time in relation to the normative standard of comparison. The first two issues will be prominent in many social research settings. The final issue is more particularly relevant to the research tradition that relies on comparison with empirically derived normative information for estimation of program effect.

Residual Regression Artifacts in Model A

A distinguishing characteristic of Model A is the requirement of a selection measure that is separate from the pretest. This was included in an attempt to avoid the commonly recognized phenomenon of regression to the mean. Before examining whether the separate selection measure in fact eliminates the regression phenomenon, it is useful to review briefly the traditional presentation of the regression artifact.

It is well known that when a group is selected from one end of a distribution of scores their mean on any other measure will appear to "regress" toward the overall mean of this other distribution. If the selection measure is a pretest and the other measure a posttest, students will appear on the average to change even in the absence of a program. The amount of regression to the mean that occurs between any two measures, x and y, can be specified. A group may be chosen from the lower end of the distribution of variable x as shown in Figure 6.2. When the standard deviations of the two distributions are equal (e.g., they are in standard score form), the correlation between the two measures is a direct reflection of the amount of regression to the mean. In fact, the symbol for the correlation, r, was originally used to signify regression in this sense. Specifically, $100(1-r_{xy})$

gives the percentage of regression to the mean for standardized variables. As illustrated in Figure 6.2, if there is a perfect correlation between x and y there is no regression to the mean (i.e., $100(1-1) = 0\%$ regression). Conversely, if there is no correlation (i.e., $r_{xy} = 0$) there is a maximum regression to the mean (i.e., $100(1-0) = 100\%$ regression). If $r_{xy} = .6$, the mean of the selected group on y will be 40% closer to the overall mean of y than their mean on x is to the overall x mean (i.e., $100(1-.6 = 40\%$ regression). If x is a pretest and y a posttest except when they are perfectly correlated, the assigned program group will appear to improve even in the absence of any program simply because of the regression artifact that results from the less-than-perfect pretest-posttest correlation and selection from the lower extreme of the pretest distribution.

Model A was constructed to avoid the regression artifact by including a separate selection test. It was thought that assignment would then be "independent" of the potential regression artifact. The fact is that this separate selection measure is likely to remove only part of the regression to the mean.[4] The regression artifact argument can be extended to Model A by considering an assignment variable, z, a pretest, x, and a posttest, y, all in standard score form and hence having equal standard deviation units. In this example, the assumption is that the program group is selected from the lower end of the distribution of variable z as is commonly done in Title I (i.e., if z is a measure of achievement those "most needy" would be chosen). If the correlation between the assignment measure and the pretest is $r_{zx} = .8$, (Figure 6.3) there would be regression to the mean from z to x of 20%. Further, if the correlation between the assignment measure and the posttest, y, is $r_{zy} = .5$, regression to the mean from z to y equalling 50% of the distance toward the overall mean of y would exist. By subtracting these two regression artifacts, the amount of regression between the pretest and posttest (in this case 30%), is obtained. The use of a separate selection measure in this example has reduced but not removed the regression artifact and one would again find that students

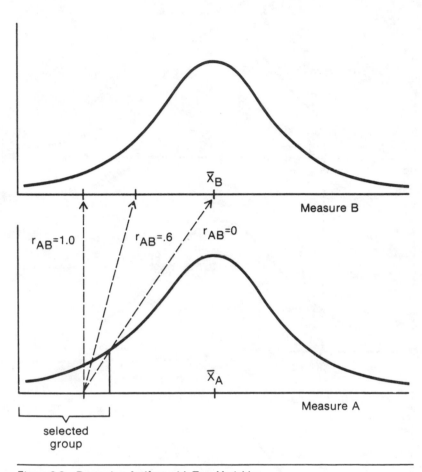

Figure 6.2   Regression Artifact with Two Variables

improve from pretest to posttest even if no program is ever given. This is termed here the "residual regression artifact" because it is the amount of regression that remains even after the attempt to remove regression by separating pretest measurement from group assignment.

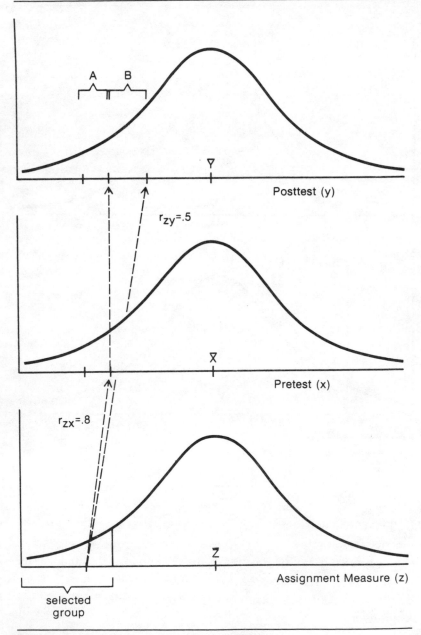

Figure 6.3   "Residual Regression Artifact" in Model A

The size of the residual regression artifact in Model A depends entirely on two correlations, r_{zx} and r_{zy}, where these are correlations between standardized variables. If $r_{zx} = r_{zy}$, there will be no residual regression unaccounted for. If $r_{zx} > r_{zy}$, some regression to the mean will be unaccounted for by the separate selection measure. If $r_{zx} < r_{zy}$, there is actually regression away from the posttest mean and the program students appear to lose ground from pretest to posttest. In order to judge whether a separate selection measure removes the regression artifact, one needs to determine which of the three patterns of correlations, if any, is typically obtained.

In general, it is reasonable to assume that correlations are higher the closer in time two measurements are taken. Thus, over time, repeated measures of the same variable tend to show progressively smaller correlations with the first measurement. The size of the correlations r_{zx} and r_{zy}, therefore, depends on two factors—the time between the measurement of x, y, and z, and the rate at which the correlations erode over time. Figure 6.4 shows a hypothetical erosion pattern and two measurement scenarios. In the first case (left side of Figure 6.4)the pretest and posttest (x_1 and y_1) are measured while their correlations with the assignment variable are eroding at a rapid rate. In the second case (right side of the graph), both measures (x_2 and y_2) are taken after the greatest erosion has occurred. In both scenarios, the same time elapses between the pretest and posttest. While a residual regression artifact occurs in both cases, it is much smaller in the second case than the first.

Theoretically, if one knows the correlations r_{zx} and r_{zy} in the absence of a program effect, it should be possible to adjust estimates of gain to account for the residual regression artifact. However, corrections of this type are hazardous for two reasons. First, they depend on the pattern of temporal erosion in the correlations and this is likely to vary for different traits, and even perhaps for different tests of the same attribute (e.g., different levels or forms of achievement tests). Second, even if the overall rate of erosion is reasonably known, accurate estimates of the

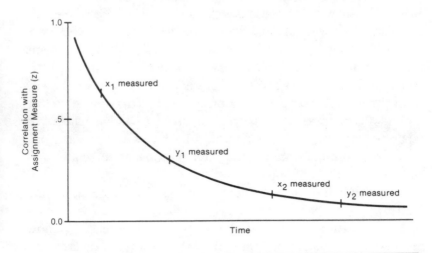

Figure 6.4 Hypothetical Correlation Erosion Pattern

correlations in the absence of a program effect are necessary. This would necessitate use of some type of comparison group or, for Model A, use of published correlations over time. In either case, the quality of such corrections would be doubtful and only serve to increase the assumptive character of the design.

The degree to which the discrepancy in results reported earlier may be due to the residual regression artifact is difficult to estimate for the same reason that it is hard to devise corrections for the residual regression bias. However, it is possible to get some empirical confirmation that a bias is occurring by examining the pattern of results obtained for Model A in Florida. This can be done by classifying the studies into NCE intervals on the basis of group pretest means. If a residual regression artifact is operating, gains for groups who scored low on the pretest should be greater on the average than gains of the higher pretest scoring groups. Table 6.1 shows the average gain for projects which are grouped into ten intervals of five NCE units each, covering a range of 0 to 50 NCEs. Six projects were excluded from the table (therefore, n = 608) because their average pretest score exceeded the mean of 50 NCE units. These results are even more striking when graphed as in Figure 6.5. The plot almost looks like a theoretical description of regression artifacts. Clearly, the results do nothing to repudiate the hypothesis that a positive bias due to a residual regression artifact occurs with Model A. Although a similar pattern would be expected if there were an interaction effect between the program and the pretest, this is considered a less plausible explanation than the residual regression artifact one.

Attrition Bias in Model A

Although Model A requires that a selection measure be administered to all potential participants, only program students are given the pretest and posttest. The required analysis for estimating gain is based on the pretest and posttest averages for only those students who took both tests. Two attrition-related problems tend to arise when dropouts are nonrandom. First, if

TABLE 6.1
Average NCE Gain for Projects Grouped by Pretest Mean NCE

Pretest Mean NCE[a]	N	NCE Gain
0-5	7	18.30
5-10	10	10.67
10-15	13	15.29
15-20	37	9.46
20-25	116	8.23
25-30	161	6.40
30-35	126	5.57
35-40	80	5.05
40-45	40	4.00
45-50	18	3.58

a. Projects with Pretest Mean NCEs that fell on interval boundaries were assigned to the lower value interval. For example, the first interval is actually 0-4.999. . . but was rounded for clarity of presentation.

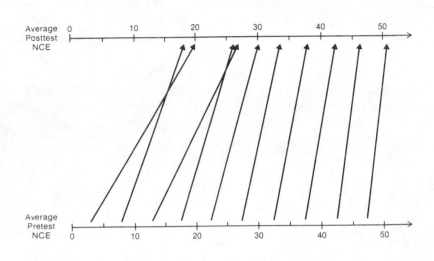

Figure 6.5   Average Posttest NCE for Projects Grouped by Pretest Mean NCE

only matched cases are used (as required) one can at least expect the positive bias due to the residual regression artifact for the matched (i.e., nonattrited) students. This may be greater or less than the bias expected for the entire original sample depending on whether attrition is disproportionately greater for higher- or lower-scoring program students. In addition, attrition of this sort obviously calls into question the use of the norming sample as a comparison standard.

The second attrition-related problem occurs if the requirement that only matched cases be analyzed is violated. This will be termed the unmatched attrition case. Here, if a program student takes one test and not the other, the available test score is still included in the group averages. While this is a clear violation of the Title I requirements, there is some reason to believe that the difficulty of matching pretest and posttest scores (Trochim, 1980) leads school districts into this practice.

The major purpose of this discussion is to determine the likely effects of unmatched attrition on estimates of gain, and ultimately, the discrepancy in results. The effects of such attrition between the selection measure and pretest, and the pretest and posttest, will be discussed.

The typical Title I program group is composed of students whose pretest scores will in most cases be below the population average of 50 NCE units. If unmatched attrition is proportionately greater among students who score below the pretest mean of the program group, a positive bias will result. This is due to two factors. First, the remaining group will consist of the higher-scoring program students. In the absence of any program, an apparent gain will occur from the observed pretest mean (which includes attrition cases) to the observed posttest mean. Second, in addition to this gain there will also tend to be a positive regression artifact bias from the remaining students' pretest mean to their posttest mean. Thus, the positive regression artifact will augment the positive bias due to the high-scoring remaining group.

The direction of bias is not easily specified when there is proportionately greater unmatched attrition from the high pretest-scoring program students. The remaining group would have a lower pretest average, indicating a potential negative bias. However, a positive regression artifact bias is also expected for this group. Thus, when attrition occurs primarily among high pretest program students, a positive regression artifact bias competes with a likely negative bias resulting from the low scoring remaining group.

Consider a hypothetical example of how a positive bias can result when attrition occurs among the higher pretest scorers. It is assumed that the entire program group had a pretest mean of 20 NCEs and that after attrition of the higher scorers, the remaining group would have a pretest mean of 15 NCEs. The observed pretest mean is therefore 20 NCEs, but the expected posttest mean in the absence of the regression artifact would be 15 NCEs for an apparent negative bias of -5 NCEs. However, if in this example the standardized $r_{xy} = .8$, there would be a positive regression to the population posttest mean of 20% (i.e., 100 (1-.8) = 20%) of the distance between the expected posttest mean of 15 NCEs and the population mean of 50 NCEs. Thus, there would be a positive regression artifact bias of 7 NCE units (i.e., .2(50-15) = 7) and there would be an overall positive bias of 2 NCE units.

Several conclusions are reasonable at this point. First, if unmatched attrition occurs primarily in the lower pretest scorers there will be a positive bias. Second, slightly greater rates of attrition among higher pretest scorers are also likely to result in a positive bias (although this would be less than for attrition of lower scorers). Finally, the attrition bias will be negative in direction only when there is a disproportionately great enough attrition rate among higher scorers so that the resulting loss due to lower-scoring retainees exceeds their gain due to regression to the mean.

Because attrition rates for various pretest levels are not routinely reported in the Title I literature, it is difficult to say what pattern of attrition is most common. With no knowledge of the distribution of attrition rates it is reasonable to conclude that attrition between the pretest and posttest will in general be more likely to result in a positive bias. One can, however, obtain a rough idea of the likely attrition pattern by examining the major sources of attrition. Kaskowitz and Friendly (1980) report several likely sources:

— students entering and leaving a school or district
— students entering and leaving a project
— students being held back or double promoted in grade progression
— absence on test dates
— invalid test administration
— loss of data in processing and editing
— deliberate omission of data

For most of these factors, it is plausible to argue that attrition would be more likely to occur at a greater rate among the lower-scoring students because these students would be more likely to miscode answer sheets, have greater absenteeism, be held back a grade, be discouraged and leave the program, and so on. If this assessment is correct, greater confidence can be placed in the likelihood of a positive bias due to unmatched attrition.

The more realistic case of attrition between both the selection and pretest and the pretest the posttest is more complex but leads to similar conclusions. Attrition bias may either inflate the pretest program group average or, less often, result in a lower pretest mean for the reasons discussed above. Because lower or higher pretest means will result in different amounts of residual regression artifact bias, attrition between the selection measure and the pretest may affect the amount of bias resulting from attrition between the pretest and posttest. However, even in this three-variable case, the direction of bias will still be positive except when there is enough attrition among higher scores to enable the negative bias of the low-scoring remaining group to exceed the residual regression artifact bias. On this basis, it is reasonable to conclude that the discrepancy in results yielded by Model A and Model C may in part be attributable to a positive unmatched attrition bias in Model A.

Time-Of-Testing Bias in Model A

Model A relies on a comparison between the program group and what is termed here a "pseudo-comparison" group, which is a hypothetical subsample of the norming group that is similar to the program students. It is important, therefore, to examine how test norms are developed in order to determine the reasonableness of such a comparison.

Typically, test publishers developed norms for a test on the basis of an annual test administration. Thus, samples of students might be tested in the fall of one year and the fall of the next or in the spring of one year and the spring of the next. In the typical

Model A scenario, the selection test consists of an annual district-wide achievement test in the spring; the pretest is based on fall administration of the test to the program students and the posttest is comprised of the annual test given in the following spring (which then becomes the selection test for the subsequent year). If a test were normed on the basis of annual test samples, the pretest or posttest in Model A would have to be compared with interpolated norms. Thus, if the test had been normed based on fall-to-fall testing, the spring norm would be an interpolation, while if the test had been normed spring-to-spring, the fall norm would be an interpolation. As Linn (1979) explains,

> Normatively derived scores for other testing dates were usually obtained by linear interpolation with the three summer months treated as a single month. That is, it was assumed that growth was linear for the nine month school year and that one additional month's gain was made during the summer.

Thus, when the test was normed based on annual administrations, either the obtained pretest or posttest in Model A is typically compared with an interpolated norm. The question here is whether the difference between an obtained and interpolated norm is the same as the difference that would be found if an actual testing were substituted for the latter.

Several attempts have been made to answer this question using data based on fall and spring norm testings. The results of these studies must be interpreted cautiously because they are often based, at least in part, on cross-sectional rather than longitudinal data. However, the general pattern of results indicates that larger gains occur between fall and spring testings (Beck, 1975; David & Pellavin, 1977; Linn, 1979), than between spring and fall testings. This is typically attributed to a lower rate of growth over the summer months.

A hypothetical graph of changes across testing times that is similar to those reported in the literature (Linn, 1979) is depicted in Figure 6.6. Such a pattern might be obtained if the same group of norm students were measured in the fall and spring for two successive years, assuming that there are no clear floor or ceiling effects at any testing. It is important to recognize that the solid line depicts the growth pattern expected in norm scores even with the typical "summer growth" correction. The dashed lines between the two fall tests and two spring tests indicate hypothetical linear interpolations that might be used to obtain estimates of norm group performance for points in time between the norm testing administrations. In general, the figure shows that when the test has been normed with fall-to-fall tests, the spring norm will be underestimated, while with spring-to-spring norming the fall norm will be overestimated.

Assuming that this pattern is accurate, it is relatively easy to determine the bias that may result from using tests that are normed on the basis of such annual testings. If the test that is used in a particular Model A design was normed with fall-to-fall testings, the spring norm will be an underestimate of the true

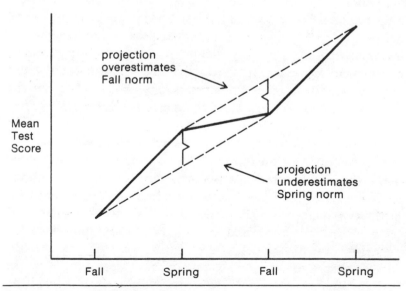

Figure 6.6 Time-of-Testing Bias

norm value. In the absence of a program effect, the program group will appear to improve from fall to spring simply because the norm posttest value is underestimated. Similarly, if the test that is used was normed using spring-to-spring testings, the fall norm will be an overestimate of the true norm value. Thus, in the absence of any program effect, the Title I group would appear to be lower than the estimated pretest norm and therefore would show pretest-posttest improvement relative to the norm sample simply because the pretest norm is an overestimate. In this hypothetical scenario, it is clear that whenever the test that is used was normed on the basis of annual testings the estimate of program effect is likely to be positively biased.

In practice, the situation is likely to be more complex. Tests may not be administered near the norm or interpolated norm testing dates and it may be necessary for a school district to attempt to construct local interpolations or extrapolations appropriate to local test administration times. In addition, in order to avoid floor and ceiling effects, it is sometimes necessary to use different levels of a test for pretest and posttest. In this case, norms are dependent on the standardized scales developed by the test producers to "vertically equate" scores from different levels of a test. In any event, it is clear that the use of normative test data in Model A relies on assumptions about change in the norming sample. In many cases these assumptions are unverified or, as in this case, actually suspect.

To some extent this time-of-testing problem can be reduced if tests are normed on the basis of fall-to-spring-to-fall longitudinal norm samples. There is some indication that test producers appreciate this fact and have modified or are considering modifying their norming procedures. Nevertheless, this is a relatively recent trend and it is a fair assumption that the majority of the 614 Model A projects that were aggregated in the analysis described earlier relied on tests that were normed on the basis of annual testings. Because of this, it is reasonable to conclude that the discrepancy in the results generated using Model A and Model C can be attributed, at least in part, to a positive bias that results from time-of-testing problems in Model A.

THREE POTENTIALLY BIASING FACTORS IN MODEL C

The discussion above demonstrates that Model A is likely to yield positively biased estimates of program effect as a result of the three factors considered. The factors that are presented next have an influence on Model C results—but in these cases, the direction of the resulting bias is likely to be negative. More specifically, these factors will tend to make programs look worse than they actually may be. It is important to recognize that the three factors—misassignment relative to the cutoff, curvilinear pre-post relationships which result from poor measurement, and errors in data preparation—are likely to arise in any implementation of the regression-discontinuity design.

Misassignment Bias in Model C

Most school districts that use Model C employ some procedure that makes it possible to challenge the assignment of a student by the cutoff criterion. Usually a challenge is initiated by a teacher, although the source may at times be a parent or school principal. A greater proportion of students tend to be challenged into the program group than out of it. In some cases, the teacher's judgment is considered sufficient evidence to warrant a change of group status, but more often the student is retested and a cutoff score on the retest is used as the criterion. Challenges can be motivated by an honest belief in the fallibility of the test instrument, by political factors or favoritism, by a reluctance to deny potentially useful training to "borderline" students, and for a number of other reasons. Trochim (1980) points out that the practice of challenging assignment is widespread, that there is often no limit put on the number of times a student may be retested, and that challenges sometimes go unreported.

The central question here is whether misassignment relative to the cutoff score might be related to the pattern of gains described above. It is useful to construct a hypothetical example to help clarify what might occur. In this example it is assumed that all of the challenges in a district are those which shift students into the program. If the challenges are reasonable, these might be students who parents, teachers, or administrators feel scored artificially high on the pretest—their true ability should have placed them in the program group. Furthermore, one might expect that these lower-ability students would on the average perform more poorly on the posttest than others who received the same pretest scores. An extreme version of this hypothetical group is indicated by the darkened portion of the graph in Figure 6.7. It is important to recognize that the graph portrays the original bivariate distribution and would be the same whether the challenge is based on teacher judgments or retest scores.

There are a number of potential strategies for analyzing data when challenges have been allowed. For example, if the evaluator is not aware of the challenges, the data would be analyzed using the assignment indicated by the pretest cutoff score. For the null case depicted in Figure 6.7 no bias would be expected. However, if the program is effective, the challenged cases should evidence this effect. If the analysis assumes that these students are in the comparison group, that group's posttest scores would be increased near the cutoff point and the slope of the comparison group linear regression line would be attenuated somewhat resulting in an underestimate of the program effect. If the challenges are reported, one might be tempted to analyze the data on the basis of actual assignment (i.e., as challenged). Here, in both the null and effect cases the slope of the program group linear regression line would be attenuated somewhat (due to inclusion of the low pretest scoring challenged students) and a negative pseudo-effect would be expected. Another strategy would be to include the challenge cases in the analysis using their

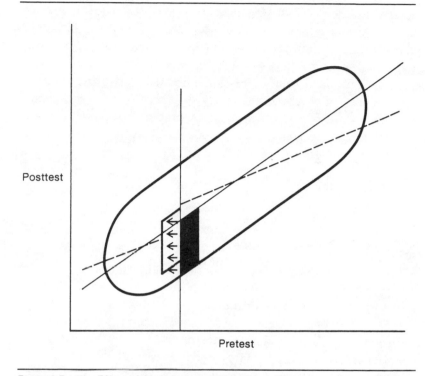

Figure 6.7   The Effect of Challenges on Within-Group Slopes

retest scores in place of the pretest. This would have the effect of increasing the number of the cases immediately below the cutoff value that also tend to fall below the linear regression line as shown in Figure 6.7. The addition of these cases in the program group and their removal from the comparison group would serve to attenuate the slopes of both linear regression lines and again one would expect a negative bias. In all of these analyses of this hypothetical "reasonable" challenge scenario, one expects that the true program effect will be underestimated.

A similar scenario can be constructed for the case of challenges that move a student out of the program. If it is assumed that these cases are most likely students who scored just below the cutoff on the pretest and would be expected to do better than average on the posttest (because their pretest score underestimates true ability), one again expects to find negative pseudo-effects because their removal from the program group and inclusion in the comparison group will always act to attenuate the slopes of the linear regression lines in each group.

These intuitions about the likely direction of misassignment bias can be illustrated through some simple simulations. First, data are randomly generated for 1000 cases using the following models:

$$x = T + e_x$$

$$TE = T + e_{TE}$$

$$RE = T + e_{RE}$$

Where T is true ability, all e's are independent random error, x is the pretest, TE is the teacher rating of student ability, and RE is the score obtained for students who are retested. Thus, it is assumed that the pretest, retest, and teacher rating are all imperfect but fairly reliable measures of true ability (e.g., achievement in reading or math). Second, assignment to program or comparison groups is constructed for three cases:

Sharp assignment:
    $z0 = 1$ if $x < 0$
        $= 0$ otherwise
Teacher challenges:
    $z1 = 1$ if $x < 0$ or $(x > 0$ and $TE < 0)$
        $= 0$ otherwise
Retest challenges:
    $z2 = 1$ if $x < 0$ or $(x > 0$ and $(TE < 0$ and $RE < 0))$
        $= 0$ otherwise

The cutoff score of zero is arbitrary and represents the theoretical pretest mean. The case of sharp assignment is included as a no-bias comparison. The program group consists of the lower pretest scorers and challenges are only in the direction of into the program. It is assumed that retests are given (i.e., can be a factor in assignment) only if a teacher recommends it (i.e., the teacher first judges that the student was misassigned). Thus, the retest challenge procedure is more restrictive in these simulations than the teacher challenge procedure. Third, posttest scores can be calculated under the general model:

$$y = T + gz + e_y$$

where y is the posttest, g is the program effect (either 0 or 3 units), and z is the dummy assignment variable (either z0, z1, or z2). Thus, the posttest is also a fallible measure of ability and is linearly related to the pretest through the common true score, T. Finally, the following analyses are applied to the simulated data:

(1) No challenges, analysis using actual assignment. This case is included as a no-bias comparison case.

(2) Teacher challenges, analysis using actual assignment. This analysis would only be feasible if teachers report the challenges and the actual challenged assignment variable (z1) is used.

(3) Teacher challenges, analysis using pretest assignment. Here it is assumed that the analyst is not aware of the challenges and that the original pretest assignment variable (z0) is used.

(4) Retest challenges, analysis using actual assignment. Again, this analysis is only feasible if the challenges are known to the analyst and the actual assignment variable (z2) is used.

(5) Retest challenges, analysis using pretest assignment. Again, it is assumed the analyst is unaware of the challenges and that the pretest assignment variable (z0) is used.

(6) Retest challenges, analysis using retest scores of challenged cases. Here the retest scores are substituted for the pretest scores of challenged cases.

(7) Teacher challenges, challenged cases excluded.

(8) Retest challenges, challenged cases excluded.

Each analysis is conducted using the following two-step procedure:

$$\text{Step 1: } y = \beta_0 + \beta_1 x + \beta_2 z + e$$

$$\text{Step 2: } y = \beta_0 + \beta_1 x + \beta_2 z + \beta_3 xz + e$$

The first step fits a straight line with the same slope in the program and comparison groups while the second step allows the slope to differ between groups. Thus, Step 1 represents the true simulated pretest-posttest relationship (in the absence of challenges) while Step 2 is equivalent to the recommended Title I analytic approach. A total of twenty simulation runs were conducted for each combination of analysis (i.e., analyses 1 to 8) and gain (i.e, 0 or 3).

The average estimates of program effect (β_2) and standard errors across twenty runs are given for both steps in Table 6.2. Of course, when there is no effect, one expects that use of the pretest assignment variable (z0) in the analysis will yield a zero effect estimate whether there were challenges or not. This is corroborated in Table 6.2 by the fact that estimates of the effect under analyses 1, 3, and 5 are the same in the null case. With this exception in mind, it is clear that all analyses involving challenges tend to result in biased estimates of effect and in every case the bias is negative (i.e., the program effect is underestimated). Confidence intervals can be constructed using the standard errors provided. In every case, the upper limit of the .95 confidence interval falls below zero (i.e., $\beta_2 + 2SE(\beta_2) < 0$). Not surprisingly, teacher challenges tend to result in a greater bias than retest challenges in part because in these simulations the latter is more restrictive and results in fewer numbers of challenged cases. Results appear to be least biased due to problems of equating the scales of pretests with retests given at a different time. In general, knowledge of challenges and use of actual assignment in the analysis yields less bias than use of the original pretest assignment.

These simulations are only intended to be illustrative. Certainly, it might be useful to add more runs, include curvilinear pre-post relationships, systematically manipulate the true score and error variances, include other possible analyses and challenge scenarios, and so on. Nevertheless, these simulations do illustrate that even under relatively "ideal" conditions (e.g., normally

TABLE 6.2
Estimates of Gain (β_2) and Standard Errors for Simulations of Several Challenge Procedures

| | True Gain $(g) = 0$ | | | | True Gain $(g) = 3$ | | | |
| | Step 1 | | Step 2 | | Step 1 | | Step 2 | |
Analysis	$\hat{\beta}_2$	$SE(\hat{\beta}_2)$	$\hat{\beta}_2$	$SE(\hat{\beta}_2)$	$\hat{\beta}_2$	$SE(\hat{\beta}_2)$	$\hat{\beta}_2$	$SE(\hat{\beta}_2)$
No challenges	.003	.030	.002	.030	3.031	.031	3.031	.032
Teacher challenge, analysis using actual assignment	-.500	.027	-.495	.030	2.511	.035	2.519	.036
Teacher challenge, analysis using pretest assignment	.003	.030	.002	.030	2.154	.042	2.163	.041
Retest challenge, analysis using actual assignment	-.375	.030	-.368	.032	2.622	.040	2.630	.040
Retest challenge, analysis using actual pretest assignment	.003	.030	.002	.030	2.551	.037	2.556	.037
Retest challenge, analysis using retest scores	-.127	.031	-.139	.032	2.881	.037	2.871	.037
Teacher challenge, challenge cases excluded	-.258	.031	-.278	.032	2.762	.038	2.744	.038
Retest challenge, challenge cases excluded	-.172	.031	-.179	.032	2.837	.037	2.831	.037

distributed variables, unidirectional challenges, linear pre-post relationships, fairly reliable measurement), misassignment in the compensatory education case tends to lead to underestimates of the program effect using Model C. Because of this, the misassignment problem must be considered a plausible explanation for at least part of the discrepancy in the results yielded by Model A and Model C.

Measurement-Related Bias in Model C

Two separate measurement issues are discussed here, both of which are likely to have an effect on the pattern of gains obtained with Model C. The first problem concerns the potential for floor and ceiling effects in the measures. These would result, respectively, from a test that is either too hard or too easy for the group in question. For example, if the test is too difficult, a number of students will receive the lowest possible scores. Their scores will not be indicative of their true ability because the test does not measure that low. Floor or ceiling effects on the pretest would tend to result in a more positive pre-post slope in the vicinity of the floor or ceiling. Conversely, such effects on the posttest would tend to attenuate the slope in the vicinity of the floor or ceiling. The situation becomes especially complicated when considering that it is possible to have a floor or ceiling effect or both on either the pretest or posttest or both.

The second measurement issue of relevance is related to the chance level of the test. The concept of chance level can best be understood through a simple example. A hypothetical multiple choice test has 100 items, each having four possible answers. If a respondent guesses on all 100 items, one would expect by random chance alone that the average test score would be 25. Thus, any student scoring in the vicinity of or lower than a score of 25 could have been guessing on the exam. If a student guesses on the pretest and either does or does not guess on the posttest, there should be no statistical relationship, or correlation, between the two tests. Assuming that a portion of the students are guessing, cases with pretest scores near the chance level are likely to exhibit a lower pre-post correlation, and consequently a lower pre-post slope, than cases having higher pretest scores.

The direction of bias that would result from either of these two measurement problems depends in general on both the nature of the problem and the placement of the cutoff. For example, if there is a chance level or posttest floor effect, the pretest-posttest relationship might be best described by a line like the one shown in Figure 6.8. With a high pretest cutoff value, the figure demonstrates that estimates of gain would be negatively biased. Conversely, with a low cutoff, estimates would tend to be positively biased.

It is possible to get some indication of the likely direction of bias in practice by examining gains in relation to typical cutoff percentiles. The median cutoff percentile for the 273 Model C cases from the State of Florida described earlier is 28.6 with a range of 7 to 50. It is difficult to know whether this median value tends to be above or below typical chance level values or posttest floor ranges without examining the specific chance levels for the tests that were used. Nevertheless, it is possible to get a rough idea of the effect of cutoff placement alone on the estimates of gain by looking at the average gain for all projects with cutoffs above and below the median cutoff percentile. When cutoff values were below the median, the average gain was .2563 (SE = .720) for the estimate at the program group pretest mean and −2.3127 (SE = .737) for the estimate at the cutoff. When cutoff values were above the median, the average gain was −1.6527 (SE = .412) and −2.4181 (SE = .334) for estimates at the program group pretest mean and cutoff, respectively. Thus, for both estimates, the average gain tended to be lower the higher the cutoff value (although the above and below median estimates for the analysis at the cutoff do not appear to differ significantly). While these results must be interpreted cautiously (at least in part because of poor reporting of or adherence to cutoffs), they do not

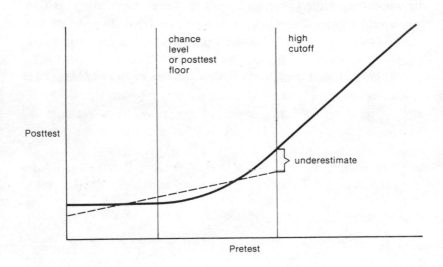

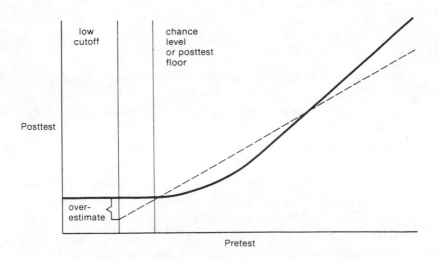

Figure 6.8   Effects of Cutoff Placement and Chance Levels or Floor Effects on Estimates of Effect

repudiate the notion that higher cutoffs may be associated with negative bias while lower ones may be linked to positive bias. In any event, the potential for bias due to the placement of the cutoff relative to the chance level of the test or floor and ceiling effects must also be considered a plausible contributing factor to the discrepancy between the results of Model A and Model C.

Data Preparation Problems in Model C

A large number of exclusions are routinely made in Title I evaluations in the process of preparing the data for statistical analysis. Cases are excluded from the analysis for lack of a pre-post match, because the student was "challenged" or misassigned, because the student moved either within the district or out of the district, and so on. Some exclusions are likely to have a consistent effect on estimates of gain and must be considered plausible sources of the discrepancy in gains.

This can be illustrated with the commonly made exclusion of grade repeaters, that is, those students who are held back a grade from one year to the next. It is certainly reasonable to expect that most of the students who repeat a grade are low achievement test scorers who are eligible for Title I service. If there are a fair number of repeaters and if these cases are routinely excluded from the data analysis, it is likely that the program group regression line, and subsequently the estimate of gain, will be distorted. Furthermore, it is not unlikely that these students come from even the lower portion of the Title I program group distribution and that they have more than the average share of disciplinary problems, learning disabilities, and so on. It is possible to conceive of circumstances in which excluding such students actually makes the Title I program look worse. A polar case is illustrated in Figure 6.9. It is assumed that the "hard-core" repeaters are low in true ability and therefore, score low on both the pretest and posttest. Hypothetically, the majority of these cases should fall in the region indicated by the blackened portion of the figure. If such students are excluded, the slope of the program group regression line would be attenuated and an apparent negative gain would result. A similar scenario can be constructed for the exclusion of students who move either within or across districts.

The effects of excluding grade repeaters can also be illustrated through simulations. Here, a pretest is constructed using the model

$$x = T + e_x$$

where x, T, and e_x are constructed as described earlier. Next, a dummy assignment variable, z, is constructed. Again, a cutoff of zero is arbitrarily selected and the low pretest scorers receive the program. Finally, the posttest is constructed

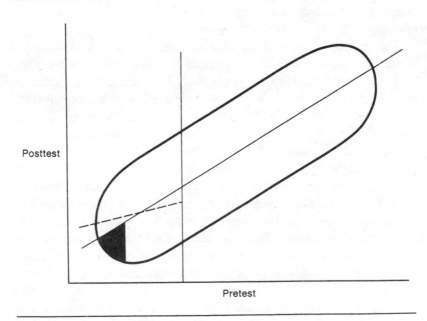

Figure 6.9   Effect of Excluding Title I Repeaters

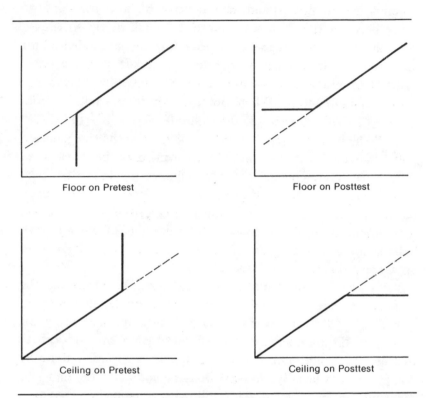

Figure 6.10   Hypothetical Pretest-Posttest Relationships or Floor or Ceiling Effect on Either Measure

$$y = T + gz + e_y$$

where the program effect, g, is either 0 or 3 units. It is assumed that grade repeaters on the average are the lowest in true ability, even within the low-scoring program group. In these situations, a hypothetical grade repeater group is excluded on the basis of their true scores. Specifically, all cases having a true score (T) less than $_{-4.5}$ units are excluded from the analysis. As in the previous simulations, there are n = 1000 cases in each run and twenty runs for each condition. The same two-step regression analysis is conducted where the first step fits the same linear function in both groups and the second step allows the slopes to differ between the groups (i.e., the Title I analytic strategy).

In the no-exclusion case, as expected, results are unbiased for all analyses. With exclusions, the Step 1 estimate of gain is $-.093$ (SE $= .026$) in the null case and 2.968 (SE $= .036$) when the true gain is equal to 3 units. When low true scorers are excluded from the Step 2 (Title I) analysis, the estimate of gain is $-.163$ (SE $= .025$) in the null case and 2.90 (SE $= .039$) when the true gain is 3 units. Obviously, these simulations can only be considered illustrative. Nevertheless, they do support the idea that even under fairly optimal conditions (e.g., fairly reliable measures, normally distributed variables, linear pre-post relationships, less than 8% exclusions) the exclusion of grade repeaters can lead to biased estimates of program effect and that the bias is likely to be an underestimate of the true effect.

Another data preparation problem that can lead to bias is the occurrence of data coding errors. For example, matching of individual pretest and posttest scores is usually made using the name or ID number for the student. Both are subject to miscoding. In addition, because matching is typically done by computer, it is usually essential that the coding of the name be identical on both tests. The following chapter on research implementation discusses a number of data preparation problems and how they typically manifest themselves.

Problems of data preparation tend to result in bias if the characteristic on which a data exclusion is based is nonrandomly distributed across pretest scores. For example, if there is reason to believe that program students move or repeat grades more frequently or are more likely to make coding errors, exclusion of these students' test scores is more likely to distort the true function and bias estimates of effect. For reasons similar to the grade-repeater case, it may be reasonable to expect that the bias would be negative in direction. Thus, data preparation problems must be considered potential contributing factors to the discrepancy in the results of Model A and Model C.

SUMMARY OF THE NEGATIVE GAIN ISSUE

We can reach a number of conclusions on the basis of this discussion. First, there is a discrepancy between the results yielded by Models A and C. On average, Model A results are slightly positive while Model C results are near zero or slightly negative. Second, examination of the major likely contributing factors indicates that Model A may be overestimating the true gain while Model C is probably underestimating it. This implies that the "truth" is likely to be somewhere between the average estimates yielded by either model. Finally, it is clear that the major factors that influence the potential for bias in the regression-discontinuity design in this context are related to poor implementation of the design. Failure to adhere to the cutoff criterion, poor measurement, data preparation errors, and other implementation problems occur frequently in compensatory education, probably occur frequently in other contexts, and have a profound effect on the validity of the results. The major implication of this chapter is that users of the regression-discontinuity design in any setting must attend to research implementation issues if the results are to be credible. Because of the importance of good research implementation for the regression-discontinuity design or any other, this topic is discussed is some detail in the next chapter.

NOTES

1. Material in this chapter is excerpted from Trochim (1982).

2. In order to remain consistent with the literature of compensatory education, the term "Model C" is used in this discussion. The reader should note that Model C is the regression-discontinuity design as described in earlier chapters.

3. An insufficient number of Model B analyses are available to make a reasonable determination of average gain and, therefore, that model will be excluded from consideration in this discussion.

4. The argument here is based on the Glass memo reported in Echternacht (1978).

7

The Implementation of Regression-Discontinuity

It should be clear from the discussion in the previous chapter that problems in the execution of the regression-discontinuity design can contribute to serious distortions in the estimate of program effect. While the design may be fine in theory, its implementation may be problematic in some settings. This chapter considers the implementation of the regression-discontinuity design in the context of compensatory education where it has been most frequently used. The reader should recognize that many of the issues discussed here will be as relevant in other research contexts. Four general categories are discussed—the implementation of the assignment, the measurement, the program, and the data preparation—in the context of Title I of ESEA.[1]

ASSIGNMENT ISSUES

One of the distinguishing features of the regression-discontinuity design and, in fact, the characteristic that sets it apart from other pretest-posttest designs, is the use of a pretest cutoff value for the assignment of students to program or comparison groups. The need for adherence to a strict cutoff poses serious administrative and political problems for a school district. The requirement of a sharp cutoff has been clearly stated within the Title I evaluation literature. The reader is referred to Campbell, Reichardt, and Trochim (1979), Trochim (1980), and Goldberger (1972) for more detailed discussion of the rationale for this requirement.

The implementation issues of primary importance in this section are:

1. The placement of the typical cutoff value.
2. The manner in which the cutoff is selected.
3. The measures that are used for assignment.
4. The degree of adherence to the cutoff criterion.
5. The effect of assignment problems on estimates of gain.

Each issue is discussed below.

PLACEMENT OF THE CUTOFF VALUE

In their annual evaluation reports to the State of Florida, all but two school districts that used the regression-discontinuity design expressed the assignment criterion in terms of a pretest percentile or stanine. Thus, a school district might report that all students scoring below the twentieth percentile on the pretest would be eligible for Title I training, while all those above that percentile would not. The other two school districts in Florida reported the pretest scale score value as the cutoff criterion. Here, the rule might be that all students scoring below a CTBS scale score value of 340 are eligible for Title I services while those scoring above that value are not. The way in which the cutoff value is reported to the state, however, is not necessarily indicative of the way in which the assignment procedure was handled within the school district. For example, a school district which reported the cutoff as its pretest percentile might actually have used a pretest scale score and simply reported in terms of percentiles for convenience. Within the State of Florida, the median pretest cutoff percentile was 28.6. The lowest percentile over the two-year period studied is 7.0 while the highest is 50.0. Thus, there never was a case reported where over half the eligible students were assigned to Title I services.

SELECTION OF THE CUTOFF VALUE

Regardless of the value of the cutoff score, it is useful to look at how a district chooses it. The majority of respondents at the local level stated that they select the cutoff value so that they will be able to have the maximum number of students served given the available resources. However, a large number of school districts reported the exact same cutoff percentile in 1978 as in 1979, suggesting that there is either a remarkable consistency in the available resources and the number of eligible students, or that school districts have some latitude from year to year in the way in which they handle allocation of funds. One school district reportedly chose its cutoff point in terms of standard deviation units on the pretest. Thus, all students scoring below, say, one standard deviation unit below the pretest mean are eligible for Title I services while all those who score above are not.

It is worthwhile to investigate in more detail how allocation procedures are managed at the district level. The remarkable consistency in the cutoff percentile from year to year suggests a fair amount of discretionary power in the allocation of funds on the part of the district or the possibility of the existence of a "reported" cutoff score that is different from the "real" cutoff used for assignment. Part of the problem may be that in order for a school district to truly allocate on the basis of the pretest distribution, they must know the test scores in advance. If proposals for Title I funds that are submitted to the state are required before a district has the time to examine this distribution, it is possible that they would give a reasonable guess for the cutoff percentile and change this if it proves unmanageable.

MEASURES USED FOR ASSIGNMENT

There are essentially three ways in which a school district can assign students to program group while adhering to a sharp cutoff. First, they can use the same test or different levels of the same test for both the pretest and posttest. Second, they can use different tests for pretest and posttest. Third, they can use a combination or composite of several tests or measures as the pretest and some other measure as the posttest.

Most school districts use the same test for the pretest and posttest, sometimes relying on different levels of this test for each. There are special cases where this is not feasible. For example, for students entering the first grade, there is not likely to be a standardized achievement test that would be appropriate. In this case, the district often relies on a "readiness" test of some sort for the pretest and a standardized achievement test for the posttest. Another case where using the same test for both testings is not feasible is when there is no readily available standardized achievement test that is appropriate. Thus, in Puerto Rico, because there is a dearth of standardized achievement tests written in Spanish, the pretest may be a measure of grade point average while the posttest will be a locally developed achievement test. One reason for reliance on the same test or different levels of the same test for pre- and post-testing is the advertised requirement of a pre-post correlation of at least .4. Although this is not technically necessary as mentioned earlier, some districts report reluctance to using different tests for pre and post-testing because of the fear that the necessary correlation would not be obtained and the analysis would be invalid.

One of the more interesting potential assignment procedures involves the use of a composite of several measures for the pretest. Since a major problem in adhering to the strict cutoff seems to be the impressions of teachers, parents, or administrators that certain children were misassigned, it would be useful to attempt to quantify their implicit assignment strategies and incorporate them directly along with a pretest. One can conceive of an assignment measure that is a weighted average of a pretest value, a grade point average, a quantified estimate of skill from the classroom teacher, and so on.

The major problems with such a procedure are that it requires a good deal extra effort, it can be arbitrary, and it makes explicit an assignment decision that for political reasons might in specific cases be difficult to justify. A respondent from one school district that investigated the possibility of a composite assignment variable claimed that the major problem occurred in trying to determine the relative weighting of different variables. Other respondents stated that it is likely, on the basis of their experience, that the assignment to program group would not differ greatly regardless of whether standardized achievement test scores or teacher's subjective impressions are used. Some work that has been done on the degree to which teachers can correctly estimate the performance of students on standardized achievement tests shows that there is a strong correspondence between the two measures (RMC Research Corporation, 1979). However, much of this work has been informal and has gone undocumented (Hill, 1979).

The possibility that subjective impressions might be quantified and subsequently incorporated into the assignment strategy offers great potential and should be investigated further. Such a strategy is not without its hazards however. One school district which has tried it cited dissatisfaction with the results primarily because of conflicting advice given to them by their regional TAC. In this case, the district attempted to combine an achievement test score with the classroom teacher's impression of each student's skill. According to local officials, the regional TAC advised them to transform the teacher rating from a continuous scale to one where all students scoring below a given value received a score of 0. When this transformed variable was added to the pretest score it obviously resulted in a nonnormally distributed assignment measure and led to nonlinearity in the analysis. In the subsequent year, the TAC corrected this advice and suggested the use of a continuous scale. This example seems indicative of the lack of experience with composite scales in the Title I system. Nevertheless, with more experience, this approach to assignment under Model C appears to hold promise.

ADHERENCE TO THE CUTOFF

Virtually every school district that was contacted initially claimed adherence to the strict cutoff value in assignment. On further examination most indicated that this "adherence" was strictly nominal. Sometimes district evaluators are aware of the extent of misassignment, while at other times this is disguised by the procedures that are used to analyze data. For example, in some cases, what was advertised as strict assignment turned out to be so only because the analyst directly excluded or disqualified cases from the analysis that were misassigned relative to the cutoff point. In some cases, the extent of the misassignment is more subtly disguised. Several districts, at the time of data analysis, simply took the pretest and posttest scores at hand, and considered all those with pretest scores below the cutoff as participants in the program group, while those above the cutoff were considered comparison students. Unless this formal decision rule was actually adhered to within schools and/or classrooms, there is likely to be some misassignment present. Classroom records of which students actually receive Title I services need to be compared with the assignment by means of the cutoff or it is impossible to detect directly the degree to which misassignment occurs. Some districts have formal procedures for comparing the students serviced with assignment by the cutoff, but even in these cases the degree to which the information agrees is seldom calculated or used.

Another problem related to adherence to the cutoff in assignment concerns the timing of feedback from the district level to individual schools and classrooms. For example, if test scores are processed at the district level and this information is not forwarded to the schools or classroom teachers prior to the beginning of Title I service, the teachers may begin service to those who they believe will be eligible, and this will often be in disagreement with eligibility by the test scores (Hill, 1979). It is difficult to assess, given the data at hand, the degree to which such problems occur within Title I evaluation.

By far, the most frequent form of misassignment is through formal procedures by which the assignment can be challenged. Almost every district has some mechanism which makes it possible for a teacher, principal, or parent to challenge the assignment by the cutoff criterion. By far the most common method for handling challenges involves retesting of the student in question. Several problems occur at this level. First, as one respondent stated, because of the number of challenges which are submitted annually in his district, as many as "600 or more among the grades" (Visco, 1980), retesting of all these students is prohibitive. Second, there is often no limit put on the number of times a student may be tested. Thus, as one respondent reported, a teacher who challenges a particular child's assignment could have that child retested again and again until the score falls below the cutoff value. Third, the time of retesting is critical. It is well known that average achievement test scores in the fall tend to be lower than those in the spring, all things being equal. As a result, if a teacher wishes to challenge the assignment of a given student by the spring pretest and administers a fall makeup test the chances are greater that the student would have a lower score and be more likely to qualify for Title I services. Along with this problem, one must consider the difficulties in equating scores given at a fall testing with those given in spring. It is not clear whether one should use the fall test scores as they are or attempt to transform these scores to a scale that is similar to the spring scale. Most likely, students who are challenged into Title I programs tend to have pretest scores just slightly above the cutoff value, (although this is not necessarily the case). One might attempt to verify the existence of such challenges by looking for distortions in the pretest frequency distribution in the vicinity of the cutoff score.

It is not always clear that the existence of a challenge is reported to the district level. For example, a challenge could theoretically be handled entirely within a school or a classroom. Thus, a teacher who challenges the original test score could administer a makeup test, grade that test, assign the student to Title I service, and never inform the district evaluator of the procedure. Part of the problem then is related to the lack of documentation of such cases, while the other part concerns how it should be handled in the analysis. In any case, most districts report using such procedures and believe that the frequency of challenges poses significant problems for the data analysis.

The existence of formal challenge procedures tends to disguise political factors related to assignment. It is not surprising that this is the case when one considers that the regression-discontinuity design tends to eliminate the discretionary power of teachers and school administrators. Only in-depth interviewing and observation is likely to turn up some of the subtle ways in which challenge procedures can be used to political advantage. This is illustrated in one example cited by Visco (1980):

> One principal apparently insisted on having (with few exceptions) only certain challenges approved, namely those submitted from a particular group of classroom teachers (the principal's old friends, I'm told). When the coordinator spoke to the principal regarding this, the principal emphasized that it was her school and she had final say. Apparently, she was right.

Misassignment relative to the cutoff point has long been recognized as a major difficulty for the analysis of the regression-discontinuity design. It is important to note that there are a variety of possible causes for misassignment, all of which might operate in the same setting. Teachers or administrators might, for example, use the challenge procedure as a vehicle for showing favoritism to certain students. Another source of misassignment is likely to be related to administrative error. Errors in test correction, score reporting, and the like, might lead to incorrect test score information upon which the assignment is based. Finally, well-intentioned teachers and administrators might be unwilling to deny service to students who they feel are deserving of that service. An unusual example of this type of well-intentioned misassignment is documented by Visco (1980):

> At least one teacher (maybe it was two) told me that she would not challenge certain students "out" of the program even though they did not require service, because if they officially left the program they were no longer eligible to receive clothing through the Title I clothing component-grant. Instead she just stopped servicing those students and never reported it to Title I administration. . . . Obviously, it affects the evaluation, but I have no way of knowing the extent to which it occurs.

ASSIGNMENT PROBLEMS AND THE ESTIMATE OF GAIN

An important question is whether program estimates are distorted due to assignment problems. Two possibilities are discussed here. First, if the pretest-posttest distribution is nonlinear, the placement of the cutoff can affect the gain. Second, the manner in which misassigned cases are treated in the analysis can distort the program effect. We can indirectly examine the effect of cutoff placement by looking at the average gains for those using a high one. When the 273 gains obtained from the State of Florida are dichotomized at the median cutoff percentile, those school districts having a cutoff below the twenty-eight percentile had an average gain of −2.31, while those who had a cutoff above the median of 28.0 had and average gain of −2.42. It is not clear then that there is any difference in the estimate of program effect for districts that differ in their placement of the cutoff. More important is the impact which including or excluding challenge cases from the analysis might have on estimates of program effect. This was described in Chapter 6 where it was shown that exclusions of this sort in compensatory education settings will tend to bias estimates of effect in a negative direction.

The issue of misassignment under the regression-discontinuity model is important, then, for a number of reasons. First, the results of the study can be distorted. Procedures need to be developed for determining the extent of this distortion. This might involve looking at the distribution of challenges relative to the pretest scores to determine whether it is homogeneous or tends to show a coincident jump in the vicinity of the cutoff score, or conducting an analysis of challenge cases separate from those which are correctly assigned, or both. Second, an investigation of the reasons for challenges and the relationship of such challenges to test distributions is essential for developing reasonable models for "fuzzy" regression-discontinuity designs. These models would be useful for the generation of simulated data for purposes of testing new and alternative analytic procedures for the "fuzzy" case such as those described in Chapter 5. Finally, it is important that the occurrence of such problems be documented routinely and that their implications be communicated to those responsible for evaluation at the school district level.

MEASUREMENT ISSUES

The assumption implicit in most research is that the data that is collected for analysis is accurate and has been collected correctly. Put in other terms, we assume that the tests or measures have reliability, validity, and are free of bias. Because most Title I evaluation relies upon the use of standardized achievement tests, issues related to who administers the test, when it is administered, which test is given, the scales on which scores are reported, and the possibility of falsified or "revised" scores are important in considering design degradation.

For convenience, these issues are divided into four topics:

(1)   Test Administration
(2)   Test Characteristics
(3)   Test Problems

(4)   Data Maintenance and Access

Each of these are considered especially in terms of their potential for distorting estimates of program effect.

TEST ADMINISTRATION

First, it is important to consider how the test is administered and the problems that might arise in the administration. School districts differ considerably in the manner of administration. In some cases, the school district requires that all schools be tested during the same week under specific conditions. This might include testing of all students within the school in the same setting, such as an auditorium or a school gym, or might allow each class to test within its classroom. Sometimes the test is administered by district personnel while at other times individual classroom teachers are in charge. Similarly, the test can be corrected by the teachers themselves, by school personnel, or at the district level. An enormous number of factors can affect the test context, but for our purposes, we are primarily interested in those which differentially affect program or comparison group students.

Any conditions other than pretest scores that serve to target students as either potential program or comparison group participants should be considered suspect. If, within a particular classroom, Title I students tend to sit in a preassigned section of that classroom, it is possible that this "segregation" can lead to differential attitudes or behavior at the time of testing. Under these conditions, for example, Title I students from the previous year, when taking the next year exam may have more anxiety because of fear of assignment into Title I training. In other ways, the teacher or test administrator might subtly communicate differently with Title I and comparison students. This can manifest itself in the instructions, in offhand comments or in any behavior that tends to confirm the segregation. Similarly, control students might display more anxiety concerning the test because of their fear of being assigned to Title I programs. Generally, any factor that creates different expectations or anxieties in the different program groups can have an adverse effect on the research that is conducted. These factors tend to change the scores for one group and not the other, and at the point of data analysis might be confused or mistaken for an effect of Title I service.

Another troubling factor concerns differences in testing conditions between classrooms or schools. Again, such factors will only affect the results if they are manifested differentially within subgroups. Thus, if those classrooms with higher proportions of Title I students also happen, through circumstances or by plan, to have systematically worse or better facilities, classrooms, and so on, the results might be affected.

Other seemingly more mundane problems related to the processing of the test might affect results seriously. This is especially true when a large number of people have responsibility for handling the test administration. Thus, when the tests are processed by classroom teachers, problems related to miscoding of information often arise. Several respondents mentioned problems of this nature such as miscoding of identification numbers, names, sex, age, and so on. Some problems, such as the occurrence of 80-year-old first graders (Visco, 1980) can be flagged at the district level, although it is not clear that most districts have procedures capable of doing this. Especially important in the case of Model C is the coding of student names or ID numbers, because it is necessary to match up pretest and posttest scores for each student. Some of these problems will be discussed in more detail later.

Another problem related to administration concerns when in the school year the test is given. It is commonly found, for example, that average achievement test scores tend to be lower for fall testings than for the previous spring testings. This is sometimes attributed to a degradation of skills due to summer vacation, lack of practice, and the like. While this is a far more serious concern under Model A because using a fall pretest instead of a spring pretest will tend to inflate gains, this problem can affect Model C results if, for any reason, the "loss of skill" is differential between the program and control groups.

TEST CHARACTERISTICS

Another problem related to testing concerns which test is given. For this study, it will be assumed that the test is an appropriate reflection of the skills that are likely to be affected by Title I training. This is an important and difficult issue, and one that lies outside the scope of this work (see for example, Linn, 1979). More germane are questions related to the level of the test, procedures for makeup testing, and so on. One issue that is important in determining the use of Model C concerns the need to administer non-English exams to some students. Because there is a lack of achievement tests in languages other than English that have been appropriately normed, such places as Puerto Rico, the Northern Mariana Islands, Guam, and so on, are more likely to use Model C, which does not explicitly require the translation of scores to norms and thus encourages use of locally developed tests. This might also be a problem in large metropolitan areas where a considerable proportion of the student population is composed of foreign-speaking students.

An issue of more widespread importance concerns the level of test that is administered. Most achievement tests that are currently marketed have several different levels or forms of the test designed to measure different levels of achievement or skill. Usually, the test maker will recommend a particular test level for a given age group or grade level. While the assigned test level is likely to be appropriate for the majority of students in any grade, it will tend to fail precisely where the most accurate information is desired for purposes of Title I evaluation, that is, at the lower end of the testing distribution.

The issue of choosing the appropriate test level is related to the potential for floor and ceiling effects, and the effect of the chance level of the test. Since most Title I students come from the lower quarter of the test distribution, if that test is too difficult, one is likely to find a floor effect differentially affecting the program group. Several suggestions have been offered to avoid test level problems, most notably, the idea of "out-of-level" or functional level testing. This is commonly implemented in one of two ways. First, if the district is concerned about the possibility of floor effects, they could simply require that each grade be tested at the next lower level of test, although this obviously increases the potential for ceiling effects. A second approach is to allow individualized testing. Here, the classroom teacher or some other appropriate and knowledgeable administrator, assigns whatever level of test is most reasonable for any given student. Within the same grade, several different levels of the same test might be used for students who are believed to have different ability. The major problem with individualized testing stems from the fact that at some point these test scores must be converted to a common scale for purposes of analysis. Thus, one must rely on "extended" standardized scales provided by the test makers and obtained from norming samples of students who received multiple levels of the test. While the use of out-of-level or functional level testing holds promise for Title I evaluation, especially when Model C is the method of choice, one must be careful to anticipate the special problems that occur when moving from on-level testing to one of these procedures.

A related question concerns the scales on which the scores are reported and on which the analysis is based. Most test makers will report test results on a variety of scales such as raw score, extended standardized score, local standardized score, and so on. The issues involved in converting scores from one scale to another for the most part are outside of the scope of this work. As a general recommendation it is probably best in conducting an analysis to rely on the raw scores for developing estimates of gain and to convert these estimates into NCE units for reporting purposes. By using the raw scores, one can for the most part avoid concerns about the quality of various standard scales provided by the test maker.

Another issue related to test characteristics stems from the finding that students first entering grade school are likely to differ considerably in their ability to read or to handle simple mathematics problems. However, after several years of education, it is more likely that the ability levels will become similar. One might expect, as a result, that estimates of program effect will be higher at higher grades where tests are more likely to reflect ability better. There is some corroboration for this notion in the analyses of Model C results from the State of Florida. Across all Title I programs (n = 273), there was a tendency for test results to be more positive for the higher grades, but whether this is due to developmental phenomena or other factors such as better measurement, better training, loss of less intelligent students, and so on, is not certain.

Another issue related to the quality of test information concerns the fact that standardized achievement tests are designed to discriminate best near the middle of the test distribution. For the most part these tests are constructed to yield good estimates of average performance for any given group. Thus, the tests are most fallible at the tails of the distributions. This is exactly where the most precise information is desired in Title I evaluation because program group cases tend to be confined to the lower end of test distribution.

TEST PROBLEMS

Some of the most serious measurement problems for Model C result from factors which distort the pretest-posttest functional relationship and consequently, estimates of program effect. Two such factors, floor and ceiling effects and chance level performance, are described here.

Floor and ceiling effects result, respectively, from a test that is either too hard or too easy for the group in question. For example, if the test is too difficult, a "floor" effect results because most students will receive a low test score and consequently the distribution will be positively skewed. The test will not sufficiently discriminate between students of different ability who all receive low scores. The issue is especially complicated here because it is possible to have either a floor or a ceiling effect or both on either the pretest or the posttest or both. In Figure 7.1, several expected pre-post patterns for various combinations of floor and ceiling effects are depicted. The figure shows that if there is a floor effect on the posttest, the program group slope would be likely to be lower than the comparison group slope. Similarly, the same pattern would result if there is a ceiling effect on the pretest. Either of these could occur in practice. To consider the likelihood of such occurrences one must look at the test or tests that are used. Assuming that the same test is used for both the pretest and posttest, it seems more likely that one will have a floor effect on the pretest and a ceiling effect on the posttest (assuming that subjects grow or gain in skill between the testings). Thus, in the case where the same test is used both times, it seems unlikely, or less likely, that floor and ceiling effects would yield the pattern of negative gains commonly attained as described in Chapter 6.

The situation becomes more complicated if different tests or different levels of the same test are used for the pre- and posttest, as is commonly the case in Title I. Here, depending upon the difficulty of either task, one could get the floor effect on the posttest or the ceiling effect on the pretest that could yield a lower program group slope and result in a negative gain. Thus, for any given analysis, the likelihood that a ceiling or floor effect results in a lower program group slope must be assessed within the context of the tests that are used. As a potential source for the observed pattern of negative gains mentioned earlier these effects cannot be ruled out.

Another measurement related problem that could result in a lower program group slope than control group slope and consequently in negative gains, is related to the chance level of the test. The chance level issue and its impact on Model C estimates are discussed in Chapter 6. It is important to recognize that there is a difference between a chance level effect and a floor effect. A floor effect occurs when there is value on a test below which students cannot score even though their ability would indicate that they should. A chance level effect occurs when students respond to questions by chance or guessing. A floor effect should be evidenced by an absolute flattening of the distribution at the floor of the test, whereas a chance level effect allows for test scores on both sides of the chance level. Thus, it is theoretically possible to have either a floor or chance level effect or both in any set of data.

The relationship of the chance level of the test to the cutoff score in the regression-discontinuity design has been investigated by Visco (1980). Generally, he finds that in most cases the cutoff score is in the vicinity of or lower than the chance level of the test. While it is impossible to say that for these cases all those in the program group were guessing, it is not unlikely that a large number of students were. In this regard, it is important to determine whether the instructions of the test explicitly encourage guessing. In addition, in the 273 Florida analyses, the median value for the cutoff was about the twenty-eighth pretest percentile and one can infer that it is quite likely that the cutoff is often very close to or even below the typical chance level for the tests that are used. Thus, in the case of Title I evaluation, it can be assumed that this phenomenon can result in the lowered program group slope and, at least in part, the resulting pattern of negative gain estimates described earlier.

DATA MAINTENANCE AND ACCESS

One area that has received little attention from methodologists concerns processing of test information. Many school districts had little experience prior to the initiation of the current Title I evaluation system with processing vast amounts of achievement test data for purposes of analysis. There are several types of problems that can occur in this context. First are problems of miscoded information that can result from the students themselves or from the test correctors. Second are errors in processing the test made by the test producer or the company that markets the test. Third are errors made at the school district level such as calculation mistakes or errors made when using tables to convert scores. Fourth are problems related to accessing the data and correctly processing the data for purposes of analysis.

Problems of coding are illustrated well by the difficulties involved with trying to match pretest and posttest scores by computer. For example, it is necessary to match the data in some districts by name of student before conducting the analysis. In one case, the test that was used allowed 12 columns for the last name, 6 columns for the first, and 1 column for the middle initial. Ideally, one would like to match students on the basis of an exact correspondence between all 19 columns of the name field on the pretest and posttest. However, in practice, there are many ways in which the name for the same student can be miscoded on different tests. Some of the problems detected when matching data include:

—Code "long" name one time, "short" name the other:
    SMITH, CATHER
    SMITH, CATHY

—Code middle initial one time, not the other:
    JONES, JOHN M
    JONES, JOHN

—Errors (keypunch or entry) leading to "unlikely" names:
    ADKINR instead of ADKINS
    ALBRECNT instead of ALBRECHT
    MAAK instead of MARK

—Different coding of name due to number of columns allowed:
    SAMANT OR SAMATH for Samantha
    JACQUL OR JACQUE for Jacqueline

—"Joking" or suspicious names:
    MOUSE M
    DUCK D

—Placing middle initial in first name field:
    TERREN A vs TERRYA

—Extension of long name into next field (e.g., if first name and middle initial are Vincent E.):
VINCEN E   VINCEN T

—Coding of abbreviation of first name:
ROBT instead of ROBERT

—Legitimate name change from one testing to another:
CLAY to ALI

At the point of actually matching the cases, problems like these can act to prevent a successful match.

One might attempt to eliminate some of these problems by reducing the amount of information used to match, but this will lead to more frequent mismatches. For example, for the first 100 alphabetically sorted cases (including both pretest and posttest) in one school district, use of a 19-column match using the complete name (last, first, and middle initial) yielded 21 matches (i.e., 42 cases were paired). When the number of columns was reduced to the first 15 (last name and first three letters of first name), 28 matches were found (i.e., 56 cases were paired). Other variables might be included to improve the match such as sex, age, race, school, and so on, but each of these will have its own errors and their addition may considerably complicate the match procedure. In general, the more information included in the match field, the greater the probability of excluding a legitimate match due to coding errors. Conversely, the less information included, the greater the chances of obtaining illegitimate matches. Perhaps the best way to deal with matching problems is to match as conservatively as possible (i.e., include many matching variables), and, for cases that do not have a match, attempt to determine the reason (e.g., did not take both tests, miscoding of answer sheet by student, error in keypunching of data), making corrections where possible.

The matching issue is important for two reasons. First, the need to match cases with Model C is often cited as a factor in favor of choosing Model A that is often incorrectly perceived as not requiring matching. Second, there is good reason to believe that matching problems related to miscoding of answer sheets will be more prominent in the treated group that is composed of lower-achieving students. This leads to differential "exclusions" between the groups that, in turn, have the potential of biasing the estimates of program effect.

A second issue related to data maintenance concerns errors that are made by the test producer or corrector. Most districts that use standardized achievement tests have them corrected by either the test producer or using automated procedures within the district itself. A number of problems can occur at this stage that have serious effects on the analysis. For instance, one respondent reported receiving the achievement data for the school district from the test company and subsequently discovering the wrong correction key had been applied in processing the data. Obviously, had this not been detected the results for that district would have been totally erroneous. In another district, pre- and posttest scores were matched up by the test producer using ID numbers that were assigned to all public school students. Those who attended private schools were not given numbers. For some reason, the test producer separated these data into two groups: those with IDs and those without. Unfortunately, only the data with ID numbers were returned to the school district. The analysis of the Title I programs for that year were conducted and it was not until the subsequent year that the evaluator realized that none of the private school data had been included. It is clear that situations of this nature must be avoided and that procedures for doing so need to be developed.

In an excellent paper, Crane and Maye (1980) examine the frequency and effect of three types of "correctable" errors made at the school district level: calculation errors, misread norms tables, and use of incorrect norms tables. The data consisted of aggregate values reported to the State of Illinois for two successive years (n = 1,788 for 1978 and n = 198 for 1979). They found that the total percentage of aggregates having at least one correctable error was 51.6% for 1978 and 57.6% for 1979). In 1979, these errors alone resulted in an overall positive bias of .74 NCE units (with a range of from .43 to 3.20 NCE units, depending on the error). In addition, "the effect of undetected errors on a single aggregate (e.g., for a grade within a project in a single school district) ranges form –24 NCEs to 41 NCEs." They suggest that statistical quality control procedures are needed to detect such errors and reduce their influence on estimates of gain.

Another set of problems concerns the school district's ability to access the data. These problems become prevalent when large amounts of data are processed and/or when the data is computerized. Sometimes the problem is exacerbated by the test producer. For example, the CTBS standardized achievement test reports scores in three different computer formats, depending on the level of the test. This is especially a problem when the format statements for the pretest and posttest differ. The application of the wrong format to a given set of scores will obviously result in erroneous results and sometimes these can be difficult to detect. Other problems in accessing the data result from the processing of magnetic tapes, errors in reading such tapes, and the like.

It should be clear that irrespective of research design, the quality of measurement is crucial. Sometimes measurement problems will occur differentially between program and comparison group students. Procedures need to be developed for assessing the extent of these problems and their effect on the statistical analysis. These should include methods for flagging "outliers," miscodings, floor and ceiling effect, and chance level problems, as well as procedures for determining the proportion of such errors in each subgroup of interest.

PROGRAM ISSUES

It is not the purpose of this work to comment on what types of treatment or program produce what types of results, or to make a statement on the substantive issues involved in Title I service. Nevertheless, there are important issues related to the program that can have a detrimental effect on the quality of the results. Three problems of this nature are discussed here:

(1)   Identifying recipients of the program.
(2)   Determining the amount of service received.

(3)   Determining the type of program received.

If unaccounted for, each of these can distort the estimates of effect.

IDENTIFYING RECIPIENTS OF THE PROGRAM

Implicit throughout the Title I evaluation system is the notion that Title I service is somehow "standardized," that is, that all students receive service that is "of a kind." This is evidenced by the existence of a system for national aggregation of gains; it would be unreasonable to aggregate gains from different types of programs. Within a particular program, students are usually divided into program or comparison group, implying that on the average they are homogeneous with respect to experiences in their condition. In practice, however, the assumption of stan-dardized programs is unreasonable and the analysis will be improved if the actual service can be more accurately described.

Many of the problems related to measuring the program are involved with the seemingly mundane task of determining who actually received service. This was mentioned above for example, in citing the difficulties that arise at the district level when one attempts to match up who actually received the program with who should have received the program according to the cutoff point criterion. The amount of error in documenting who actually received the program is difficult to determine given the data at hand. However, several respondents cited examples of cases where the assignment to program was incorrectly reported. For example, a student who was assigned to program by the cutoff and who is listed as having received the program, may not have received it because the classroom teacher felt that it was not warranted and never informed the evaluator. Similarly, some Title I teachers may simply have too many students assigned to them and may, as a result, have to resort to putting some on a "waiting list" to be serviced later in the year, if at all. Often these cases go undocumented and it is assumed that all students designated as receiving Title I service were given the same amount and type of program. Equally difficult to detect and identify are those students who did not receive service. For example, those students who began the school year in a designated Title I school but transferred to a non-Title I school may have been eligible for service on the basis of their pretest score, and may be listed as receiving such service, even though they did not. As of many other problems in this context, the extent of the problem is unknown and its effect on the analysis is undocumented.

AMOUNT OF SERVICE RECEIVED

Even if all students could be correctly identified as having either received Title I service or not, the amount of service that is received is difficult to determine. Most districts report that students receive service for a given number of minutes or hours per day or week. This figure is usually illusory and in fact the amount of service received tends to differ from student to student. For example, a Title I teacher is likely to show favoritism or give special instruction to those students who most need or appreciate it. Little, if any, attempt is made to document the degree to which students do not receive service due to such factors as absenteeism, holidays, cancelled sessions due to school plays, field trips, weather, and so on (Visco, 1980). In addition, there are systematic factors that tend to reduce the time available for instruction such as transportation time, set-up time, clean-up activities, and so on.

In general, it would be desirable to document the degree of the program received and to incorporate this information directly into the analysis. Some guidance on how program implementation information can be incorporated into the analysis is provided by Boruch and Gomez (1977).

TYPE OF PROGRAM RECEIVED

A major problem in documenting program implementation involves determining what type of specific instruction students received. While it is fairly reasonable to assume, for instance, that students who are supposed to be receiving reading instructions are in fact getting some type of instruction related to reading, the type of instruction might differ considerably from one class to another. Any attempt to document the differences in instruction or to standardize them within a school district is likely to improve the quality of the evaluation, although it may pose political and managerial difficulties.

Another problem related to type of instruction concerns the setting in which instruction is given. The State of Florida, for example, requires each district to report the setting under one of five classifications: self-contained classroom, regular classroom, pull-out small group, pull-out individual instruction, and other. This is certainly an improvement over no information at all, but falls short of a good description of the setting for instruction.

The most common setting is the in-class approach that involves the Title I teacher providing service to Title I students in the back or corner of a room while regular classroom activities continue. Several respondents indicated that although this might be the accepted practice it may or may not be popular with any given Title I teacher. The essential problem is whether one should provide instruction within the classroom (in which case the instruction is likely to be intrusive or disruptive of classroom activities), or whether one should pull out students for instruction in another room (in which case students are more likely to be labeled or stereotyped in a negative way). In any event, issues related to the program setting have important implications for the analysis and should be documented where possible.

Another problem related to the type of program received concerns the instruction given to comparison students while Title I students are receiving service. Obviously, the students do not remain "fallow" while Title I students receive service and this time is often dedicated to additional instruction in social sciences, the arts, and so on. The level of instruction may, in fact, be raised due to the removal of the least advanced pupils. The problem that arises here concerns whether any skills related to those being communicated to Title I students are also being communicated to the comparison students. This would tend to diminish their comparative quality and reduce the differences that one might expect between the two groups. For example, if comparison students are receiving instruction in social sciences and this instruction also serves to improve their skills in reading, one would expect that the Title I students as a group would gain less relative to the amount the comparison students would gain had they not received such instruction.

Because of the nature of the subject matter, one might expect that this would be a greater problem for reading programs than for math programs. This is because other skills tend to generalize to reading ability more readily than to math skills. On the basis of this alone we might expect that the gains found for Title I math programs might be more positive than those found for the reading programs. In fact there is evidence for this proposition in the results from the State of Florida. There, the average gain at the cutoff for all reading programs was -3.32, while for math programs it was $-.56$. One must interpret such differences cautiously as they could possibly be attributed to other factors such as better test reliability for math than for reading. Nevertheless, it is important to recognize how the existence of the competing forms of the program or instruction might tend to degrade the comparison.

Another problem in this same vein concerns the existence in many school districts of state or locally supported compensatory education programs (Visco, 1980; Parkes, 1980). For the most part, districts attempt to keep such programs separate from Title I programs by incorporating them into different grade levels. Nevertheless, there are occasions where these programs overlap in the same grade level, school, and classroom. In one such case, students were assigned Title I service if their pretest score was below a given cutoff, but those students within this eligible group who scored at the lowest end of the pretest distribution were often put into more intensive locally funded compensatory education programs. Unfortunately, no second lower cutoff was used to assign these eligible students to the local programs. As a result, while assignment to group may have been sharp relative to a cutoff value, assignment to different levels of the program was not, and the analysis was consequently complicated.

The determination of the type of program that is received needs to be studied in more detail. In fact, this was a sentiment that was seconded by many of the respondents, although viewed in slightly different terms. Many respondents felt that the emphasis within the Title I evaluation system on outcome evaluation or on the estimate of gain was misplaced and that more work should be done on studying the process of Title I training. This would involve a more careful look at the type and amount of the program that is administered and is to be encouraged especially if this information will be coupled or incorporated into the analysis of gains.

DATA PREPARATION ISSUES

In conducting a data analysis, it is often necessary to exclude or disqualify certain cases for a variety of reasons. Sometimes the cases "exclude" themselves through attrition from the program, that is, for one reason or another it is impossible to obtain both a pretest and a posttest score. In other cases, the data analyst decides to exclude certain subgroups from the final analysis because they do not represent the target group of interest or for some reason their data is suspect. Thus, what is included here under the title "Data Preparation" includes those groups that are disqualified for one reason or another, as well as a discussion of the process of defining the final data that will be used in the analysis.

Three types of issues are considered here:

(1)   Background and Prevalence of Exclusions
(2)   Common Exclusions
(3)   Data Processing Issues

Very little formal work has been done on the systematic effects of such exclusions, and in fact the wide variety of decisions that must be faced by a school district evaluator suggests that the task at times can become overwhelming. Many respondents, especially at the local level, reported that problems of this nature pose tremendous difficulty and that there was little formal guidance on how they should proceed.

BACKGROUND AND PREVALENCE OF EXCLUSIONS

The office of Education along with the RMC Corporation has indirectly commented on the issue of data exclusions, most often within the context of attrition. A recent draft of the Policy Manual (USOE, 1979) states that:

> some units (students, schools, etc.) will no longer be available when the second measurement (posttest) is made. The loss is referred to as *attrition*. If a large percentage of units has been lost, the effects of this attrition should be checked to see if the data are still representative.

> As a general rule, if the posttest includes fewer than two-thirds of the students that were pre-tested, the data should be considered probably not representative. The evaluator can check the representativeness of the data by determining whether:

>> —the mean score of students having both measurements is significantly different from the mean score of students having only one measurement.
>> —certain subgroups in the project (e.g., the lowest or highest scoring students, the lowest or highest socio-economic status) tend to have only one score.

> In its evaluation plan the LEA may wish to consider whether attrition has been a problem in the past. If certain types of students have been lost to previous evaluations, the evaluator may be able to develop a plan to locate those types of students for posttesting.

It is clear that attrition is a primary concern of the Title I evaluation system.

Attrition technically only pertains to those cases where it was impossible to obtain a pretest and posttest score. As will be shown below, there are many other data cases that are routinely excluded from the final analysis even though both pretest and posttest scores are obtained. While a district may have more than two-thirds of its cases with a pre and posttest, this does not necessarily mean that two-thirds of the eligible cases will finally be used in the data analysis. Little guidance is provided to aid the local evaluator in deciding which data must be used in the final analysis. Some guidance is implicit in the definition of who is eligible for Title I service. Thus, the Office of Education Annual Report for 1979 (USOE, 1979) states that:

> Exceptions to serving the most needy students are: continuation of services to educationally deprived students no longer in greatest need; continuation of services to educationally deprived children transferred to an eligible area in the same school year; skipping children in greatest need who are receiving services of the same nature and scope from non-federal sources; and a school with 75% or more if its students from low-income families may have a project for all of its students (called a school-wide project).

This statement provides some idea of students who may or may not be eligible for Title I services, but does not indicate whether or not these cases should be included in the data analysis if treated.

We can begin to determine the extent of the problem by looking at estimates of attrition for the data obtained from the State of Florida. The annual report for the State of Florida (Florida Department of Education, 1979) states that the "unduplicated participant count" (that is the number of students estimated statewide for the 1978 school year) was 173,477 while the total number unaccounted for in reporting Title I analysis was 40,145. This means that approximately 76.8% of the data was present and that there was a loss of about one quarter of all these cases. This was significantly less than in the previous year and tended to occur, according to the report, primarily in kindergarten and first grade.

Some attempt was made to verify this information by individual school districts. The annual evaluation report for each school district requires a listing of the number of participants in Title I evaluation programs broken down by subject area. Although this is listed as a "duplicated count," it might still serve to allow estimates of the percentage of missing data and at worst is likely to yield conservative estimates. The procedure followed here was to total up the number of participants listed and to compare this to the number of students listed as included in each analysis. Thus, a ratio can be formed with the number of students in the analysis as the numerator and the number of participants as the denominator. While one must be cautious about interpreting these results because of the possibility of faulty or missing information in the annual report, it is nevertheless instructive to compare these estimates of missing data with those reported by the state. This tabulation indicated that the median amount of missing data is 32% with a range from 1% to 91%. While this range suggests the possibility of inaccuracy in reporting, the median value of 32% does not differ considerably of the value of 25% as reported by the state. It is obvious from this information that a good deal of the data falls into the category of attrition. What is not clear is the degree to which additional exclusions are made on the data that are not reflected in these figures.

One reason for calculating within-district estimates of missing data is so that it might be possible to compare the effects of various amounts of missing data on the estimates of program gain. Thus, when the estimates of missing data are dichotomized at the median, that is, all districts having less than 32% missing data are considered in one group while those having more are considered in the other, it is possible to see whether there are differences in gains under these conditions. In fact, the differences do not appear to be great. Those estimates of gain based on relatively little missing data yielded an average gain at the cutoff point of −2.02 while those districts with evidence of higher percentages of missing data had an average gain at the cutoff point of –2.61. While no difference appears to be present when the data is aggregated for the state, it is not clear how the exclusion of data might affect a given analysis. One study (Kaskowitz & Friendly, 1980) shows that while national aggregates of gains are not likely to be seriously biased due to attrition, individual project estimates can sometimes be distorted by as much as ± 15 NCE units. What is clear is that a significant percentage of the data does not reach the final analysis.

COMMON EXCLUSIONS

The list of subgroups that might be excluded from any given data analysis reads like a list of "special problems" that tend to arise in the process of conducting research. The most common exclusion, as recognized above, is due to what is traditionally considered attrition, that is, the lack of both a pre- and posttest score for a given student. Several factors may responsible for this. First, it may in fact be the case that students do not take both tests. This could be due to factors such as absenteeism or the movement of students either into or out of the school district. It is often the case that these standardized achievement tests take several days to administer, and as a result, a student missing class on one particular day may not have both tests depending upon whether the students were retested or whether test data was available from the district that they previously attended. Another source of attrition cases has to do with the inability to match successfully the pretest and posttest for given students. Thus, the problems mentioned above concerning the miscoding of such items as identification numbers, name, and so on, will result in an inability to successfully match pre- and posttest score.

A second exclusion that tends to occur is the result of misassignment relative to the cutoff score. One respondent noted that it was discovered that schools within the district were not sending in cases that were misassigned relative to the cutoff score. When school administrators were asked why these scores were not sent, their reasons usually had to do with the desire to comply with the requirements for strict adherence to a cutoff score. Sometimes this exclusion is made by the data analyst in order to insure that the requirement of a sharp cutoff appears to be met.

Data is often excluded because of the mobility of the students. Generally, there are two types of mobility of concern here. First, students may transfer into and/or out of schools within the same district. Second, students may transfer into or out of the district itself. Within a given school district, a distinction is often made between Title I and non-Title I schools. The Title I allocation procedures require at the district level that schools be ranked according to some measure that is an indicator of poverty. Most often, schools within a district are ranked according to a measure, such as the number of free lunches that are served, which is a readily available measure and is thought to be a reasonable proxy for the degree of poverty. Depending upon the size of allocation to the district, it is often the case that some schools will receive no Title I funds at all. The schools that receive funds are usually determined by a cutoff point on the measure of poverty. Problems occur for the data analysis when a student who is eligible to receive Title I service begins the school year in a Title I school and transfers to a non-Title school or vice versa. It is possible in this situation that eligible students will receive total service, partial service, or no service. Often, the documentation is poor and it is difficult to know whether or not such cases should be included in the final analyses. Along with this is the difficulty in tracking any kind of transfers within the same school district. Illustrative of such difficulties is an example cited by Visco (1980):

> A child started out at School A transferred to School B and then transferred to School C all during the fall. All three schools are Title I and the child qualified for service in each. Thus, she was dropped at A and added at B, dropped at B, and added at C, (so far, that is).

In this case, even though the student might have received service throughout the year, she was excluded from the analysis. This may or may not be justified depending upon how one wishes to interpret the effect of the individual circumstances.

The second type of mobility that occurs involves transfers into and out of the school system. Depending upon the time of year the student transferred, it may or may not be possible to obtain the necessary data. Thus, students transferring into the school district for the fall semester who did not receive the spring pretest may be able to be pretested and included in the analysis. Obviously, in cases such as this, one runs into the administrative difficulties posed by such additional pretesting, as well as the problems associated with equating scores from tests given at different points in time.

Another problem related to mobility concerns the situations where students simply "drop out of sight" for a time only to reappear later somewhere within the school district. This occurs with alarming frequency, especially in school districts in Florida in orange-growing regions. Especially unnerving is the case of the prime harvest season being coincidental with the administration of district-wide tests. Given that it is not unreasonable for many school districts to have mobility rates as high as 25% or 30%, it is clear that the problems posed in trying to track such students can rapidly become formidable. Even if a certain percentage of this "mobile" population can be identified for both the pretest and posttest, it is not clear whether their score should be included in the analysis.

Another exclusion that is commonly made is of the repeaters or those students who are held back a grade from year to year. This exclusion offers a particularly clear illustration of the detrimental effects that exclusions in general can have on the data analysis. It is certainly reasonable to expect that most of the students who are required to repeat a grade come from the group of students who are eligible for Title I services. If there are a fair number of repeaters and if these cases are routinely excluded from the data analysis, it is likely that the program group regression line and subsequently the estimate of gain will be distorted as described in Chapter 6. There, it was shown that exclusions of this sort act to bias estimates of effect in a negative direction.

Another set of exclusions is made for students who graduate from or drop out of the Title I program. Some respondents reported that when the Title I teacher perceives a student to have "caught up," the teacher will sometimes remove the student from the program without recording this information. Excessive absenteeism may also cause a child to be dropped or not depending upon whether or not this information was duly noted. Title I students are also sometimes "picked up" by other programs such as English As A Second Language, Special Education, local compensatory education, and so on. Again, depending upon how accurately this information was recorded and the view of the individual data analyst, such cases may or may not be excluded.

Cases are also excluded from the final analysis if it appears that they are "outliers." These exclusions are often made without any clear rationale to guide them. Thus, an analyst may, in viewing graphs of the univariate and bivariate distributions, decide that certain cases lie well outside the normal range for the distribution and on this basis exclude these cases. The question in such cases often revolves around whether the observed score is legitimate or whether it is the result of some processing error or miscoding. Sometimes it is possible to investigate such cases in-depth, but often this is difficult or too costly. More rational guidelines for excluding outliers have been suggested and analytic procedures less sensitive to their presence have been recommended (Fleming & White, 1980).

It is legitimate within the Title I system to allow students who received services in one year to continue to receive services in subsequent years even if they no longer qualify in terms of their pretest score. This provision is largely left to the discretion of individual district administrators. In cases where school districts decide to take advantage of this option, two problems tend to occur. First records of which students got serviced in previous years tend to be spotty and/or nonexistent and thus it is difficult to determine which cases fall into this category. Second, even for cases that do not fall into this category, whether they should be included in the analysis or not is not clear.

It is obvious from the above discussion that a large number of exclusions or disqualifications are considered or are incorporated prior to the statistical analysis. While any one exclusion may have only a minimal effect on the analysis, the combination of several can pose formidable difficulties. Further work needs to be conducted to determine the extent to which such exclusions are made and the effect they have on the analysis.

DATA PROCESSING ISSUES

Another class of problems related to exclusions or disqualifications concerns the order in which these are made and the variables that are used to select the excluded cases.

In the large amounts of data analyzed by computer, it is often difficult to know which variables should be used to select subgroups for the analysis. For example, if one wishes to perform a task as simple as dividing students into those who were in Title I or non-Title I schools, it is not clear whether it is better to use information available from the school at the time of the pretest, the posttest, or a match between the two. Similarly, students are often selected for the analysis of a particular grade level by selecting on the posttest grade. This seemingly simple rule would include in the final data setup all students who repeated the grade. This may or may not be desirable.

Generally, one of two strategies is followed by a school district in the processing of its data. The first strategy involves creating successively smaller data sets by excluding certain subgroups from the analysis. The second strategy involves creation of a comprehensive data file, including all cases and the application of a multiple if-statement for purposes of selecting the appropriate subgroups. When all exclusions are considered together, the process of selecting the appropriate subgroup is seen to be a formidable task. Visco (1980) provides an illustration of the complications that can occur in an example of the multiple if-statements that might be used to select the data for an analysis of a fourth grade reading program:

> If Title I school on pretest
> If Title I school on posttest
> If school has reading service
> If grade 4
> If not repeater
> If Title I service in reading
> If below cutoff in reading
> If not challenged in reading
> If no makeup in reading
> If stationary (no add-drop)

These are the statements that might be used to select the program group cases assuming that these cases have already been success-fully matched on the pretest and posttest and assuming that other exclusions (such as of Title I program repeaters) are not desired. Other sequences might be designed to achieve the same subgroup of interest and, in fact, the order in which the selections are made might significantly affect the cases that are finally included.

SUMMARY OF RESEARCH IMPLEMENTATION ISSUES

The litany of implementation problems listed in this chapter serves to illustrate the wide variety of these problems and their potential impact upon the data analysis. One would be naive to believe that these problems could be considered minor or that they are not likely to affect the data analysis seriously. On the basis of the investigation documented above it is possible to list the major goals of a complete implementation analysis. These would include:

(1)   An identification of the major problem areas in implementing the design. Four general areas were identified in this chapter, with each area containing subcategories of potential problems.

(2)   A determination of the prevalence or frequency of each problem for purposes of prioritizing the expected seriousness of their effects upon the data analysis. Although this task was addressed to some degree, one can conceive of carrying it out in a more formal manner. This could take the form of frequency counts of the number of times the problem occurs in various settings; or with percentage estimates, as with the estimates of the amount of missing data; or by charting the distribution of the problem as when one looks at the percentage of grade repeaters for different pretest values. Because it is unreasonable to believe that all problems can be identified and accounted for, the purposes of this step would be to determine which are the major or most frequent problems that need to be addressed.

(3)   An assessment of the effect that the major implementation problems have on the estimates of program effect. There are several procedures that might be used to accomplish this. First, one might simply look at pretest means for various subgroups of interest. This is especially appropriate if posttest data is missing and one wishes to determine whether for those cases there is any likely bias. Thus, if one finds that the pretest mean for students who do not have a posttest is not in the vicinity of the overall pretest mean, one might suspect that this subgroup differs from the overall population of interest. In other cases, one may be able to look at the bivariate relationship between an estimate of a particular problem and either the pretest or the posttest. For example, if one is interested in attrition, it would be useful to plot the percentage of attrition cases for various pretest scores. One would expect that if attrition has no serious effect upon the results, this percentage would be evenly distributed across all pretest values. It is especially useful in the case of the regression-discontinuity design to determine whether there is a coincidental jump in this distribution near the cutoff, as well as whether there are a proportionately greater number of cases in the program group range than in the control group. Probably the best way to determine the effects that various implementation problems have on program effect estimates is to conduct multiple analyses. For example, one could conduct the analysis with or without grade repeaters, transfers, and so on. If the results do not differ significantly, one would feel more confident in including such data in the final analysis. Similar strategies might be applied to determine the effect of measurement problems such as floor and ceiling effects. If, for example, a ceiling effect is thought to exist, one might do a series of analyses where various amounts of data at the

upper end of the distribution are systematically excluded. If a ceiling effect is present, the estimates of gain under such a series of analyses should change systematically. One must be careful, of course, to avoid misinterpreting such analyses. In this case, for example, a true quadratic relationship, if interpreted and analyzed as a ceiling effect, could lead to erroneous conclusions.

The analysis presented in this chapter illustrates the importance of implementation issues. Such study tends to degrade the distinction that is often made between process and outcome evaluations. While the conduct of an implementation investigation is similar to the types of activities often involved in process evaluation, the goal is primarily to improve the quality of outcome studies. Nevertheless, much of the information that is gathered would be useful to administrators and researchers for understanding better how their programs work and improving procedures for future applications. The reader is referred to Trochim (1982) and Trochim and Visco (1983) for more extensive discussions on how techniques adapted from accounting, auditing, industrial quality control, and other fields might be used to study and improve research implementation.

The results of this investigation of the implementation of regression-discontinuity in compensatory education can be summarized briefly in terms of the major topics considered in this chapter:

(1) *Assignment.* Misassignment occurs routinely in many districts as part of formalized "challenge" procedures. In typical Title I programs, misassignment is likely to produce biased estimates of effect regardless of how these cases are handled in the analysis. Including challenges in their original group (disregarding their retest score), including them in the group indicated by their retest score, or excluding them from the analysis altogether will not in many cases remove the bias.

(2) *Measurement.* Floor and ceiling effects and chance level problems can induce curvilinearity in the data and result in biased estimates of gain when using the Title I Model C analysis. The differences between chance level problems and floor effects have been underinvestigated and deserve further study.

(3) *Program.* The assumption that all program (or comparison) students experience standardized conditions is unrealistic. This is acknowl-

edged in the Title I system by use of gross categories for differentiating program types (e.g., reading versus math, in-class versus pull-out, etc.). Nevertheless, more accurate descriptions of program and comparison group experiences (based perhaps on a detailed process analysis of the program) will improve the quality of the statistical analysis and the estimates of gain.

(4)   *Data Preparation.* Significant amounts of data are routinely excluded prior to analysis. Cases are excluded because they are perceived as coming from "special" groups (e.g., Title I repeaters or graduates) or because of attrition (e.g., due to absenteeism, migrancy, transfers, and so on). Any combination of exclusions can act to distort estimates of program effect. Multiple analyses may be useful for assessing the extent of these problems.

Overall, a major problem is poor documentation that makes it impossible to determine the extent and influence of implementation problems. Even where documentation exists, there can be doubts as to its accuracy. Improvements in documentation are needed so that implementation problems can be ranked accurately by order of importance and procedures, or analyses can be devised to deal with them.

It is appropriate that this volume conclude with a strong statement of concern regarding the implementation of the regression-discontinuity design. The little experience we have in applying the design indicates that implementation issues can act to corrupt a well-conceived research plan. Work must continue simultaneously on both the theoretical methodological design considerations and the problems encountered when applying the design if we are to ever realize the full potential of the regression-discontinuity design in applied social research.

NOTE

1. The reader is referred to Chapter 2 for an overview of Title I evaluation. This discussion is based on Trochim (1980). Much of the material comes from interviews and site visits conducted as part of that project. For confidentiality reasons, most persons involved in that study are not identified by name but are rather referred to as respondents. The reader will find a more detailed description of the procedures used to gather this data in Trochim (1980).

APPENDIX A

COMPUTER ANALYSIS OF
REGRESSION-DISCONTINUITY DATA

This appendix briefly outlines some considerations for using standard statistical programming packages to analyze regression-discontinuity data. Two statistical software packages, SPSS (Nie et al., 1975) and MINITAB (Ryan et al., 1976) are explicitly discussed. Readers who are familiar with other statistical packages (e.g., SAS, BMDP, Datatext) should have little difficulty in adapting the instructions offered here for those contexts. The analysis of the basic regression-discontinuity design as outlined in Chapter 5 simply requires use of any standard least squares regression analysis program. It is assumed that the reader is familiar with regression analysis on computers.

The discussion here will deal only with the basic three-variable regression-discontinuity case. Minimally, one needs a pretest variable, assignment variable (i.e., a dummy-coded program indicator), and a posttest variable, labelled x, z, and y respectively. There are three basic steps involved in the computer analysis:

(1) *Data Input.* The three variables x, y, and z must be input to the program. This can be accomplished by punching the data onto cards, entering them into an online data file or, with some programs, entering them interactively. It is assumed that the reader knows how to accomplish this for the program of interest. In the SPSS and MINITAB presentations below, it will be assumed that the three variables have already been entered.

(2) *Transformations and Recoding.* There are two major transformations or recodings that must be done in order to carry out the analysis as

outlined in Chapter 5. First, one must subtract the cutoff value from each pretest value (if the estimate of gain is desired at some point other than the cutoff, then that point must be subtracted). Second, one must construct polynomials of the pretest and interaction terms to the degree of polynomial that is desired.

(3) *Model Specification.* This step involves specifying to the computer program the appropriate regression model. As outlined in Chapter 5, one should specify a forward stepwise regression procedure that fits lower-order terms earlier.

The next two sections describe how one can accomplish steps two and three in MINITAB and SPSS.

MINITAB ANALYSIS OF REGRESSION-DISCONTINUITY DATA

The MINITAB language is an interactive statistical package that is ideal for teaching and demonstrations of statistical techniques, and for exploratory analysis of data. It does not offer sufficient precision in calculations to be appropriate for a high accuracy analysis of regression-discontinuity data.

It is assumed that the analyst has read the three variables, x, y, and z, into columns C1, C2, and C3, respectively. The reader should note that if assignment to group has been sharp relative to the cutoff, one need only reading in the pretest and posttest. The dummy-coded assignment variable can be constructed by recoding the pretest (as shown in the simulations in Appendix B). Once the data have been read in, one needs to conduct the appropriate recodings. First, the cutoff needs to be subtracted from the pretest:

let c4 = c1 − (cutoff value)

Where the analyst substitutes the cutoff score in the above command. Next, the polynomials and interaction terms are constructed. To begin, construct the treatment x pretest interaction:

let c5 = c3 * c4

One can then construct the quadratic term and its interaction:

let c6 = c4 * c4

let c7 = c3 * c6

Similarly, one then constructs the cubic terms and interaction:

let c8 = c6 * c4

let c9 = c3 * c8

Notice that for each higher-order term, all one does is to multiply the next lowest polynomial term by the adjusted pretest (i.e., pretest minus the cutoff) variable. To obtain the interaction term for that order of polynomial, one simple multiplies the dummy assignment variable by the polynomial term. One can continue constructing polynomials and their interactions to any degree desired as described in Chapter 5.

Because the current version of MINITAB has no facility for conducting stepwise regression analysis, the analyst must conduct separate regression analyses for each step in the model. The procedure suggested here involves adding in all terms of the same order, beginning with first-order terms, one step at a time. Thus, the first analysis that would be run would be:

regr c2 3 c3 c4 c5

which simply calls for the regression of the posttest (C2) on three variables: the group assignment variable (C3); the adjusted pretest (C4); and, the assignment x pretest interaction term (C5). The next step (analysis) would add in the quadratic term and its interaction:

regr c2 5 c3 c4 c5 c6 c7

which simply adds the squared adjusted pretest (C6) and its interaction with assignment (C7). One then adds in the cubic terms:

regr c2 7 c3 c4 c5 c6 c7 c8 c9

The analysis proceeds in steps until all terms desired have been included. The reader should examine the simulations in Appendix B for further details on the use of MINITAB with regression-discontinuity data.

SPSS ANALYSIS OF REGRESSION-DISCONTINUITY DATA

SPSS is a high-quality statistical package appropriate for professional analysis of research data. As above, it is assumed that the analyst has already read the data into an SPSS program. Here, the variables will be named X (for the pretest), Y (the posttest), and Z (the dummy group assignment variable). The first step in the analysis is to subtract the cutoff value from the pretest, which can be accomplished with:

COMPUTE   X1 = X − (cutoff value)

where the analyst substitutes the value of the cutoff in the above statement. Next, the assignment x adjusted pretest interaction is constructed:

COMPUTE   I1 = Z * X1

The quadratic term and its interaction are computed with:

COMPUTE   X2 = X1 * X1

COMPUTE   I2 = Z * X2

and the cubic term and its interaction by:

COMPUTE   X3 = X2 * X1

COMPUTE   I3 = Z * X3

One can continue generating higher-order polynomials and their interaction terms to any degree desired as outlined in Chapter 5.

SPSS allows for stepwise multiple regression and therefore, the complete analysis can be run using one regression specification statement. For a first through third-order polynomial analysis, one could use:

REGRESSION   VARIABLES = Y,Z,X1,I1,X2,I2,X3,I3/

REGRESSION = Y WITH Z(6),X1(6),I1(6),

X2(4),I2(4),X3(2),I3(2)/

The VARIABLES = portion of the regression statement simply tells the program what set of variables will be considered for inclusion in the analysis. The REGRESSION = statement specifies the regression of the posttest (Y) on the assignment variable (Z), adjusted pretest (X1), and higher-order terms and their interactions (X2 through I3). The numbers in parentheses after each variable specify the order of inclusion, that is, the step at which the variable will be entered. The value of the number is arbitrary (i.e., one could use values of 24, 12, and 2 instead of 6, 4, and 2, respectively), but all variables having the same inclusion value are entered on the same step and the higher the inclusion value, the earlier the step of entry. Thus, the specification above indicates a three-step analysis with the variables having an inclusion value of 6 (i.e., Z, X1, I1) being entered on the first step, those with an inclusion value of 4 (i.e., X2 and I2)being added on step two, and those with an inclusion value of 2 (i.e., X3 and I3) being added on the third and final step. The reader is encouraged to consult Nie et al. (1975) for a detailed description of the regression ststement specification.

CONCLUSION

Obviously, this appendix only outlines the simplest analysis. Variations of the regression-discontinuity design that were presented throughout the text are, for the most part, straightforward extensions of these procedures. In addition, any analysis of regression-discontinuity data should include descriptive statistics and graphic analysis. Some simple procedures for plotting the data using MINITAB are presented in Appendix B. Both SPSS and SAS have excellent high-quality plotting procedures that would enable the analyst to examine the data, especially when trying to assess visually the degree of polynomial that will be fitted in the analysis.

APPENDIX B

REGRESSION-DISCONTINUITY
SIMULATION EXERCISES

This appendix consists of two computer simulation exercises in the MINITAB language that illustrate some of the major statistical issues in regression-discontinuity analysis. In addition to their use as classroom exercises when teaching the regression-discontinuity design, these simulations are similar in structure to many of the simulations reported in this volume.

The write-up assumes that the reader has access to a computer that implements MINITAB and knows how to get into the MINITAB language. In most institutions, users can consult their local computer operation office to determine whether MINITAB is available and how it can be accessed. The exercises have been written in a conversational tone and require no prior knowledge of MINITAB to be interpretable (although such would be helpful, of course). The author has used these exercises in undergraduate level research methods courses with reasonable success.

THE REGRESSION-DISCONTINUITY DESIGN
PART I

In this exercise, we are going to create and analyze data for a regression-discontinuity design. Recall that in its simplest form the design has a pretest, a posttest, and two groups, usually a program and comparison group. The distinguishing feature of the design is its procedure for assignment to groups—persons or units are assigned to one or the other group solely on the basis of a cutoff score on the preprogram measure. Thus, all persons having a preprogram score on one side of the cutoff value are put into one group and all remaining persons are put in the other. We can depict the design using the following notation:

C O X O

C O   O

where the C indicates that groups are assigned by a cutoff score, the first O represents the pretest, the X depicts the administration of some program or treatment, and the second O signifies the posttest. Notice that the top line represents the program group while the second line indicates the comparison group.

In this simulation we will create data for a "compensatory" program case. We will assume that both the pretest and posttest are fallible measures of ability (where higher scores indicate generally higher ability). We will also assume that we want the program being studied to be given to the low pretest scorers—those who are low in pretest ability. To begin, log on as usual and then get into MINITAB:

minitab

It is convenient to turn off extended printing and statistical output with:

noprint

brief

The first step is to create two hypothetical tests: the pretest and posttest. Before we can do this, we need to create a measure of true ability and separate error measures for each test:

nran 500 50 5 c1

nran 500 0 5 c2

nran 500 0 5 c3

Now we can construct the pretest by adding true ability (C1) to pretest error (C2):

let c4 = c1+c2

Before constructing the posttest it is useful to create the variable that describes the two groups. The pretest mean will be about 50 and, arbitrarily, we will use 50 as the cutoff score. Because this is a compensatory case, we want all those who score lower than or equal to 50 to be program cases, with all those scoring above 50 to be in the comparison group. The following two recode statements will create a new dummy variable (C5) with a value of 1 for program cases and 0 for comparison cases:

reco 0 50 c4 1 c5

```
reco 50 100 c5 0 c5
```

To check on how many persons you have in each condition do:

```
table c5
```

Notice that you probably don't have exactly 250 people in each group (although in the long run, that is how many you would expect if you divide a normal distribution at the mean). Now you are ready to construct the posttest. We would like to simulate an effective program so we will add in 10 points for all program cases (recall that we accomplish this by multiplying 10 by the dummy-coded variable—for all program cases this product is 10, for comparison cases, 0—this is then added into the posttest):

```
let c6=cl+c3+(10*c5)
```

It is convenient to name the variables:

```
name cl='true' c2='xerror' c3='yerror'
```

```
name c4='pretest' c5='group' c6='posttest'
```

To get some idea of what the data look like try:

```
table c5;
    means c4 c6.
```

And don't forget to put the period at the end of the second line. This command gives pre and post means for the two groups. Note that the program group starts off at a distinct disadvantage—we deliberately selected the lower scorers on the preprogram measure. Notice also that the comparison group actually regresses back toward the overall mean of 50 between the pretest and posttest. This is to be expected because we selected both groups from the extremes of the pretest distribution. Finally, notice that the program group scores as well or better than the comparison group on the posttest. This is because of the sizeable 10 point program effect that we put in. You might also want to examine pre and post histograms, correlations, and the like. Now, let's look at the bivariate distribution:

```
plot c6 c4
```

You may want to reset the HEIGHT to get the plot to fit on your terminal screen. You should be able to see that the bivariate distribution looks like it "jumps" at the pretest value of 50 points. This is the discontinuity that we expect in a regression-discontinuity design when the program has an effect (note that if the program has no effect, we expect a bivariate distribution that is continuous or does not jump).

At this point we have finished creating the data. The distribution that you see might be what you would get if you conducted a real study (although real data seldom behaves as well as this). The first step in analyzing this data is to examine the data to try to determine what the "likely" pre-post function is. We know that the true function here is linear (that the same straight-line fit in both groups is appropriate), but with real data it will often be difficult to tell by visual inspection alone whether straight or curved lines are needed. Therefore, while we might think that the most likely function for this distribution is linear, we will deliberately over-fit or over specify this likely function a bit to be on the safe side. The first thing we need to do to set up the analysis is to set up a new variable that will assure that the program effect will be estimated at the cutoff point. To do this, we simply create a new variable that is equal to the pretest minus the cutoff score. You should see that this new variable will now be equal to zero at the cutoff score and that all program cases will have negative preprogram scores while the comparison group will have positive ones. Since the regression program would automatically estimate the vertical difference or "jump" between the two groups at the intercept (i.e., where the pretest equals 0), when we create this new variable, we are setting the cutoff equal to a pretest value of 0 and the regression program will correctly estimate the jump at the cutoff. We will put this new variable in C7:

let c7 = c4–50

name c7 = 'pre-cut'

and name it appropriately. You will see that we always substitute this variable for the pretest in the analyses.

Now we need to set up some additional variables that will enable us to overspecify the "likely" true linear function:

let c8 = c7*c5

This new variable is simply the product of the corrected pretest and the dummy assignment variable. Thus, C8 will be equal to zero for each comparison group case and equal to the corrected pretest for each program case. When this variable is added into the analysis we are in effect telling the regression program to see if there is any interaction between the pretest (C7) and the program (C5). This is equivalent to asking whether the linear slopes in the two groups are equal or whether they are different (which implies that the effect of the program differs depending on what pretest score a person had). Now, let's construct quadratic terms:

let c9 = c7*c7

let c10 = c9*c5

For C9, we simply square the pretest. When this variable is entered into the analysis, we are in effect asking whether the bivariate distribution looks curved in a quadratic pattern (consult an introductory algebra book if you don't recall what a quadratic or squared function looks like). The second variable, C10, allows the quadratic elements in each group to differ, and therefore, can be considered a quadratic interaction term. We should name the variables:

    name c8 ='i1' c9 ='pre2' c10 ='i2'

Where I1 stands for "linear Interaction." PRE2 for the "squared pretest," and I2 for the "quadratic interaction." We could continue (and normally would) generating even higher-order terms and their interactions (cubic, quartic, quintic, etc.), but these will suffice for this demonstration.

We are now ready to begin the analysis. We will do this in a series of REGRession steps, each time adding in higher-order terms. In the first step, we fit a model that assumes that the bivariate distribution is best described by straight lines with the same slopes in each group and a jump at the cutoff:

    regr c6 2 c7 c5

The coefficient associated with the GROUP variable in the table is the estimate of the program effect. Since we created the data ourselves, we know that this regression analysis exactly specifies the true bivariate function—we created the data to have the same slope in each group and to have a program effect of 10 points. Is the estimate that you obtain near the true effect of ten? You can construct a 95% confidence interval (using plus or minus 2 times the standard deviation of the coefficient for the GROUP variable). Does the true effect of ten points fall within this interval (it should in most cases)?

With real data we would not be sure that the model we fit in this first step includes all the necessary terms. If we have left out a necessary term (for instance, if there was in fact a linear interaction), then it would be likely that the estimate we obtained would be biased (you will see this in the next simulation). To be on the safe side, we will add in a few more terms to the analysis in successive REGRession steps. If we have already included all necessary terms (as in the analysis above) then these additional terms will be superfluous. They should not bias the estimate of program effect, but we will have less precision. For the next step in the analysis, we will allow the slopes in the two groups to differ by adding in I1, the linear interaction term:

    regr c6 3 c7 c5 c8

The coefficient for the GROUP variable is, as usual, the estimate of program effect. We know that the new variable, C8, is unnecessary because we set up the simulation so that the slopes in both groups are the same. You should see that the coefficient for this I1 variable is near zero and that a zero value almost surely falls within the 95% confidence interval of this coefficient. Because this term is unnecessary, we should still have an unbiased estimate of the program effect. Is the coefficient for GROUP near the true value of 10 points? Does the value of 10 fall within the 95% confidence interval of the coefficient? You should also note that the estimate of the program effect is less precise in this analysis than in the previous one—the ST. DEV. OF COEF. for the GROUP variable should be larger in this case than in the previous run. Now, we will add in the quadratic term:

    regr c6 4 c7 c5 c8 c9

Again, you should see that the coefficients for the superfluous terms (I1 and PRE2) are near zero. Similarly, the estimate of program effect should still be unbiased and near a value of ten. This time, the standard error of the GROUP coefficient will be a little larger than last time, again indicating that there is some loss of precision as higher-order terms are added in. Finally, we will allow the quadratic terms to differ between groups by adding in the quadratic interaction term, I2:

    regr c6 5 c7 c5 c8 c9 c10

By now you should be able to see the pattern across analyses. Unnecessary terms will have coefficients near zero. The program effect estimate should still be near ten, but the 95% confidence interval will be slightly wider, indicating that there is a loss of precision as we add in more terms.

In an analysis of real data, you would by now be more convinced that your initial guess that the bivariate distribution was linear was a sensible one. You might decide to continue fitting higher-order terms or you might stop with the quadratic terms. This whole procedure may strike you as somewhat wasteful. If we think the correct function is linear, why not just fit that? The procedure outlined here is a conservative one. It is designed to minimize the chances of obtaining a biased estimate of program effect by increasing your chances of overspecifying the true function. In the next exercise, you will see what can happen if you underspecify the true function. Variations for this exercise are included at the end of the next one. When you are finished, be sure to get out of MINITAB:

    stop

and then logoff as usual.

THE REGRESSION-DISCONTINUITY DESIGN
PART II

This exercise will illustrate what happens when we don't fit the correctly shaped regression line to the data in a regression-discontinuity design. It is assumed that you have already completed the previous exercise that outlined the general analytic strategy for regression-discontinuity. To begin, logon as usual and then get into MINITAB:

```
minitab
```

We will begin with commands that are similar to the ones used in the previous exercise. Recall that we are simulating data for a "compensatory" case:

```
noprint
brief
nran 500 50 5 c1
nran 500 0 5 c2
nran 500 0 5 c3
let c4 = c1+c2
reco 0 45 c4 1 c5
reco 45 100 c5 0 c5
name c1= 'true' c2 ='xerror' c3 ='yerror'
name c4= 'pretest' c5 ='group
```

So far, this is pretty much what was done in the previous exercise. Variable C4 is the pretest and C5 is the dummy assignment variable (where 1 = program participant; 0 = comparison participant). It is important for you to note that this time we have used a pretest score of 45 units as the cutoff. This will be discussed more at the end of this exercise. In the next step, we will create the pretest minus the cutoff (C7) and the linear interaction term (C8) before creating the posttest (because we will need them to create the posttest):

```
let c7=c4–45
```

```
let c8=c7*c5
```

```
name c7= 'pre-cut' c8='i1'
```

Recall that we name variable C8 with "I1" to signify the linear (i.e., first order) interaction.

In this simulation, we will construct a posttest that has both a main effect (a jump at the cutoff point) and an interaction effect (a difference in linear slopes between groups):

```
let c6 = c1+c3+(10*c5)+(10*c8)
```

And, of course, we should name the posttest:

```
name c6 ='posttest'
```

Notice that just as in the previous exercise we have put in a 10-point jump as the main effect for group (C5). This time, however, we also put in a 10-point interaction effect. Although we might not expect this big an interaction effect in a real study, we deliberately chose a large effect so you can clearly see what happens when we misspecify the pre-post function in regression-discontinuity analysis. You should see in the bivariate distribution that we have a much more steeply sloped line. In fact, the slope should be 10 times greater for the program group than for the comparison group:

```
plot c6 c4
```

The 10-point jump at the cutoff point may not be visually apparent in this graph because of the steep slope in the program group. Sometimes it is useful to plot only a portion of the distribution so that we can see it more clearly. For instance, we can plot all scores between 30 and 60 on the pretest and between 0 and 80 on the posttest with the following:

```
plot c6 0 80 c4 30 60
```

At this point, we have created the pretest, posttest, assignment variable and the corrected pretest. You might want to examine some of these more carefully. For example, you might try:

```
table c5
```

```
hist c4
```

```
hist c6
```

Notice that because we used a cutoff score (45) which is below the pretest mean (50), we have considerably fewer persons in the program group. You might also list the means and standard deviations for the pretest and posttest with the table subcommand procedure:

```
table c5;
  means c4 c6;
  stdev c4 c6.
```

and of course, don't forget the semicolons and the period at the end.

Now, as in the previous exercise, we need to construct the variables that we will need for the analysis:

```
let c9 = c7*c7
```

```
let c10 = c9*c5
```

```
name c9 ='pre2' c10 = 'i2'
```

We are now ready to proceed to the analysis itself:

```
regr c6 2 c7 c5
```

As always, the estimate of the program effect is the coefficient for the GROUP variable in the regression table. Is it near the true value of 10 points that we put in? Here you should clearly see that the estimate is biased. What is wrong? When we created the data, we put in both a main effect (a jump) and an interaction (a difference between slopes). The model that you put into the above analysis fits straight lines that have the same slope in both groups. This is obviously wrong and leads to a biased estimate of the jump. You have underspecified the true model because you have not included all the necessary terms (in this case, you haven't included the linear interaction term, C8). The next step would be to add this term in:

```
regr c6 3 c7 c5 c8
```

Now you should observe that the estimate for the program effect (the coefficient for GROUP) is near the true value of 10 points. At this point, you have exactly specified the true model (that is, you have included all the necessary terms that went into making up the posttest). You should also find that the estimate for the linear interaction term, I1, is near the true value of 10 units. At this step in the analysis you have exactly specified the true model—you have included all of the terms that you used when you created C6, the posttest (remember that you have included C1, the true score, when you put the pretest into the regression). With real data, however, you would probably not know at this point whether you have included all necessary terms yet. So, to be on the safe side, you would estimate the next step:

```
regr c6 4 c7 c5 c8 c9
```

When you add in the quadratic term, C9, you should find that the estimates of the program effect and linear interaction remain near 10, but that the standard errors for these coefficients (and hence, the width of the 95% confidence interval) are larger—precision is lost as you add in more terms. But here, because the quadratic term is not a necessary ingredient in the posttest, there is no bias as a result of this overspecification error. Finally, we will add in one more term:

```
regr c6 5 c7 c5 c8 c9 c10
```

Again, the addition of the quadratic interaction term, C10, will not bias the estimate of program effect although precision will be lost.

By now you should understand that the central purpose of a regression-discontinuity analysis is to obtain an unbiased estimate of the program effect. If we know what the true bivariate function is in advance, there is no difficulty in doing this. We simply specify a regression model that exactly fits this true function. However, in real data analysis we will seldom, if ever, know what the true function is. We do know that if we underspecify the true function in the analysis, we are likely to get a biased estimate (you should have seen this in the first regression analysis above). We also know that if we overspecify the true function, we will get an unbiased estimate, although it will be less precise than with exact specification. Therefore, we want an analysis where specification errors will tend to be in the direction of overspecification (although exact specification is, of course, always best). About the best we can recommend is that you start by estimating what you think is the most likely true function. Then, to be safe, add several terms to this model. If it looks like these terms may be needed (this is a nontrivial decision process that is outside the scope of this presentation) then you will be safer in terms of bias if you opt for the more specified model.

There are a number of variations of this basic exercise that would increase your understanding of this design:

— Rerun the simulation using a cutoff point of 50 units on the pretest (i.e., equal to the mean). In this case it may not appear that underspecifying the true function leads to bias—you may get an estimate for the main effect that is very close to 10 points. Why does this happen? The key to the answer lies in the fact that when you split a normal distribution in the middle, you create a type of "symmetry" in the regression lines across groups. You might be able to see what happens if you draw a graph of the bivariate distribution and then visually fit regression lines with the same slope in both groups. If you are not particularly adept at doing this visually, you might try plotting the residuals and the regression lines for the first two steps in the analysis using the following commands:

```
regr c6 2 c7 c5 c20 c21 c22
plot c20 c4
plot c21 c4
regr c6 3 c7 c5 c8 c20 c21 c22
plot c20 c4
plot c21 c4
```

The first plot under each REGR statement is the residuals against the pretest. If the line you have fit is a good one, we expect that this bivariate plot will be circular in shape. Notice that it is not for the first regression and is for the second. The second plot is a rough sketch of the regression line that you have fit. You may be able to use these graphs to help you figure out why this "special case" of the regression-discontinuity design does not appear biased even with underspecification.

— Rerun the simulation for the "meritorious" (that is, noncompensatory case). To do this, just change the recode statements used to create C5 so that the higher pretest cases are in the program group (and remember to make the cutoff higher than 50, for instance, 55).

— Put in a negative rather than a positive effect.

— Alter the reliability of the measures by changing the proportion of true score to error variance in the original NRAN statements.

— Those of you who are really ambitious might like to try playing around with higher-order true functions (quadratic, cubic) or even some nonpolynomial ones (e.g., logarithmic). In these you must be very careful. For example, observe what happens when your true function is only a quadratic term (i.e., C9) and your cutoff is at the pretest mean. Can you graph the situation out and convince yourself that even underspecification in this special case will not generally lead to bias? You should see that this is similar to the first variation above.

When you are finished, don't forget to get out of MINITAB:

stop

and then logoff as usual.

References

Advisory Committee on Intergovernmental Relations (ACIR). *A catalog of federal grant-in-aid programs to state and local governments: Grants funded FY 1978. The intergovernmental grant system: An assessment and proposed policies.* Washington, DC: U.S. Government Printing Office, 1978.

Barnow, B. S., Cain, G. C., & Goldberger, A. S. *Issues in the analysis of selection bias.* Unpublished manuscript, University of Wisconsin, August 1978.

Beck, M. D. *Developments of empirical "growth expectancies" for the Metropolitan Achievement Tests.* Paper presented at the annual meeting of the National Council on Measurement in Education, Washington, DC, 1975.

Bentler, P. M., & Woodward, J. A. A head start reevaluation: Positive effects are not yet demonstrable. *Evaluation Quarterly,* 1978, 2, 493–510.

Berk, R. A., & Rauma, D. Capitalizing on nonrandom assignment to treatment: A regression discontinuity of a crime control program. *Journal of American Statistical Association,* 1983, 78, 21-28.

Blair, C. Personal communication, 1980.

Boruch, R. F. *Regression-discontinuity designs revisited.* Unpublished manuscript, Northwestern University, 1973.

Boruch, R. F. *Regression-discontinuity designs: A summary.* Presentation at the annual meeting of the American Educational Research Association, May, 1974.

Boruch, R. F. On common contentions about randomized field experiments. In R. F. Boruch & H. W. Riecken (Eds.), *Experimental Tests of Public Policy.* Boulder, CO: Westview Press, 1975, 108-145. (a)

Boruch, R. F. Coupling randomized experiments and approximations to experiments in social program evaluation. *Sociological Methods and Research,* 1975, 4, 31–53. (b)

Boruch, R. F. *Double pretests for checking certain threats to the validity of some conventional evaluation designs or, stalking the null hypothesis.* Unpublished manuscript, Northwestern University, 1978.

Boruch, R. F., & DeGracie, J. S. *Regression-discontinuity evaluation of the Mesa reading program: Background and technical report.* Unpublished manuscript, Northwestern University, November 1975.

Boruch, R. F., & Gomez, H. Sensitivity, bias, and theory in impact evaluations. *Professional Psychology.* 1977, 8, 411–443.

Boruch, R. F., Wortman, P. M., & Cordray, D. S. *Reanalyzing program evaluations.* San Francisco: Jossey-Bass, 1981.

Bridgeman, B. *A practical alternative to Model A.* Unpublished manuscript, Princeton, NJ: Educational Testing Service, 1979.

Campbell, D. T. Reforms as experiments. *American Psychologist,* 1969, 24, 409–429.

Campbell, D. T., & Boruch, R. F. Making the case for randomized assignment to treatments by considering the alternatives: Six ways in which quasi-experimental evaluations in compensatory education tend to underestimate effects. In C. A. Bennett & A. A. Lumsdaine (Eds.) *Evaluation and experiment.* New York: Academic Press, 1975.

Campbell, D. T., & Erlebacher, A. How regression artifacts in quasi-experimental evaluations can mistakenly make compensatory education look harmful. In J. Hellmuth (Ed.) *Compensatory education: A national debate.* New York: Brunner/ Hazel, 1970.

Campbell, D. T., Reichardt, C. S., & Trochim, W. *The analysis of the "fuzzy" regression-discontinuity design: Pilot simulations.* Unpublished manuscript, Northwestern University, 1979.

Campbell, D. T., & Stanley, J. C. Experimental and quasi-experimental designs for research. In N. L. Gage (Ed.) *Handbook of Research on Teaching.* Chicago, IL: Rand McNally, 1963.

Chow, G. C. Tests of equality between sets of coefficients in two linear regressions. *Econometrika,* 1960, 28, 591–605.

Conner, R. F. Selecting a control group: An analysis of the randomization process in twelve social reform programs. *Evaluation Quarterly,* 1977, 1, 195–244.

Cook, T. D., & Campbell, D. T. *Quasi-experimentation: Design and analysis issues for field settings.* Chicago: Rand McNally, 1979.

Cordray, D. S. *Making the case for the use of "patchwork" analyses in quasi-experimental evaluation research.* Unpublished doctoral dissertation, Claremont University, 1978.

Crane, L. R., & Maye, R. O. *Effects of correctable errors on Title I NCE estimates and implications for statistical quality control.* Paper presented at the annual meeting of the American Educational Research Association, Boston, April 1980.

David, J. L., & Pellavin, S. H. *Research on the effects of compensatory education programs: Reanalysis of data.* SRI Project Report URU-4425, Menlo Park, CA: SRI International.

Echternacht, G. *A summary of the special meeting on Model C held in Atlanta in January 1978.* Unpublished manuscript, Princeton, NJ: Educational Testing Service, 1978.

Echternacht, G. *The comparability of different methodologies for ESEA Title I evaluation.* Paper presented at the annual meeting of the American Psychological Association, New York, 1979.

Echternacht, G. *Model C is feasible for Title I evaluation.* Paper presented at the annual meeting of the American Educational Research Association, Boston, April 1980.

Echternacht, G., & Swinton, S. *Getting straight: Everything you always wanted to know about the Title I Regression Model and curvilinearity.* Paper presented at the annual meeting of the American Educational Research Association, San Francisco, 1979.

Eidenberg, E., & Morey, R. D. *An act of Congress: The legislative process and the making of educational policy.* New York: W. W. Norton, 1969.

Fleming, P. D., & White, J. W. *Comparison of several schemes to estimate the treatment effect under Model C of the ESEA Title I evaluation system.* Paper presented at the annual meeting of the American Educational Research Association, Boston, April 7-11, 1980.

Florida Department of Education. *Title I evaluation report.* Tallahassee, FL, 1979.

Goldberger, A. S. Selection bias in evaluating treatment effects: Some formal illustrations. Discussion Papers, 123–72. Madison: Institute for Research on Poverty, University of Wisconsin, 1972.

Gujarti, D. Use of dummy variables in testing for equality between sets of regression coefficients. *American Statistician,* 1970, 24, 50-52.

Hampel, F. R. (1974) Influence functions. *Journal of the American Statistical Association,* 1974, 69, 383-393.

Hansen, J. B. *Problems and suggested procedures related to the regression model for Title I evaluation (Model C).* Paper presented at the Technical Assistance Center Director's Conference, Atlanta, January 19–21, 1977.

Hansen, J. B. *Report on the Committee to Examine Issues Related to the Use of the Norm Referenced Model for Title I Evaluation.* Portland, OR: Northwest Regional Educational Laboratory, 1978.

Hardy, R. *Comparison of Model A and Model C in Florida.* Atlanta: Educational Testing Service (Memo), 1978.

Hill, R. Personal communication, 1979.

Hocking, R. R. The analysis and selection of variables in linear regression. *Biometrics,* 1976, 32, 1–49.

House, G. D. *A comparison of Title I achievement results obtained under USDE Models A1, C1 and a mixed model.* Paper presented at the annual meeting of the American Educational Research Association, San Francisco, 1979.

Judd, C. M., & Kenny, D. A. *Estimating the effects of social interventions.* New York: Cambridge University Press, 1981.

Kaskowitz, D. H., & Friendly, L. D. *The effect of attrition on the Title I evaluation and reporting system.* Paper presented at the annual meeting of the American Educational Research Association, Boston, 1980.

Kidder, L. H. *Sellitz, Wrightsman and Cook's Research Methods in Social Relations.* New York: Holt, Rinehart & Winston, 1981.

Linn, R. L. *Measurement of change.* Presented at the Second Annual Johns Hopkins University National Symposium on Educational Research entitled, "Educational evaluation methodology: The state of the art." Washington, DC, November 2, 1979.

Long, J., Horwitz, S., & Pellegrini, A. *An empirical investigation of the ESEA Title I evaluation system's no-treatment expectation for the special regression model.* Paper presented at the annual meeting of the American Educational Research Association, San Francisco, 1979.

Maddala, G. S., & Lee, L. Recursive models with qualitative endogenous variables. *Annals of Economic and Social Measurement,* 1976, 5, 525–545.

Magdison, J. Towards a causal model approach for adjusting for pre-existing differences in the non-equivalent control group situation: A general alternative to ANCOVA. *Evaluation Quarterly,* 1977, 1, 399–420.

McNeil, K. *NTS/TAC Responses to Model C questions raised at Region III Model C workshop on October 21, 1977.* Unpublished memorandum, 1977.

McNeil, K., & Findlay, E. A. *Evaluating Title I early childhood programs: Problems, the applicability of Model C and several evaluation plans.* Unpublished manuscript, NTS Research Corporation, July 1979.

Murray, M. *Models A and C: Theoretical and practical concerns.* Paper presented at the Florida Educational Research Association Convention, Daytona Beach, January 21, 1978.

Murray, S., Arter, J., & Faddis, B. *Title I technical issues as threats to internal validity of experimental and quasi-experimental designs.* Paper presented at the annual meeting of the American Educational Research Association, San Francisco, 1979.

NCES (National Center for Education Statistics). *Quick Survey on Title I evaluation models.* Washington, DC: Department of Education, 1979.

Nie, N. H., Hull, C. H., Jenkins, J. G., Steinbrenner, K., & Bent, D. B. *SPSS: Statistical Package for the Social Sciences.* New York: McGraw-Hill, 1975.

Office of Management and Budget (OMB). *1979 catalog of federal domestic assistance.* Washington, DC: U.S. Government Printing Office, 1979.

Parkes, J. Personal communication, 1980.

Reichardt, C. S. *The design and analysis of the non-equivalent group quasi-experiment.* Unpublished doctoral dissertation, 1979.

Riecken, H. W., Boruch, R. F., Campbell, D. T., Caplan, N., Glennan, T. K., Pratt, J. W., Rees, A., & Williams, W. *Social experimentation: A method for planning and evaluating social intervention.* New York: Academic Press, 1974.

RMC Research Corporation. *Out-of-level testing.* Unpublished collection of materials, Portsmouth, NH, 1979.

Rubin, D. Assignment to treatment group on the basis of a covariate. *Journal of Educational Statistics,* 1977, 2, 1–26.

Ryan, T. A., Joiner, B. L., & Ryan, B. F. *MINITAB Student handbook.* North Scituate, MA: Duxbury Press, 1976.

Sacks, J., & Ylvisaker, D. *Linear estimation for approximately linear models.* Discussion paper Number 9, Center for Statistics and Probability, Northwestern University, October 1976.

Seaver, W. B., & Quarton, R. J. Regression-discontinuity analysis of Dean's list effects. *Journal of Educational Psychology,* 1976, 68, 459–465.

Spiegelman, C., H. *Two techniques for establishing treatment effect in the presence of hidden variables: Adaptive regression and a solution of Reiersøl's Problem.* Unpublished doctoral dissertation, Northwestern University, 1976.

Spiegelman, C. H. *A technique for analyzing a pretest-posttest nonrandomized field experiment.* Florida State University, Statistics Report M435, 1977.

Spiegelman, C. H. Estimating the effect of a large scale pretest-posttest social program. *Proceedings of the Social Statistics Section,* American Statistical Association, 1979, 370–373.

Stewart, B. L. *Investigating the technical adequacy of Model C in Title I evaluation.* Paper presented at the annual meeting of the American Educational Research Association, Boston, April 1980. (a)

Stewart, B. L. *The regression model in Title I evaluation.* Unpublished manuscript, Mountain View, CA: RMC Corporation, April 1980. (b)

Strand, T. *Who said what about Title I evaluation at the AERA/NCME Annual Meeting, San Francisco, April, 1979: Summaries of selected papers.* Unpublished manuscript, Evanston, IL: Educational Testing Service, August 1, 1979.

Sween, J. A. *The experimental regression design: An inquiry into the feasibility of nonrandom treatment allocation.* Unpublished doctoral dissertation, Northwestern University, 1971.

Sween, J. A. *Regression discontinuity: Statistical tests of significance when units are allocated to treatments on the basis of quantitative eligibility.* Unpublished manuscript, April 1977.

Tallmadge, G. K. *An empirical assessment of norm-referenced evaluation methodology.* Unpublished manuscript, Mountain View, CA: RMC Corporation, 1980.

Tallmadge, G. K. *Selecting students for Title I projects.* Mountain View, CA: RMC Research Corporation, 1978.

Tallmadge, G. K., & Horst, D. P. *A procedural guide for validating achievement gains in educational projects.* Number 2 in a series of monographs on evaluation in education. Washington, DC: U.S. Department of Health, Education, and Welfare, 1976.

Tallmadge, G. K., & Wood, C. T. *User's guide: ESEA Title I Evaluation and reporting system.* Mountain View, CA: RMC Research Corporation, 1978.

Thissen, D., Baker, L., & Wainer, H. Influenced-enhanced scatterplots. *Psychological Bulletin,* 1981, 90, 1, 179-184.

Thistlethwaite, D. L., & Campbell, D. T, Regression-discontinuity analysis: An alternative to the ex post facto experiment. *Journal of Educational Psychology,* 1960, 51, 309–317

Trochim, W. *The regression-discontinuity design in Title I evaluation: Implementation, analysis, and variations.* Unpublished doctoral dissertation, Northwestern University, 1980.

Trochim, W. Resources for locating public and private data. In R. F. Boruch, P. M. Wortmann, & D. S. Cordray (Eds.), *Reanalyzing program evaluations.* San Francisco: Jossey-Bass, 1981.

Trochim, W. Methodologically based discrepancies in compensatory education evaluations. *Evaluation Review,* 1982, August.

Trochim, W., & Spiegelman, C. H. The relative assignment variable approach to selection bias in pretest-posttest group designs. *Proceedings of the Social Statistics Section.* American Statistical Association, 1980.

Trochim, W., & Visco, R. *Quality control in educational research.* Paper presented at the annual meeting of the American Educational Research Association, April 1983.

U.S. Department of Commerce. *Report on Statistics for Allocation of Funds: Statistical Policy Working Paper I.* Prepared by the Subcommittee on Statistics for Allocation of Funds, Federal Committee on Statistical Methodology, Washington, DC: U.S. Government Printing Office, March 1978.

U.S. Office of Education (USOE). *Policy Manual: Subpart F—Evaluation.* Unpublished manuscript, October 20, 1979.

U.S. Office of Education (USOE). *ESEA Title I Annual Report,* 1979. Washington, DC: Author.

Visco, R. Personal communication, 1980.

Wick, J. W. *Title I elementary and secondary education acts: Formation, function and purposes, 1965-1978.* Unpublished manuscript, City of Chicago, Department of Education, August 1978.

Wood, C. Personal communication, 1979.

About the Author

William M. K. Trochim is Assistant Professor in the Department
of Human Service Studies in the College of Human Ecology at
Cornell University. He received his Ph.D. from the Department
of Psychology program in Methodology and Evaluation Research at Northwestern University. In addition to his work on
the regression-discontinuity design, he has investigated experimental and quasi-experimental designs more generally, and has
written on strategies for improving the implementation of
research methods. His current work includes investigations of the
applications of methodological and statistical computer simulations in teaching and research, and the development of strategies
that help to define and scale the conceptual framework for a
research project.